Advance

"Marie-Nathalie Beaudoin and Gerald Monk are both veterans of the 'first generation' of narrative therapy practitioners, theorists, and educators. As is often the case when you amalgamate two traditions of practice and theory, you are in for surprises. There are surprises aplenty in *Narrative Practices and Emotions*—and who better than these authors to have integrated these two seemingly disparate approaches?"

—**David Epston**, co-originator of narrative therapy

"Marie-Nathalie Beaudoin and Gerald Monk incorporate knowledge from neuroscience and positive psychology into narrative practices with curiosity and open-mindedness. I especially like how they explore the 'landscapes' of affective physiology and the embodiment of emotions, as well as their inquiries about clients' experiences of relational flow and mindfulness in their lives. Their ideas are refreshing and inspiring and represent an emergence of a flourishing identity for narrative work itself."

—**Margarita Tarragona**, PhD, director, ITAM Center for Well-Being Studies, Instituto Tecnológico Autónomo de México, Mexico City

"A significant contribution to a burgeoning body of literature. The authors weave together the diverse strands of the postmodern narrative worldview with the recent developments of interpersonal neurobiology. Beaudoin and Monk invite us to journey with them into new territories of possibility that crackle with innovation. By artfully intersecting narrative practices with generously particularized practices from interpersonal neurobiology and embodiment, they offer many fresh options for fostering the emergence of preferred and robust identities. This timely volume is a must-read."

—**Jim Duvall**, MEd, codirector of JST Institute, editor of Journal of Systemic Therapies, and coauthor of *Innovations in Narrative Therapy: Connecting Practice, Training, and Research*

"With remarkable finesse, the coauthors draw from decades of study, practice, and teaching narrative therapy to carefully venture into pioneering territories that integrate their clinical work with current research findings about the brain, body, and emotions. Each chapter offers novel therapeutic practices accompanied by transcripts and associated therapeutic questions. If you are a narrative practitioner wishing to broaden the scope of your work with uniquely intense problems, this trailblazing book is for you!"

—**Peggy Sax**, PhD, psychologist and founder of Re-Authoring Teaching

"*Narrative Practices and Emotions* provides a great wealth of knowledge and new ideas for narrative practitioners. Beaudoin and Monk write with a level of lucidity that underscores the vital role of emotions in narrative practices. Through a series of vignettes from clinical practice, the authors demonstrate how emotions expand clients' narratives. Attention to local knowledges and historically disregarded healing practices offers a breath of fresh air. Indeed, this is a very well-written book that weaves narrative therapy with interpersonal biology, mindfulness, and embodiment approaches. A must-read!"

—**Hugo Kamya**, PhD, professor, Simmons University,
School of Social Work

NARRATIVE PRACTICES
AND EMOTIONS

Narrative

Practices

and

Emotions

40+ WAYS TO SUPPORT
THE EMERGENCE OF
FLOURISHING IDENTITIES

MARIE-NATHALIE BEAUDOIN
GERALD MONK

Norton Professional Books

An Imprint of W. W. Norton & Company
Independent Publishers Since 1923

Note to Readers: Standards of clinical practice and protocol change over time, and no technique or recommendation is guaranteed to be safe or effective in all circumstances. This volume is intended as a general information resource for professionals practicing in the field of psychotherapy and mental health; it is not a substitute for appropriate training, peer review, and/or clinical supervision. Neither the publisher nor the author(s) can guarantee the complete accuracy, efficacy, or appropriateness of any particular recommendation in every respect. As of press time, the URLs displayed in this book link or refer to existing sites. The publisher and author are not responsible for any content that appears on third-party websites.

For all the people who have weathered tempests of emotions, fierce and wild, and are striving to emerge with kindness and light.

Contents

Acknowledgments

We would like to thank Deborah Malmud for her interest in this combination of ideas bridging narrative therapy with interpersonal neurobiology, mindfulness, and embodiment approaches. We are also grateful for the support of the Norton team: Sarah Johnson, Mariah Eppes, Jamie Vincent, Olivia Guarnieri, and Sara McBride Tuohy, who contributed in so many ways to the fine-tuning and publication of this book.

Marie-Nathalie Beaudoin

I have been extremely fortunate to have developed as a person and professional immersed in the narrative community since the 1990s. There are so many people I could thank: mentors, students, interns, workshop participants, and in particular, the clients who have trusted me with their stories. My thinking has been enriched by countless meaningful interactions—you know who you are, thank you!

This book would not have been possible without the support of my coauthor Gerald Monk, who graciously accepted the idea of embarking on this writing journey. I had been experimenting with new practices for over a decade and was so impressed by Gerald's coauthored landmark paper "Narrative Therapy and the Affective Turn" (Monk & Zamani, 2019) that the idea churned in my mind to invite him to cowrite this book. Knowing Gerald only through his eloquent and engaging writings, I first checked out his reputation with a few trusted colleagues and, interestingly, always got the same response: "Gerald Monk? He's a rrrrrrrreally good person . . . I rrreally mean it!" or "Oh! Gerald is such a gooooooood person, you can't go wrong working with him." I can now attest firsthand that Gerald is very kind, patient, and flexible. He's an encyclopedia of scholarly knowledge. Not only did he actively contribute to the rise of narrative therapy in the 1990s, but he is also open minded to progressive views in our contemporary world. I'm grateful for his heartwarming support of new ideas, his savvy editing and questioning of certain concepts, and his fascinating contributions to the book. As a first-generation narrative therapist involved in these ideas since their conception, his complex knowledge of the practices, coupled with his passion for social justice and culturally respectful approaches, allowed us to include challenging subjects in this book, rarely discussed elsewhere.

I'm grateful to David Epston for generously agreeing to answer my questions on the history of narrative therapy's relationship to emotions. His stories and genuine explanations were eye-opening. I also immensely appreciate his review and skillful editing of several chapters of this book. His vocabulary is so precise and fine-tuned that he added many important nuances to my writing.

I am also thankful for the generous editing of Chapter 5 by Robert Maclennan, who excels at perfecting a text and offers his own rich knowledge on the topic of trauma, and by Esther Beaudoin, who has unparalleled eagle eyes to find typos and redundancies.

Last but not least, I would like to acknowledge the unconditional support of my loving husband, daughter, and son, who graciously accepted seeing me disappear into my office almost every evening for the past nine months to work on this project, and for my husband's cup of tea late in the night, which warmed my heart and body. Paul is always there to fly with me when I have wings, and to help steer my flight back to values, when winds get tough.

Gerald Monk

I want to thank Marie-Nathalie for inviting me to join her vision for this book, which she has nurtured for at least a decade. The writing of this book has been an exciting adventure to take with you, Marie-Nathalie. I had known of you only through your gifted writing over the past 15 years or so, and now our paths have finally connected. What I didn't know earlier and know now is you are an enormously talented clinician, teacher, and supervisor. I truly believe that your writing and your teaching of narrative therapy are bringing a new generation of therapists back to the creative impulse set in motion by Michael White and David Epston over 40 years ago. I have learned a lot about narrative therapy from you over this past year. I have most appreciated your warmth and kindness in our communications as we navigated the challenges of writing the book during the COVID-19 pandemic.

I too want to thank David Epston for his mentorship, guidance, and wonderful inspiration, which dates back to that unforgettable workshop conducted with Michael White at the University of Canterbury, Christchurch, New Zealand, in August of 1984.

I want to thank from the bottom of my heart my beautiful and lovely partner in life, Stacey Sinclair, who has always been so understanding and supportive of my writing, teaching, and clinical work over these past few decades. You are always there for me in supporting my journey both personally and professionally and keeping me on track with navigating the process of life itself!

Introduction:
A Historical Overview

We would like to invite you for a brief moment into the 1980s and 1990s. Imagine the rise of Blockbuster, movies and music videos, an explosion of consumerism, the commercialization of the Rubik's Cube, and the Walkman (ancestor of the iPod). It was also a decade of powerful social movements, in part stirred by the end of the Vietnam War. These included advancements in and backlashes against the feminist movement, protests in Tiananmen Square in China, the destruction of the Berlin Wall, the collapse of the Soviet Union, the Civil Rights Restoration Act, the AIDS crisis, international rallies against nuclear weapons, and pro-environment concerts. In some countries, Indigenous peoples were mobilizing against their government and the societal status quo to seek redress for stolen land and lost language.

During this period of protest for human rights, two wonderful social workers, Michael White and David Epston, met at a conference. They shared many passions, in particular, a desire to depathologize the mental health system of the time and develop respectful, collaborative, and dignifying therapeutic conversations with clients reporting serious burdens. They disliked a dominant professional mindset of the time, which conceived of people seeking counseling as "disordered beings," degrading them instead of restoring their dignity and agency.

Michael and David agreed on an important concept: If people were born into different cultural contexts or life situations, they would not have the same struggles. For example, a teen girl who struggles with anorexia might not develop that problem if she was born into a Polynesian community where large body frames instead of thinness are a sign of high status, strength, and beauty. Michael and David saw both problems and desirable outcomes as intimately associated with the contexts in which people developed. The deficit-based approaches used by many mental health services seemed to create issues or make problems worse for people rather than help them.

Along with their partners, Cheryl White and Ann Epston, who held to a strong feminist approach (Chamberlain, 2012), they were mobilized by issues around power and gender inequities. Contextual factors such as trauma, social isolation, or challenging family dynamics negatively affected by patriarchy were often ignored in the mental health system of the time, which tended to be reductionist and dismissive of many important social influences. On a personal level, Cheryl and Ann witnessed the devastating negative effects of these cultural biases in their own lives. Michael White commented about his childhood that "almost every adult man I knew was abusive. . . . It was a terrible thing" (Duvall & Young, 2009, p. 68). The aftermath of domestic violence in his neighborhood was visible on a regular basis, with women covering their faces and men diminishing the severity of the matter. Michael grew up sensitized to these injustices by an "incredibly loving and caring" mother who gave him a sense that "there has got to be more than this" (Duvall & Young, 2009, p. 68).

David Epston described growing up with the most kind and loving parents he could imagine (Epston, 1998), yet found himself cornered in humanistic trainings where participants were intensely pressured to express anger at their mothers, whether they wanted to or not (David Epston, personal communication, October 15, 2022). The climate of Western psychiatry—blaming people for their problems, failing to address destructive expressions of anger, and using emotions to pathologize vulnerable people or find a pseudoliberation through catharsis—further led Michael and David away from the favored counseling styles of the time. They became increasingly concerned about the harmful effects of theories with no accountability to clients' well-being. Eventually, they both recoiled from mainstream approaches, and this included moving away from using the word "emotion" altogether and discussing the subject of feelings in their trainings and practices. Later, this recoiling was further exacerbated by how emotional expressions were being monopolized and "fetishized" by a highly visible group of humanistic psychologists in New Zealand who were eventually found guilty of abusing and exploiting clients (David Epston, personal communication, October 15, 2022).

Michael and David turned to innovative thinkers in the humanities and social sciences of the 1960s, 1970s, and 1980s. They immersed themselves in the reading of literary theory, poststructural philosophy, and psychology (Bateson, 2000, 2002; J. S. Bruner, 1990, 2009; Derrida, 1972, 1981, 2001; Foucault, 1982, 1990, 2012, 2013), education (Vygotsky, 1987), cultural anthropology (Geertz, 1988, 2008; Myerhoff, 1988), and ethnography (E. M. Bruner, 1984, 1986). Acutely aware that people are multifaceted and that many aspects of experience are invisible to observers, they began offering therapeutic services in an innovative way. They introduced the idea of externalizing problems by acknowledging linguistically that people's problems are not a representation of internal deficiencies. Rather, human problems are a result of interactions between aspects of people's experiences and their social environment. So, if a woman is seeking help for "self-doubt" or "self-hatred," she is not choosing to feel this way, was not born this way, and does not necessarily have something "wrong inside of her." Rather, her experience could be the result of feeling stuck in a relationship harmed by domestic or sexual violence. The narrative therapy founders were concerned with this question: How can we, as therapists, respectfully communicate to people that they are more than a problem, more than a traumatic event, and that they are immensely more than whichever issues are occupying their lives? The best way Michael and David found to be congruent with this idea was to externalize problems (Epston, 2020b; White & Epston, 1990). A further example of externalizing might include, What are "depressed feelings" doing to your life? They found this linguistic shift opened up new therapeutic possibilities instead of being guided by a totalizing and internalized label such as "depressed person." They found that such labels often eclipsed the resiliency and vitality of other dimensions of people's lives. Externalizing increased people's capacity to change problematic patterns and realigned their lives according to their values and preferences. They had uncovered an utterly powerful clinical practice that would spread around the world to community service agencies and therapists' offices alike.

Narrative therapy was born (White & Epston, 1990).

Michael and David's clinical wizardry lay in constructing potent clinical innovations and impactful practices by combining ideas from various disciplines, which brought forth preferred stories of value, hope, possibility, and agency. Michael and David created an entirely new approach where the focus was not on pathologizing an emotion or a behavior, but rather on the development of preferred identities in specific sociocultural environments (Epston, 1993; White, 2007). They would ask clients to state their own objections to the problem's pattern, and their clients would give examples of moments when they behaved according to their preferences, which could then be articulated explicitly and with invigoration. These clinical practices were highly effective and still are. They have improved the lives of thousands of people and been taught by the Dulwich Centre and many well-known narrative practitioners, impossible to list all here (for instance: Duvall & Beres, 2011; Freedman & Combs, 1996; Madsen, 1999; Monk et al., 1996; Zimmerman & Dickerson, 1996).

Fast-forward 40 or 50 years, and the world is different. Social movements have continued to rise and fall. The importance of considering culture and context in therapy, addressing inequity, and protesting problems such as domestic violence is no longer a radical notion held by a few rebels. Social justice movements have reached the ears of many Western doctors and psychiatrists, who have now changed their rhetoric about mental health issues being due solely to internal deficiencies. The invention of the fMRI in the mid-1990s has revolutionized our understanding of what happens in the brain when people are subjected to various experiences and ways of regulating emotions. New understandings of neuroplasticity have confirmed the value of many narrative practices. Emotions are no longer *systematically* pathologized and their expression imposed on people regardless of their context. Positive psychology has dramatically enriched our knowledge of how people can attain well-being and flourish (Fredrickson, 2009). Interpersonal neurobiology (IPNB; Siegel, 1999, 2012, 2023) stands out as acknowledging the powerful impact of the relational environment on shaping people's personal narratives, the many possible ways of being, and that people can embrace life despite challenges and setbacks. Mindfulness, which in the 1980s was considered an exotic Eastern practice, has become acclaimed for its powerful ability to dramatically influence many areas of people's lives, including emotion regulation and people's experience of their identity (Germer, 2014; Kabat-Zinn, 1990, 2005; Kornfield, 1993; Salzberg, 2015; Winston, 2019). Embodiment and somatic therapies are emerging with fascinating observations about the body's role in healing trauma (Levine, 2010; Ogden, 2021a; van der Kolk, 2014). So much has been discovered in the fields of brain science and emotion; yet there are only a few practitioners who have begun to expand upon foundational narrative ideas to spark new innovations (Beaudoin, 2010, 2015; Beaudoin & Duvall, 2017; Beaudoin & Maclennan, 2021; Beaudoin & Zimmerman, 2011; Duffy, 2012; Maclennan, 2019; Monk & Zamani, 2018, 2019; Percy & Paré, 2021a, 2021b; Zimmerman, 2018; Zimmerman & Beaudoin, 2015). A number of narrative therapy practitioners are intrigued by new possibilities but unsure of how to integrate the new knowledges inspired by interpersonal neurobiology, positive psychology, and the emerging fields of affect studies in their practices. Many narrative practitioners want more complex and effective ways to address clients' complaints of being emotionally hijacked by problems, while at the same time respecting narrative therapy's foundational commitment to a contextual and client-centered lens.

As coauthors of this book, we believe that practitioners of narrative therapy can remain consistent with its foundational origins while being open to new ways of working with emotions and personal narratives. Michael White and David Epston were avid readers and selectively "poached" ideas in other domains (Epston, personal communication, 2022). David feels that all ideas have a "shelf life," and he is against orthodoxy, which is in opposition to the very origins of narrative therapy and its spirit of adventure. He invites practitioners to "call back Michael's irreverent, maverick, spirit of adventure. . . . The original meaning of maverick refers to unbranded cattle that have gone astray. Applied to a person, it means 'one who thinks in an unorthodox manner'" (Epston & White, 1992, p. 9; White & Epston, 2020b). He has invited the narrative community to "reimagine narrative therapy" (Epston, 2016; Heath et al., 2022) and go beyond the sentiments in the book *Maps of Narrative Practices* (White, 2007). Michael White himself was interested in the study of memory before he passed (White, 2004, Part 3) and was intrigued by different streams of consciousness, a subject very different from his classical writings. David Epston believes in the prospect of "amalgamating with other paradigms" as long as the ideas translate into respectful practices actually dignifying people in ethical ways, and as evidenced through accounts of such ideas in practice (Epston, personal communication, 2022).

We have been immersed in narrative ideas for 25-plus years and have become compelled to explore new ideas. Reading about IPNB has allowed us to try new paths in therapeutic conversations, and then try to understand the process by which these worked so well in order to replicate these steps with other clients. By selectively using relevant research discoveries and innovative scholarship, we have refined our practices, developed new ones, and assisted a greater variety of people in more effective ways.

This book offers a collection of new clinical material to better address clients' embodied experiences of affect and emotions, which play a fundamental role in every aspect of life and are particularly relevant in therapeutic conversations. Clients usually seek our help to gain relief from emotional experiences that are problematic to them or their loved ones. Being more intentional about integrating considerations of emotions in narrative practices can open up new ways to observe, describe, and work with emotions more intentionally, and tap into their powerful potential to support flourishing identities. By doing so, we can alter therapeutic outcomes, sometimes significantly. While Michael's and David's therapeutic conversations were visibly attuned to people's affective experiences, their practical descriptions of clinical work did not offer clear directions on engaging with affect and emotion directly, because of the sociopolitical context of their time. In general, narrative therapists compassionately attend to affect when it is expressed. However, in the absence of a framework guiding a more focused attention, specific work addressing emotions remains limited.

We are delighted to invite readers into an exploration of the new territory of working with narrative practices and emotions. This book is organized into eight chapters, each with multiple stories of therapeutic practices and transcripts.

Chapter Overviews

Chapter 1. A Biopsychosocial View of Emotions: Rich Therapeutic Possibilities

This chapter offers novel therapeutic practices that show the value of attending to the biopsychosocial dimensions of emotions in narrative work. This fresh approach offers original therapeutic possibilities exemplified by sixteen different affective activity and embodiment markers and associated therapeutic questions for deconstructing and de-storying problems or consolidating flourishing identities.

Chapter 2. Scaffolding Preferred Emotions: A Conversation Map

In this chapter, we describe a step-by-step conversational map to help a client move away from problematic emotional experiences associated with an inability to find employment and help her develop a sustainable preferred identity. This new conversational map can contribute actively to the well-being of self and others, and augment advances in socially just outcomes when relevant.

Chapter 3. Centered, Decentered, and Co-Centered Postures

Many narrative practitioners take a decentered and influential posture in therapeutic conversations. While such a posture provides an important starting place to avoid an expert and all-knowing position with clients, we argue that there is value in embracing what can be called a "co-centered" posture, which fosters connectivity, attunement, and trust. This proposed therapeutic posture considers verbal and nonverbal expressions.

Chapter 4. Neutralizing Intense Problematic Emotions
With Ideas From Interpersonal Neurobiology
A considerable amount of neuroaffective research published in the past two decades has shed light on many ways of helping clients regulate intense emotions, which often hijack preferred ways of being. This chapter sifts through relevant findings and offers readers unique ways of considering ideas from interpersonal neurobiology (IPNB), a field of medicine interested in how people construct personal narratives based on their experiences, relationships, and context of life. An innovative set of practices, which can rapidly neutralize troublesome and unwanted emotions in times of crisis, is described and illustrated by transcripts of conversations with a man crippled by intense sadness.

Chapter 5. Working With Traumatic Experiences:
Bodies, Stories, and Identities
Working with traumatic experiences benefits from a keen understanding of the physiological ramifications encoded with life-threatening memories. In this chapter, we draw clear distinctions between empowering and retraumatizing conversations about distressing life experience, paying special attention to working with states of hypoarousal-disconnection and hyperarousal-distress.

Chapter 6. Working With the Five Primary Senses:
Unexpected Solutions
The current research on the brain and body is a new frontier in mental health. Tapping into embodied aspects of experience provides clients with a completely new method to activate and strengthen preferred ways of being, especially when faced with struggles. This chapter offers many micropractices illustrated by the stories of five clients, with whom using a specific sense was pivotal in their transformative journey.

Chapter 7. The Importance of Collectivist Practices
Mental health healing practices performed in collectivist contexts are embedded in rich and ancient histories. Much of this rigorous knowledge,

handed down over centuries, has been eclipsed or diminished by modernist evidence-based work that is thrust upon diverse communities, sometimes in patronizing ways. The chapter works at building bridges between the delivery of mental health services that have emerged in modernist and postmodernist contexts and collectivist therapeutic practices.

Chapter 8. Harnessing Bodily Resources With Specialized Practices

In this final chapter, we move beyond verbal and nonverbal conversational practices to discuss other unique pathways to overcoming debilitating emotional problems. We expand on the value of combining narrative therapy with mindfulness, breathing exercises, and EMDR. These practices offer additional clinical skills that allow practitioners to work with uniquely intense problems and provide space for emergent neural pathways associated with preferred ways of living.

Limitations

We are drawn to a variety of fields, including neurobiological studies, to broaden the scope of our work, enrich our practices with new ideas, and continue increasing our abilities to support the development of flourishing preferred identities. However, unlike Western medicine and attachment theory, which may fix problems into unchangeable traits, we uphold narrative therapy's unshakable belief in human beings' abilities to overcome hardship and constantly evolve. We share Michael White's and David Epston's deep reverence for complexity, mystery, and trust in people's adaptability. Knowing that each person holds an immense repertoire of ways of being, stories, and memories, this stance fuels our collaborative partnership with clients toward co-constructing preferred identities, even in the face of what may appear to be insurmountable problems on a physiological level. We are aware that some of the material may not fit with classic anti-essentialist and poststructural traditions and are not seeking a consensus. We locate our work in the emerging discursive–affective practice proposed by Margaret Wetherell (2012) and recently recognized by some narrative therapy scholars and practitioners (Cromby, 2012; Duffy, 2012; Monk & Zamani, 2019;

Percy & Paré, 2021a, 2021b; Strong, 2017; Zimmerman, 2018). We find that dialogue across fields allows for a generative engagement of personal experience and is valuable in supporting the emergence of flourishing identities in our therapeutic conversations. We hope your interest will be sparked by one or more of our stories.

NARRATIVE PRACTICES
AND EMOTIONS

CHAPTER 1

A Biopsychosocial View of Emotions: Rich Therapeutic Possibilities

We wish to explore some introductory ideas on the relationship between brain, body, emotion, and narrative. In doing so, we acknowledge the great limitations of these descriptions of human experience but find their contributions to narrative practices and clinical work worthy of consideration. Studying affect and emotion can be helpful, given their significant impact on human experiences and stories of identity.

The distinction between affect and emotion is widely confused and much of the literature uses these terms interchangeably. We use Siegel's (2012, 2020) definition of *affect* as a basic, raw sense of feeling that is precognitive and precedes awareness. It is an important concept when working with the lingering effects of trauma and will therefore be discussed further in that section.

We adhere to the view of *emotions* as biopsychosocial constructions (Barrett, 2017), and this multidimensional understanding opens the door to a wealth of possible clinical practices at each of these three levels. Below we explain the influence of the social, psychological, and physiological dimensions shaping our emotional lives, followed by their implications for clinical practice. The chapter ends with the transcript of a therapeutic conversation with a man struggling with loneliness, which exemplifies a portion of these new ideas.

Emotions as Social Constructions

Emotions are inextricably tied to sociocultural forces. As stated by Lisa Feldman Barrett: Emotions "are not universal but vary from culture to culture . . . you create them" (2017, p. xii). This is in line with the findings of many social science researchers who have studied diverse ethnic communities from around the globe and concluded that we do not interpret, experience, and express emotions in the same way across diverse cultural communities (Crivelli et al., 2016). For example, according to a study by Gendron et al. (2014), many people identifying with the ethnic group Himba in South Africa *interpret* a wide-eyed, mouth-open expression as "paying attention," whereas this same facial expression is interpreted by many Westerners as an expression of "fear."

There are a number of ethnic groups around the world who don't have an internalizing, individualistic bias so characteristic of many communities in the West (Barrett, 2017). Many Indigenous communities do not use emotional words to describe an inner state of being or have words in their language for "self." Rather than see a person as happy, sad, nervous, or belying some internal trait, these individuals view emotions as an action just as eating is considered an action. As an example, a person would be "doing anger" instead of "feeling angry." This way of responding to emotions offers opportunities to engage with ourselves or others without characterological judgment.

The words used in various ethnic communities to convey affective experiences elect which bodily sensations receive meaning, attention, connotation, and action. When no words exist to describe an experience within different ethnic communities, the affective state receives little attention and may be considered inconsequential. For example, if you are Arabic speaking, the word *tarab* is used to describe a musically induced state of ecstasy, and if you speak Dutch, the word *uitwaaien* conveys the revitalizing feeling that comes from walking in the wind. These experiences don't translate well into English and are essentially imperceptible to a person occupying a different linguistic register. Consider the limitations for English-speaking people when learning about the emotions experienced by other linguistic communities in the following phrases (Lomas, 2020, 2021; Robson, 2017):

> *natsukashii* (Japanese): nostalgic longing about the past, with a combination of happiness (for its occurrence) and sadness (for its ending)
>
> *mbuki-mvuki* (Bantu): irresistible impulse to shrug off your clothes while dancing
>
> *gigil* (Tagalog): the intense urge to squeeze someone because you love them
>
> *sukha* (Sanskrit): lasting happiness independent of situational factors
>
> *dadirri* (Australian aboriginal): state of contemplative and reflective listening
>
> *rasmia* (Spanish): eagerness, tenacity, activeness, and gracefulness
>
> *liget* (Ilongot): a state of high voltage that can lead to cutting someone's head off, howling, or making love

Emotions are shaped by the social and linguistic environment in which they emerge, and this typically includes the influence of discourses such as individualism, collectivism, patriarchy, matriarchy, heterosexism, racism, and so on. Children born in any society are quickly enculturated by their communities to learn local vocabulary, meanings, and expressions, which in themselves will shape their experiences, choices, and actions in all areas of life, including emotions. Fernald et al. (2013) findings show that children from privileged communities develop a more expansive vocabulary than children from underprivileged environments, and this becomes apparent at a very young age. A more expansive vocabulary is often helpful for naming embodied feelings and helps to regulate emotion and fine-tune solutions to problems. The linguistic capacity to name and differentiate experience is referred to as "emotional granularity" (Barrett, 2017). Underprivileged children whose only labels for their identity are being "good" or "bad" are often at a disadvantage compared to those who are able to discern nervousness or fear and their preferred self as being bold and outspoken. A granular analysis tends to provide people with richer descriptions and consequently greater resources to overcome problems (Tugade et al., 2004).

In sum, language and culture determine what receives meaning, attention, and expressive options. Since emotions are profoundly shaped by social and linguistic constructions, bodily sensations and experiences are more clearly articulated when high granularity exists.

Emotions as Psychological Constructions

Emotions are constructed based on what members of a community emphasize, notice, and ascribe meaning to. "A person is a person through other persons," as represented by the South African concept of *ubuntu* and popularized by Archbishop Desmond Tutu (His Holiness the 13th Dalai Lama et al., 2016, p. 60). Our stories and experiences are shaped by others. The influence of people in our psychological construction of meaning is visible in the stories and scripts that are readily available for making sense of experience and are passed down from one generation to the next, as well as being repeated in mainstream media. As an example, in the United States, it is widely assumed that if one works hard, one will be successful. This cultural story is repeated in movies, magazines, and schools. People who work very hard and remain unsuccessful because they belong to a marginalized group may feel hopeless and interpret their failure as a personal deficit.

Just as stories are created in the wider societal context, stories can also be constructed based on personal and familial experiences. For example, a woman once shared that she couldn't understand why her dog was always trying to "separate her" from her husband when they were standing and giving each other a hug. She was regarding her dog's joyful joining in the exchange of affection from the lens of her personal childhood story where she felt her little brother was always "interfering" with her mother's expressions of affection for her. As a result, she was perturbed, and scolded her dog when the animal, being a gregarious creature, wanted to participate in the affectionate exchange. The stories available in one's life can skew interpretations and lead to actions that unnecessarily create emotional problems.

Interpersonal neurobiologists, mindfulness researchers, anthropologists, psychologists, and many philosophers have proposed that creating stories seems to be a central way in which humans understand the world (J. S. Bruner, 1990; Gergen, 2015a, 2015b; Myerhoff & Metzger, 1992; Siegel, 2012; Wallace, 2007). As stated by Daniel Siegel (2012, p. 84): We store "and then recall experienced events in story form." Confronted with free time, people's minds wander as they construct endless stories and attempt to either understand past experiences or predict future events. Often dubbed the *default network* of the brain, the "chatting mind" seems to narrate everything, and its activity even increases when people are asked to relax in fMRi studies (Christoff et al., 2009). The default network stands in contrast to the *experiential network*, which is a unique pattern of activation cultivated by long-time mindfulness meditators and is associated with a reduction of firing in the language and emotion centers of the brain (Hölzel et al., 2011; Lutz et al., 2016; Siegel, 2007). The default network and experiential network are inversely correlated. One cannot sustain mental engagement in thinking (default network) and not thinking (experiential network) at the same time. Just as a child would never learn how to read unless taught to do so, the *experiential* network will likely remain an undeveloped potential in most people unless they receive mindfulness training. It is the diligent experiential practice of this skill that ultimately allows people to become capable of pausing involuntary thinking and narrating. This will be further discussed in other chapters of this book.

We can work with problematic stories either by reducing their influence through mindfulness meditation, or through narrative practices, which do not seek disengagement from mental activity but instead facilitate a different relationship to thoughts, meanings, possibilities, and sense of identity.

In sum, emotions are associated with a psychological meaning-making process that leads to noticing and linking selected life events in narratives. These stories can be understood as either problem saturated or preferred and can contribute to stifling or supporting certain emotional experiences. Problem stories and their associated emotions can be addressed by mindfulness meditation and, differently, by narrative practices.

Emotions as Biological Constructions

The fact that emotions are tied to embodied sensations has often been neglected in many styles of traditional therapeutic conversations. Have you ever experienced an emotion that didn't involve your body? Emotions involve a bidirectional relationship with the body. An experience such as anger might elevate one's heart rate, which in turn will amplify the interpretation that there are reasons to be angry. Antonio Damasio, in his well-known book *Descartes' Error* (1994), described how bodily sensations can often (if not always) come first, challenging traditional understandings in psychotherapy about the primacy of cognition. For example, interesting research on the gut brain (neurogastroenterology) revealed that the gut is influencing the brain more than the other way around. This is because sensory information from the outside world goes unfiltered to the gut, while information directly sent to the brain tends to be interpreted by the filters of experience before reaching conscious awareness (Hadhazy, 2010).

Many narrative practitioners are accustomed to asking questions such as, "When anxiety gets you to be preoccupied, where do you feel it in your body?" This assumes the mental activity comes first. Rarely do we examine the fact that the body can also be the first manifestation of an affective issue, followed by subsequent interpretation and labeling.

Understanding the significance of bodily reactions might encourage us to ask a different question, such as, "What was the first sign in your body before you wondered if this was a depression relapse?" Giving attention first to our clients' sensations can be more effective in many problematic experiences, especially when the embodied emotional landscape is salient, as in the example at the end of this chapter. A strange, embodied sensation with no name and no understanding is destabilizing and people are often motivated to interpret their physiology with their most available stories to escape from the distressing feelings that accompany such uncertainty.

Many areas of the body can be mobilized during the experience of a strong emotion, ranging from the general body (face, throat, limbs, etc.) to visceral organs (gut, heart, etc.) to senses (hearing, touch, sight, etc.), all of which have important ramifications, as will be discussed later. The body plays a significant part in the production of emotions, and choosing to address this embodied dimension can make a difference between a successful and an unhelpful therapeutic outcome. For example, there are many situations where clients live with intense problematic emotions but rely unsuccessfully on rationalizations to sustain their preferred accounts. They might say, "I know rationally that I shouldn't be with him because of the abuse, but I can't help it and still feel love and attraction for him." Since emotions can be enormously influential in shaping behaviors, intense troublesome emotional reactions can overshadow a preferred story that is built upon a purely cognitive foundation. When narrative practitioners co-construct a story that is disembodied from the emotional landscape of the client's world, it doesn't take much for that newly emerging preferred story to be bowled over by a habitual problematic and intense emotion. This leaves our clients in a very vulnerable position. As discussed elsewhere (Beaudoin, 2010; Beaudoin & Zimmerman, 2011; Zimmerman, 2018), the development of the preferred story benefits from being inextricably woven into an affective landscape, which is a buttress against the triggering of the older problematic emotion.

Sixteen descriptors, organized into a landscape of affective physiology and a landscape of affective embodiment, can be used to introduce narrative questions that explore and highlight clients' valuable emotional resources (Beaudoin, 2020). Questions illustrating the use of each of these markers are listed in Appendix 1 and illustrated in the case example at the end of this chapter.

Landscape of Affective Physiology

For practitioners, it can be helpful to think about how emotional experiences in the brain and body can be therapeutically addressed by exploring different levels of activation, such as

- speed of onset: time taken to attain a recognizable peak of intensity;
- intensity: level of affective arousal in the brain and body;
- frequency: number of occurrences of an affective event during a certain period of time;

- duration: length of time activation occurs in the brain and body;
- recovery time: length of time taken to reduce the problematic emotion back to a neutral or functional state;
- range: the recognition of subtle variations in different emotions;
- valence: quality of activation that in neuroaffective research is typically labeled as positive or negative (see discussion below); and
- action potential: intensity of the motivation to seek or avoid something.

These concepts are only briefly described here but will be discussed further and their use exemplified throughout the remainder of the book.

The idea that emotions would be positive or negative may seem simplifying, polarizing, and narrowing of the richness of human experience. However, a large body of research has demonstrated that different areas of the brain become activated during the generally positive versus generally negative experiences (Vytal & Hamann, 2010). We will occasionally use this positive/negative language with the understanding that words imperfectly describe experience and, as usual, limit precise understandings. We would have preferred that patterns of activation be labeled as *A* and *B* rather than being embedded in connotations associated with positive and negative valence. A so-called negative emotion, such as anger, can be helpful and have positive effects, depending on the context. Still, developing knowledge of how these physiological dimensions affect a person's body is an important asset, as it

- widens possibilities of understanding problems and moving toward preferred experiences;
- provides a valuable vocabulary for expanding and deepening therapeutic conversations;
- helps therapists target interventions addressing specific aspects of the problem that may have been otherwise unnoticed; and
- fosters agency and hopefulness by measuring progress in smaller observable chunks. For instance, a parent may complain that a child's tantrum problem is not being addressed as fast as they would like. When asked if there might be a difference on the level of intensity,

duration, or frequency, they might suddenly realize that the problem seems to occur as frequently but as an afterthought, is less intense, and abates more quickly.

Again, additional questions using this physiological landscape when working with problem issues and preferred self-identity narratives are described in Appendix 1.

Landscape of Affective Embodiment

Affective experiences can be expressed in many ways and therapists are accustomed to paying attention to both verbal elements (content, tone, volume, speed of speech, coherence, pitch) and nonverbal elements (facial expression, posture, movement, etc.). However, many more interesting and helpful categories exist (Beaudoin, 2020). Affective embodiment also includes two types of information (Craig, 2002): *exteroception*—attention to information coming from the external world through our senses; and *interoception*—attention to information about our inner world, such as hunger, fatigue, and heart rate (Critchley & Garfinkel, 2017). Interoceptive awareness in particular has been found to be significantly associated with one's ability to organize the different elements of experience (body, thoughts, and feelings) into a coherent sense of self (Craig, 2015). As an example, a person might recognize that being hungry contributes to feeling impatient, and refrain from blaming a friend or developing a personal story of being socially inadequate.

Below is a list of the main categories of embodied experiences reported in the literature (Fosha, 2009; Griffith & Griffith, 1994; Kabat-Zinn, 2003a; Levine, 2010; Porges, 2017; van der Kolk, 2014), which can be helpful to explore in therapeutic conversations:

- kinesthetics, such as muscle movements or tightness in the face, jaw, throat, limbs, and hands
- visceral organ activation in the chest or abdomen, such as heart, stomach, and gut
- sensory dominance, such as sight, hearing, taste, olfaction, touch

- spatial awareness, such as place, posture, movement, relative size of self
- relational attunement, such as that arising from co-regulation with another person or sense of synchronicity
- aesthetic sense arising from felt metaphors and meaning, such as light, weight, images, color, density
- time, as in the subjective experience of passing time (slow, stopped, or accelerating)
- presence, such as a person's inward versus outward focus

Developing embodied literacy for both problems and preferred experiences can contribute significantly to therapeutic progress. People can be encouraged to notice, for example, that when they are driving too fast, their belly and jaw might subtly tighten, their heart rate increases, and the likelihood of a panic attack is greater.

There is compelling research evidence for a link between people's interoceptive awareness and emotion regulation (Price & Hooven, 2018). As discussed earlier with linguistic granularity, people who are better able to detect their physiological reactions to events tend to identify affective cues earlier and are generally afforded the option to regulate their emotional experiences more effectively. In many situations of life, fraught with intense emotions and rapidly shifting relational interactions, logical thought and good intentions alone are sometimes insufficient to make preferred decisions. Complexity, uncertainty, speed of reaction, and lack of information can hinder the possibility of deliberating on preferred choices before one is required to respond to a situation. In such contexts, important decisions are strongly influenced by automatic, affective, embodied, and intuitive impulses (Kahneman, 2003) along with well-developed, intricate, embodied preferred stories.

In sum, emotions are physiologically produced in the body with different areas and organs forming networks of activation. Since patterns of affective activity and embodiment are intrinsically tied to problem stories and associated emotions, it is important to match embodied experiences when highlighting preferred narratives and identities.

Biopsychosocial Implications for Therapeutic Conversations

Since emotional states are influenced by biopsychosocial interpretations, they can be deconstructed and reevaluated during therapeutic engagement. Finding alternative explanations for experiences can shift clients' understanding of emotions away from negative identity conclusions about themselves or others and make visible the combined influence of these three factors (social contact, psychological stories, bodily experiences). This is exemplified in the clinical implications below.

Context to Emotions

Social context has a powerful role in shaping which emotions are possible, normative, and expressed. Clinically, we can reveal the influence of contexts that contribute to problematic emotional experiences in a way that frees people to feel or act differently and define who they prefer to be. This may involve shedding light on macro (cultural) and/or micro (local) contextual factors. For example, young people in high school wishing to come out as being LGBTQ often struggle with self-hate because they feel they do not fit into the heteronormative society. The problem with self-hate can be examined not as something being wrong with them but rather as resulting from the narrow specifications arising from the dominant heterosexist culture. Once this macrocontextual factor is exposed and named, individuals' emotional experience of self-hate can abate, actions to address social inequities can be taken, and connections to alternative communities developed. Foundational practices of deconstructing the taken-for-granted heterosexist dominance, externalizing the problem, and inviting clients to examine the meaning ascribed to their experience allow preferred identities to emerge. This foundational practice is illustrated in the following questions:

> "How do you understand that most teens who wish to come out have a moment of feeling some self-hate, or fear? Would that be because of the environment in which we live, rather than because of something being wrong in each of these people?"

"What difference does it make if the problem is about the world
outside, rather than inside of you?"

"Does self-hate make feeling different more salient than feeling
similar?"

Rather than pathologizing and confirming something wrong with youth,
this externalizing conversation can help clients become much clearer about
the cultural nature of the problem and this, in turn, can alter their emotional experience.

The role of contextual influence in emotions can also be exposed on a
smaller scale, in families or communities (microlevel). For instance, Elizabeth, a 20-year-old college student, had been hospitalized numerous times
for suicidality. While being heavily influenced by suicidal ideation, she also
contradicted these suicidal thoughts by expressing a strong wish to be alive.
The problem had started her first month as a freshman after reading a news
article about college students who struggled with their course load and committed suicide. She wondered, *"Could I do something like that if I become
overwhelmed?"* Over time, this client, who had previously enjoyed a quiet
life with her parents and two younger siblings in a rural area of Canada, had
increasingly become consumed by worry and surveilled her own mood as
she met intense academic pressure. Within a few months, she found herself
creating all sorts of scenes in her mind about how she might lose control
of herself and commit suicide. Ironically, it was this young woman's intense
desire to live that fueled the intensity of the worries. When she sought
help at the college counseling center, the issue was taken very seriously by
psychologists, leading to several counterproductive hospitalizations, where
she was further exposed to young people actively attempting suicide. These
hospitalizations massively amplified the worries, and since she was given
psychological labels such as obsessive compulsive disorder (OCD) and gener-
alized anxiety disorder (GAD), she became increasingly distrustful of herself,
and made demands on her friends to never leave her alone.

As her life became progressively intolerable, she decided to seek a
therapist unaffiliated with her college to address what she called her "mental disorder." After hearing her story, Marie-Nathalie examined where

the worries originated and inquired whether her mind would have independently invented this option had it not been generated by the newspaper. Elizabeth exclaimed that she probably would have never thought of that, since she had generally been an optimistic person all her life prior to reading the news article. The separation of what came from the context versus from her own mind was reassuring to Elizabeth, and helped richly describe the history of her preferred self. The source of the problem was now located in the microcontext of her life rather than in her own identity. We then further externalized "worrying" and "intrusive thoughts," mapped their effects, and examined biological contributions to the problematic emotions. In particular, intense emotional reactions were discussed and explained as acting like superglue in the brain, strengthening thoughts on a neural level. This was very interesting for Elizabeth and opened new vistas of understanding. Namely, the chronic thoughts could become physiological manifestations, without personal meaning, and therefore be "de-storied" from her identity.

This new conceptualization of the worries—as originating from a context outside of her and being inadvertently reinforced as a biological habit of the mind—created the metaphor of worries as a form of spam. With regular observations, it became clear that the spam was filling her mind with unwanted and fallacious material. She became able to develop a strategy of "not opening the spam" and, importantly, not giving it any emotional importance. Awareness and understanding of her body allowed her to more easily ignore the mental spam. Since, neurally, "attention gives power to the object of its gaze" (Beaudoin & Maki, 2020, p. 76), starving the worries of attentional and emotional fuel slowly contributed to these unhelpful thoughts fading away. Her values, preferences, and reasons to live were then given meaningful attention and, importantly, strengthened with preferred emotions. Her enthusiastic and lively preferred self became free to shine brightly with her peers again, and she resumed investing her free time in sports, nature adventures, and playing her violin. Helping people recognize the powerful interactions between problematic cultural messages and the biological encoding of repeated unwanted thoughts is crucial in our media-saturated world. At its worst, this problem can manifest itself in acts of violence, as revealed by the 15-year-old who perpetrated the December 2021 Michigan high school shooting after writing the note: "The thoughts won't stop. Help me" (Healy, 2021).

Stories to Emotions

Dominant stories about our emotions easily contribute to problem-supporting interpretations of life experiences. For instance, people who struggle with panic attacks can easily slip into misinterpreting a rising heart rate associated with an array of experiences, such as excitement, quick movement, a hot shower, or an action movie, as anxiety creeping up on them. Over time, this problem story becomes imposed on any experience of physiological activation and limits the emotional range of a person, as everything progressively becomes labeled "anxiety." Helping clients embrace and normalize a variety of emotions and better discern a complex array of bodily sensations is important to address in a therapeutic conversation. As an example, a middle-aged man had developed a struggle with panic attacks over the summer. A couple of months later, he went on his first ski trip of the winter season to Lake Tahoe, in California, which offers downhill skiing on slopes between 6,000 and 10,000 feet in elevation. While sitting on the chairlift, he was devastated to experience what he called an "anxiety spike." He felt all the signs of anxiety were building up and for the first time in his life, instead of admiring the mountain scenery, he started taking notice of how high the chairlifts were and all the reasons to be nervous when dangling from a metal wire 20 to 40 feet above the ground. He worried he was going to have a panic attack. He was troubled that this problem was now infiltrating his favorite sport and that nervousness might prevent him from enjoying his special weekend. The anxiety bias got him to interpret the normal increase in heart rate associated with altitude as a sign of an imminent panic attack, effectively disconnecting him from the precious enjoyment of his passion and instead causing him to look at his surroundings as a threat rather than a peaceful landscape. Luckily, he had learned a few embodied practices in therapy that helped him keep a lid on the escalation, and upon his return, therapeutic conversations could address the misinterpretation he was previously plagued by. Had Marie-Nathalie not been aware of the sweeping tendency of anxiety to become a default interpretation of any increase in heart rate, the session would have discussed questions such as: *"What did the anxiety get you to focus on?"* or *"How do you understand that anxiety got to you at that moment?"* or *"What effects did anxiety have on you in the chairlift?"* A problem story could easily have been created about him having never noticed before how high the chairlift was and believing anxiety was more crippling than he had initially thought. This kind of thinking would have been deeply discouraging. Such analysis could have taken up the whole session, inadvertently strengthening the neural network for anxiety and broadening its constructed sphere of influence. Instead, the embodied experience was delinked from the problematic interpretation, and the process of granularization increased. Helpful questions to foster the discernment included: *"If we were to put aside the label of anxiety for a moment and purely observe what was happening in your body, what were you specifically noticing?"* *"I wonder if something else, like altitude, could also have contributed to the increased heart rate?"* The client exclaimed joyfully, *"That's so true! I hadn't thought of understanding it that way! That means I can keep on skiing and don't have to give that up because of anxiety!"*

Fostering discernment and questioning the belief that physiological activation automatically means the problem is present, are important practices with all people struggling with anxiety, and this delinking may need to be revisited many times. For example, with the same client in a later interpretive situation where he was concerned about another wave of so-called anxiety, Marie-Nathalie asked, *"When you were about to reconnect with your girlfriend after the trip, is it possible that it was excitement accelerating your heart rather than anxiety?"* He answered, *"Oh, yes, that is probably it! I keep on forgetting how anxiety makes me interpret those sensations in a skewed way."*

Dominant interpretative stories contribute to creating emotions, and emotions in turn contribute to supporting these problem stories. Such patterns form self-reinforcing loops, which are important to address in therapeutic conversations to help clients reclaim their emotional range. With a little knowledge of the physiological domain, we can empower clients to examine their meaning-making process and more readily free their preferred self from the grip of problem stories involving emotions.

Body to Emotions

The body can sometimes have physiological reactions that are not induced by problems or cultural stories. Such a realization can liberate a client from self-deprecating personalized meanings. This would be evident with a client who has endured an assault and whose body froze out of fear rather than fighting back, which would have been their preference. Helping clients understand on a physiological level why their bodies may have responded to a situation in a particular way can de-story this event from their identity, freeing them from a problem interpretation and painful emotions.

In general, having a variety of descriptors and available meanings to make sense of embodied experiences makes it possible to create completely new perspectives and highlight a client's progress across multiple dimensions, such as intensity, frequency, duration, and range. The transcribed conversation below provides examples of the application of some of these concepts.

Clinical Example of Narrative Work Using a Biopsychosocial Understanding

Ken, a middle-aged European man from an underprivileged industrial area, sought therapy for loneliness. The past year had been spent in a rocky relationship with a woman, Cassandra, who took much of his free time outside of his online job, until she left him for his best friend, John. Ken was a kind, caring, generous, gentle soul and he had appreciated both Cassandra's and John's company in an otherwise quiet life, especially during the COVID-19 pandemic. He became very isolated. He had few activities aside from fishing, bird-watching, and online video gaming.

Loneliness was conceptualized as emerging from cultural, psychological (story), and biological influences. From a *social context* angle, U.S. dominant culture tends to portray a long-term heterosexual relationship as associated with happiness. When a long-term relationship ends, people hurt by the separation can feel they are missing out and fear being labeled a misfit even though the divorce rates in the United States tend to be high. From a *psychological-storying* angle, loneliness for Ken was fed by a story of himself as being "clumsy relationally," a consequence of middle and high school bullying. From a *biological* angle, the physiological responses arising from his initial story of himself as somehow inadequate and "less than" led to tightening sensations in his chest and throat.

Much of the initial clinical work focused on extricating him emotionally from the relationship with Cassandra, which he felt had been exploitative, explosive, and a constant roller coaster. Cassandra would have episodes of rage involving breaking objects or threatening self-harm if he wasn't giving her the level of intense attention she demanded. She regularly claimed to have had a car accident, or to have an unknown life-threatening medical illness, which required a hospitalization. Following these statements, she would disappear from his life for sometimes a week, leaving Ken to worry about her. When she left him, Ken was depressed but also exhausted and mentally clear that it was probably better for his sanity to not be in this relationship, especially since he now had evidence that she had been lying to him.

Marie-Nathalie externalized the loneliness and proceeded to rebuild Ken's sense of integrity, preferred identity, and relationships with people who respected him. By the end of the therapeutic journey, Ken had reconnected with important values shared with his deceased parents, and even joined a cycling club, an activity he used to enjoy as a young person.

About six months later, Ken urgently wanted to talk about a situation that concerned him deeply. While online, he had unexpectedly come across a message sharing that Cassandra was about to be hospitalized for one week because of a life-threatening condition. His first reaction had been, "*Oh! No! She's in trouble*," and he had a wave of compassion and concern for her health, wondering how he could help. He had then abruptly stopped this impulse, frustrated at himself for believing this story when he knew she was probably lying again. Ken had spent the next few hours feeling foolish, mad at himself, and defeated in his progress. He struggled to make sense of this old reaction coming back.

The conversation with Marie-Nathalie shifted the focus from scrutinizing himself, and the self-deprecating meaning ascribed to his reaction, to an understanding that was simply biological and unrelated to his identity or progress.

Marie-Nathalie: *What did it mean to you that you had that reaction?*

Ken: *That's what I've been trying to figure out. I can only think that it means I'm still hooked. (Angrily) What's wrong with me? I thought I was past that. It's been months since we're not together, and I know she lies. This relationship caused me so much harm. Why is that attachment fucking with me all over again? It's so frustrating.*

With foundational narrative therapy, I might have externalized the frustration, mapped its effects, asked whether this event could be interpreted differently, and separated this reaction from his value as a person.

Paying attention to Ken's physiology opened another valuable therapeutic path, which I chose to take. I hypothesized that Ken's reaction was just a reactivation of an old neural network that had been strongly encoded in the brain because of its associated intense emotions. Such understanding implied that his caring reaction, which he angrily interpreted as a relapse and something being wrong with him, might not have any meaning other than a biological one. To him, the event represented a setback because the thoughts, feelings, and impulse to act were the same as during the relationship. I assumed the setback was mostly due to the ingrained biological encoding of this reaction, and that the progress might still be visible if we examined his response using affective activity markers such as intensity, frequency, duration, and recovery time. Conceptualizing the problem in this way and highlighting biological understandings might reduce his emotional upset, so I invited him in the following conversation to *de-story* the meaning of this event from his identity.

Marie-Nathalie: *Tell me more about that moment, when you read that she was going to the hospital and had a reaction. How intense was it on a scale of 1 to 10?*

Ken: *It was really intense, like a 7 out of 10, as if I had been suddenly kicked in the chest. Then I told myself, "What the fuck was that?"*

Marie-Nathalie: *It was a 7 out of 10 intensity, and it sounds like it surprised you. How long did it last?*

Ken: *Only 30 seconds, because then I told myself, "Wait, this is*

> Cassandra, it's probably not true and not something I should be concerned about!"

Marie-Nathalie: *So the reaction was short-lived, and telling yourself "It's Cassandra and probably not true" and "I should probably not concern myself with this" helped. I wonder if it would have taken 30 seconds three months ago?*

Ken: *Heck no! I would have assumed it was true for a while and been stuck worrying for the rest of the day, or maybe a week. I might even have contacted a few people to check on her, or worse, contacted her myself to offer help and maybe have been sucked right back in again. Phew, I'm glad I didn't do that!*

The contrast introduced with intensity and duration questions, along with commenting on what he avoided, elicited joy and a reacknowledgment of his progress.

> **Marie-Nathalie:** *So there is progress on how quickly you recovered from that information after the unexpected surprise? (Yep.) And telling yourself a few reality checks helped. Did you do anything else?*
>
> **Ken:** *Yeah, I paced for hours because I was so mad at myself. Why did I have that first reaction? Will I always have it?*
>
> **Marie-Nathalie:** *Well, I wonder if that reaction could be seen as an old emotional habit, like a neural network in your brain that was encoded strongly and hasn't completely faded away. How many times have you lived this scenario with Cassandra?*
>
> **Ken:** *Oh! A lot! At least 15 times!*
>
> **Marie-Nathalie:** *So at least 15 times. What were the specific emotions you experienced during those events?*
>
> **Ken:** *It was awful. I would go from worrying to sadness, hurt, fear of never talking to her again, feeling empathy for her pain, and wanting to help but I couldn't. There was nothing I could do. I felt so helpless.*
>
> **Marie-Nathalie:** *So, you endured a lot of those intense emotions, which can act as glue in people's memory. For how long did you typically endure these emotional states?*

Ken: *Usually at least 12 hours, and much longer when she disconnected for several days.*

Marie-Nathalie: *So that means you spent a minimum of 15 × 12 = 180 hours in that state of intense empathy, worry, and wanting to do something to help?*

Ken: *Yeah, probably a lot more, probably several hundred, now that I think of it.*

Marie-Nathalie: *Would it make sense, then, that this reaction would be strongly programmed in your brain and body?*

Ken: *I guess. I hadn't thought about it that way.*

Ken now understood the problem reaction he experienced as located in his brain and body, and no longer a representation of his progress or identity. As I proceeded with therapy, I continued to scaffold this view by bringing forth a contextual perspective of what had taken place in his relationship with Cassandra.

Marie-Nathalie: *I also wonder if you were busy with something when you saw the information and had the reaction?*

Ken: *Yeah, I was scrolling Twitter and was in a stream chat at the same time.*

Marie-Nathalie: *So, there was a context where you were busy with two things, and all of a sudden that information appeared unexpectedly. Is it possible that your brain went on automatic pilot, just repeating what it did so many times before?*

Ken: *Yeah, I guess it makes sense, maybe I was just conditioned to have that reaction, and I was so startled by the unexpected news. I had been just relaxing and scrolling.*

Ken was now seeing it as solely a "conditioned" reaction that happened in a specific context and was no longer about what was wrong with him. Our conversation continued in this vein, now shifting to use the word "conditioned," which was experience-near and a fit with his unique sociocultural background. Understanding his reaction as a physiological construction reduced the self-deprecating problem story he had about himself. This real-ization alone was not enough, however. Given that intense emotions act as glue in the brain, every moment of frustration at himself when thinking about Cassandra reinforced the very neural pathways (reaction) he was try-ing to erase. The emotional reaction when he thought of Cassandra needed to be replaced by something else that would be more supportive of his pre-ferred self.

> **Marie-Nathalie:** *Since you were "conditioned" to have that reaction, and it's not your fault, what could replace the frustration afterward if it ever happened again? Is there something you might tell yourself, or a gesture you might do?*

Asking for a movement of the body that could support the preferred reaction tapped into kinesthetic memory and thickened the reauthoring process.

> **Ken:** *Probably something like, "Eh (waving his hand backward), it just hap-pened; it sucks but it's not a problem."*
>
> **Marie-Nathalie (repeating the sound and gesture):** *So,"Eh (waving her hand backward), it just happened; it sucks but it's not a problem." What feeling might go with that? What could we call that?*
>
> **Ken:** *Detachment.*

Identifying detachment as a preferred response was a valuable step; however, it was generated intellectually and was not currently connected to lived experience. A few more questions were needed to create an embodied link to a way of being that felt familiar and doable and could easily be replicated. This would increase the likelihood that he could actually use this strategy.

> **Marie-Nathalie:** *So, detachment; have you experienced that elsewhere in your life?*
>
> **Ken:** *Yeah, watching the news, I get tired of politicians and everything that happens.*
>
> **Marie-Nathalie:** *Okay, so detachment toward the information about Cas-*

> *sandra and your conditioned reaction to it, like when watching the*
> *news. Does the detachment then leave more room to acknowledge your*
> *progress and be patient with your efforts?*
>
> **Ken**: *Yeah, it's much easier if I see it that way.*

We now had a valuable alternative state of detachment, which was connected to lived experience and therefore much easier to replicate given
the memory of its embodied sensation. However, the action potential of
"detachment" was low in terms of physiological activation. Given that the
initial problem reaction was associated with compassion and frustration,
which both have strong affective action potentials of "going toward" people
and a momentum to do something, I explored the possibility of using that
physiological energy to fuel a more intense preferred affect and associated
identity.

> **Marie-Nathalie**: *So, the detachment makes it easier. I wonder, too, if there's*
> *a possibility of acknowledging how difficult the situation was for you*
> *when you were in that relationship a year ago, and maybe even flipping*
> *the compassion you had for her toward yourself?*
>
> **Ken (smiling and thinking)**: *Hmmm! That's a good idea! After all, having*
> *a moment of compassion is not bad. I can turn it toward a person who*
> *deserves it and has really struggled, someone who could use it these*
> *days . . . like me!*

As the conversation came to an end shortly after, Marie-Nathalie invited
Ken to describe the embodied sensations of compassion, which he observed
as coming from his chest being warm, and his throat *"feeling wide open and*
clear." We summarized the session and when Ken was asked what he was
taking away, he said:

> **Ken**: *I like turning compassion toward myself and not feeling helpless again.*
> *Also, I want to remember not to worry if something old jumps out, it's*
> *just a conditioning that will fade away eventually.*

This transcript illustrated many practices discussed so far: how to use contextual, storied, and physiological understandings, as well as work with action potential, intensity, duration, frequency, recovery time, and kinesthesis. This process exemplified how to shift the meaning of an event from being related to a problem story of identity to a simple biological reaction, a process that could be called "de-storying." Two weeks later, the follow-up conversation confirmed how helpful this conversation had been for Ken. He had engaged in what he called "self-care choices he had never done before," such as putting on music and allowing himself to dance and sing alone in his apartment "without feeling weird."

Conclusion

Emotions are constructed based on cultural contexts, psychological storying, and embodied experiences, all of which provide abundant territories for clinical work. The malleable nature of emotions and the remarkable complexity of life imply that a variety of affective solutions are always possible. People's lives are so rich and multidimensional that drawing attention to experiences easily remembered, through physiological and embodied descriptions, can greatly enhance access to preferred experiences of identity.

CHAPTER 2

Scaffolding Preferred Emotions: A Conversation Map

Most people seek help when their emotional suffering is reaching a threshold that can no longer be sustained, or when their life is not progressing in the direction they hoped for. Practices that thoughtfully address emotional aspects of experience can facilitate the therapeutic journey, especially when people are interpreting their struggles as representing something being wrong with their identity. Using a narrative, IPNB, and mindfulness framework, we understand that many stories of identity are possible. People make sense of what happens in their lives by linking specific events through time, explaining them with culturally available interpretations, and making assumptions about themselves and others. In this selective process, many events are forgotten or perceived as meaningless, when they could offer a completely different insight into people's values and skills. A person can tell the story of being shy in one context, outgoing in another, and resourceful during a crisis.

Typically, only a handful of identity stories are more salient, receive attention, and thus become a strong source of meaning making. The map described in this chapter demonstrates a series of therapeutic practices to address problematic emotions and support the emergence of flourishing identities. While the map is presented in a numbered sequence, readers are encouraged to attend to the client's responses to therapeutic questions instead of the mapping order. Each section of the map is described theoretically first, and then illustrated by clinical work with Bianca, a 24-year-old woman.

> Bianca, who identifies herself as Latinx, sought help for a depression that had been slowly building for a few years. Over the past 14 months, these depressive feelings had significantly intensified because of a work environment she increasingly hated. She had submitted applications to an average of five jobs per week, and participated in countless interviews, only to get rejection after rejection. The dread of going to work every day and feeling stuck in this job led her to cry regularly and feel overwhelmed. She was starting to have "meltdowns" at work and was losing sight of herself, which prompted her to seek therapy.

1. Elicit Preferred Emotional Experience

Many practitioners see the introductory portion of the first meeting as a moment for small talk to build rapport. While this is clearly essential, it is possible to accomplish a lot more by not only developing a safe relationship but also creating a foundation for clients' experiences of competency. Doing so involves being intrigued by clients' skills, talents, passions, hopes, dreams, satisfying relationships, and what David Epston calls the "wonderfulness" of a person (Marsten et al., 2016). This is an extraordinary opportunity to bring forth rewarding emotions and gain an understanding of the preferred versions of this person. Spending time exploring a person's preferred self and their successes at managing a problem provides the foundation for single-session therapies and affects physiology in measurable ways, as shown by a reduction of salivary cortisol measured before and after (Young et al., 2017). Questions in this segment might include: "What's going well in your life?" "What do you like to do in your spare time after work?" "What activity makes you feel good?" "If you had extra free time in your week, what would be enjoyable?" "Are there people you particularly appreciate spending time with?"

In this initial greeting, paying attention to a few dimensions of emotional expressions described in Chapter 1, particularly covering intensity, range, frequency, and duration, can provide valuable information. Sometimes rich possibilities of joy coexist alongside struggles, but the problem interferes with clients' abilities to fully experience those preferred aspects of their lives. This was the case with Bianca.

> At our first telehealth meeting, Bianca presented as a charming young woman and it was easy to engage with her. When asked what was going well in her life, she described a mutually loving relationship with a longtime partner with whom she shared common interests such as caring for bonsai trees and orchids. Bianca expressed her appreciation for these aspects of her life with kindness, liveliness, and warmth. She generally kept good relationships with her family and had many cherished friends. Her mother and closest friends were all concerned about her well-being and the loss of her usual joyful, spontaneous ways of being. In these first interactions, it was possible to gain a glimpse into the kind of person she had been and could be, including knowing her more on an emotional level. Clearly, she could enjoy various positive emotions, but the frequency and duration of those experiences were hampered by the current struggles.

2. Address Problem-Related Emotions

Once clients feel safe and comfortable, the conversation can move to discussing concerns. A few important factors benefit from consideration when exploring clients' emotional struggles.

A. Externalizing Conversations

Foundational narrative therapy typically aims for what has been coined an "experience-near" externalization of the problem or its meaning, using the client's language to make sure it is evocative and an accurate representation of the issue. It can be argued that externalizing a distressing emotion often accomplishes this task and offers the benefit of easily including embodied dimensions of problems. However, there is an art to choosing an externalization. One that is too intense, such as "self-despise," loses the opportunity to capture the very first signs of a problem episode. An externalization that captures the early phase of a shift toward a problem episode, such as a not-good-enough-feeling (NGEF), can broaden the scope of our work to include the moment when activation is less intense and therefore easier for clients to manage. Valuable questions in this segment involve focusing clients on a problematic moment and helping them describe very specifically what was going on internally and in their bodies. Questions that elicit such descriptions include: "Can you share a recent example when the discouragement was there? I'd like a description of a one-minute scene when you were really feeling it and how you tried to manage. Let's start with a description of where you were and what was generally happening" (DEL).

An externalization that is not visceral enough may not be meaningful and has a reduced action potential. As described in Chapter 1, "action potential" refers to the intensity and directionality of the urge to do something, which can be an impulse to go toward a problem, such as attacking or facing a problematic issue head-on; or the opposite, such as moving away from a problem and withdrawing. When there is a choice, emotional externalizations can be very effective because they include an action potential. Since all emotions are valuable in some contexts, it is beneficial to engage in conversations that help clients delineate when specific emotions are helpful versus when they have deleterious effects.

A nonemotional externalization may be necessary and valuable with some people. The example of a young man from Thailand who consulted Marie-Nathalie about never feeling joy or happiness comes to mind. Upon succeeding in getting a dream promotion he had been working on for years, he was startled to realize that he felt only one minute of a faint joy that didn't last. Cultural specifications of masculinity, in his family and as a Thai man, had trained him to not express any emotion, except anger, which progressively turned into depression when he was alone in his room. Acknowledging the anger and depression was a source of shame, so we externalized "the negative mindset," which he actively related to and openly talked about. Deconstructing the limiting effects of specifications of masculinity and externalizing the negative mindset paved the way for a successful therapeutic journey. The work required a significant amount of attention to his body and mindfulness training. After several weeks of being on the lookout for very subtle sensations of satisfaction, he slowly noticed and felt small moments of contentment, which he came to cherish. This was at first possible only when he was eating, discerning moments of enjoying some tastes, but eventually was extended into relational areas of his life and social events.

A nonaffective externalization can also be valuable with children, who are mostly aware of their behavioral manifestations, such as a pushing habit or procrastination. This would also apply to working with children who have been labeled ADHD (attention-deficit hyperactivity disorder) and have no understanding of the link between this description and their embodied experience. Helping children recognize moments that lead up to what adults call ADHD (often boredom or bouncy energy) can be really valuable. Linking problems with felt experiences in the body can facilitate recognition of moments when a problem habit is shifting into gear and starting to alter the direction of one's day. Such awareness empowers people to make different choices.

When a client has a keen self-awareness and readily talks about many problematic experiences, several words can become effective externalizations. We can either ask the client to choose one that appears more intense, work with two or three externalizations, or use a metaphor that will represent all of them.

Bianca readily talked about self-doubt, depression, overwhelm, insecurity, anxiety, sadness, frustration, and dread before going to work. "Dread" was definitely the most intense, but it applied only to a narrow slice of her experience, that is, the morning before work, or before certain interviews. "Depression" was a commonly used descriptor, but it was also associated with a mental health label given by a psychiatrist, and not very specific. "Insecurity" was a strong possibility for externalization because it applied to many contexts, was present at the onset of many episodes of depression, and could potentially be traced back to past histories of feeling this way. In the end, those different externalizations were all used following her lead until we summarized the conversations and introduced the idea that these all formed a "program" in her brain, which was bringing her down. When Bianca was asked, after a summary of all the effects, to think of a metaphor that would capture this program, she exclaimed that it was like an "Eeyore program" (a cute but sad and pessimistic donkey in the children's classic, *Winnie the Pooh*). This image became a useful externalization that cemented the separation of the problem experience from her identity. Once that was accomplished, Bianca used the Eeyore program externalization, but also continued to mention the specific names of problem emotions when describing various specific aspects of her experiences. This was a helpful development, as separation from the problem had occurred and she no longer experienced the insecurity as something that was wrong with her, but rather as a separate mental habit or program in her mind.

B. Window of Tolerance (WOT)

Discussing suffering is usually best accomplished by keeping emotional experiences as close as possible to what people can manage, which is described as "within the window of tolerance" by interpersonal neurobiologists (IPNB; Siegel, 1999, 2010, 2021). Daniel Siegel explains:

> Each of us has a window of tolerance in which various intensities of emotional arousal can be processed without disrupting the functioning of the system. For some people, high degrees of intensity feel comfortable and allow them to think, behave, and feel with balance and effectiveness. For others, certain emotions (such as anger or sadness), or all emotions, may be quite disruptive to functioning. (Siegel, 2012, p. 280)

Allowing a therapeutic conversation to trigger too much emotional intensity runs the risk of retraumatizing clients, leading to states of extreme overwhelm (hyperarousal) or dissociation (hypoarousal), neither of which is helpful. Daniel Siegel (2012) states that outside of the WOT, *"function becomes impaired as we move towards chaos or rigidity"* (p. 280). In other words, allowing therapeutic conversations to reach extreme affective states can leave clients feeling more disempowered and incompetent than they did before meeting us. Working specifically at the border of the WOT can illuminate strategies clients have developed to skillfully contain more intense experiences. While IPNB has offered explanations for why this is important on a physiological level, foundational narrative practices have given us concrete ways to accomplish this clinically by exploring unique outcomes, such as paying attention to formerly unnoticed skillful moments that contradict the story of clients being incapacitated by a problem.

Working at the border of the WOT can take the form of gently broaching the subject of a traumatic experience, but only through the lens of how a client was able to take self-protective actions. Another example would be finding a moment when the client could have lost control of her anger but didn't and managed to contain the experience before it led to destructive actions. When discussing unique outcomes, practitioners shed light on the brain's existing "brake mechanism" and associated skills. This process bolsters emotion regulation by making clients more aware of and confident in their abilities. Since every activation of an emotional experience strengthens it neurally, such narrative conversation increasingly encodes a sense of being competent. Many classic narrative questions accomplish this purpose, such as, "Was there a time this week when the problem could have completely taken you over but you didn't let it?" or "On a scale of 1 to 10, how intense could those feelings have become if you hadn't controlled them?"

Inquiring about successful moments of regulation is particularly important with children, who are more vulnerable to reliving overwhelming emotions during a discussion of the upsetting event. Clinical work in hospitals, schools, group homes, or situations of violence and natural disaster may require practices to help clients who have traversed into the hypo- or hyperarousal zones; these will be discussed in the trauma-focused chapters.

The only time to intentionally work on the outer side of the WOT is when clients are disconnected from crucial information, consequently endangering themselves or others. In such unusual situation, intensifying discomfort might increase their motivation to act (i.e., action potential, defined in Chapter 1). For instance, Marie-Nathalie once worked with a woman who was casually talking about her husband attempting to strangle her, and in the recounting completely minimized the violence and its effects. Asking questions that required tolerating the discomfort involved in revisiting the event, and articulating the repercussions of the violence on her and her baby, was essential for this client to shift toward choosing remedial actions other than simply wanting to learn how to avoid triggering her husband's wrath.

> With Bianca, working at the border of the WOT unfolded smoothly. Her strongest affective wave was when she mentioned losing herself, remembering how she used to be spontaneous, loving, and kind. Discussing ongoing evidence of this preferred self, even though less present, and establishing that it was still there, but temporarily buried under the problems, seemed to reassure her. During our sessions, she mostly remained within her WOT, never completely becoming overwhelmed by tears, partly because we always discussed problem events with a focus on how she managed to comfort herself. She described intense waves of overwhelm and insecurity after what she considered poor interviews for dream jobs. We practiced a breathing exercise (Beaudoin & Maki, 2020) to help her reset her body on an embodied level and help her transition more intentionally into the "accepting" state she wished to live. Bianca started telling herself: "This job interview was probably not as bad as the insecurity is making it out to be." Bianca really liked the breathing exercise and practiced it diligently every time unpleasant emotions threatened to take over, reducing the intensity, frequency, and duration of episodes of sadness.

C. Past Emotional Experiences

Narrative therapy has historically focused on present-time occurrences of problems and inquired about memories of the past only when these are directly linked to current issues (Zimmerman, 2018). This is in contrast with theoretical orientations that engage in one or two thorough intake sessions about clients' lives, often going through protocoled lists of questions scanning for histories of pathology and hardships. The intent in narrative therapy is to recognize that people have immense possibilities of surmounting problems and that spending time analyzing a troublesome past is not necessarily useful in helping clients move forward. Spending time on "thick" problem stories from another period of people's lives may diminish clients' self-perception of competency, and limit their sense of hopefulness and possibility. While we are in agreement with these intentions, there are also reasons to inquire specifically about past *emotional* experiences connected to presenting problems. Making visible past influences allows clients to realize that their present-time experience may in fact be from the past (more on this subject and implicit affect will be discussed further in Chapter 5). For our work to be thorough and solid enough to endure through time, there is great value in deconstructing, delinking, and processing some of the roots of problem stories, or unprocessed flashes of memory that constantly resurface.

Neuroaffective studies have revealed interesting phenomena such as "state-dependent recall" (Lewis & Critchley, 2003), which refers to a person's increased likelihood of remembering events encoded in the same emotional state. For example, if you feel angry at your partner, your memory will more easily recall a whole plethora of other moments when you felt like this. This finding that emotional context influences recall can dramatically shape the outcome of a reauthoring journey, and practitioners benefit from being intentional when choosing the affective direction of a conversation. Once a problematic emotion is slightly elicited in the therapeutic space, it becomes easier to ask a few simple questions such as, "Does this jealousy remind you of anything from your past?" "Have you ever lived such an intense self-doubt at another time?" "You mentioned feeling very small and your shoulders slouching forward; did you ever feel something similar, when you were a child or teenager?" Bodily postures and sensations easily bring back memories of events that may have created a foundation for a problem experience (Veenstra et al., 2015).

Since the Eeyore program regularly got Bianca to feel "not-good-enough," it became a reasonable question to ask if those feelings were present when she grew up. Such information provides an indication of the extent to which the problem story has been established over time, and whether implicit affect may need to be addressed. It also indicates the extent to which we will have to intensify the preferred story for it to become sustainable. Bianca answered, "Not at all, quite the contrary, my parents were always very supportive and always told me I could do it!" This was welcome information and revealed a high probability of uncovering many values and memories that could be used to bolster the preferred story in a short amount of time.

D. Map of Effects

Once an externalization has been identified and seems to fit with the client's experience, it is really helpful to use the foundational narrative practice of mapping effects, developed by White and Epston (1990). Mapping the effects of an externalized problem on a person's thoughts, feelings, relationships, bodily sensations, and identity facilitates an increasingly clear separation of identity from the influence of the problem. Once these particular aspects of externalized problems are recognized, it becomes easier to discern relational, contextual, and cultural understandings that support the problem.

Bianca shared examples of being overtaken by the Eeyore program and how it got her to think: "I'm not smart, I'll be stuck in this job forever, I'm ungrateful since I have a job when many don't; it is pointless to apply to new jobs, I'll be rejected again, my résumé 'sucks,' people at work don't care about me," and so on. We highlighted how the Eeyore program made these demeaning statements about her "feel so true" and how it negatively overfocused on a few seconds of each interview, and that there were many other pieces of information excluded. Understanding the narrow focus of the Eeyore program helped her mentally consider skillful answers during her interviews and a greater number of factors that could explain the absence of job offers, namely, the large number of people unemployed in this community and being interviewed concurrently.

E. Social Context

When clients develop some agency over their emotional experience, and separate the problem from their identity, it can be easier for them to add an extra layer of perspective about contextual factors, which early on might feel insurmountable. In some situations, moving too quickly to explore equity issues at the beginning of the therapeutic conversation can accentuate the sense of powerlessness beyond the WOT. Once the problem is differentiated from their sense of identity, people are in a better position to deconstruct the social injustices contributing to the issue (White, 1991). Questions eliciting such deconstruction might include: "I wonder where the idea of 'thin is beautiful' comes from. Are babies born with this?" "Might there be messages in the media that make it harder for teens to express their preferred gender identity? If so, is the problem 'inside of you' or 'inside the culture'? Which one should we doubt?" "Do you have any concerns about potential racism being at play here?"

> With Bianca, we explored all the contributors to the dissatisfaction at her current work and the challenge in finding new employment. We co-created a contextual understanding of these two problems. Regarding work, she concluded that her environment was toxic because the manager behaved in rude and uncaring ways with all employees, so she felt it had nothing to do with her personally. Bianca saw this boss as struggling with overachievement issues, stress, and potentially racism, although she didn't think it was the main issue given that everyone was mistreated regardless of race and gender, and most of her initial group of employees had found new jobs already, except her. Regarding her search for new employment, we concluded that the job rejections had more to do with the economic climate, the rarity of this type of job, people being hired because of connections, and the Eeyore program making her underestimate her competencies and apply only to very specific types of positions. When prompted about potential discrimination concerns, she stated that the Eeyore program made her wonder sometimes whether her Hispanic name got in the way. She responded, "It isn't helpful for me to think about that, and if racism does get in the way, I don't want to work with these people anyway." In the end, we examined patterns of interaction involving the Eeyore program and pleasing behaviors, and how those habitual responses might inadvertently enhance

employers' rudeness rather than elicit appreciation. Bianca rectified this pleasing demeanor almost immediately after.

3. Contrast Emotions

The practice of contrasting involves bringing forth two or three different experiences and juxtaposing them side by side. This offers a powerful possibility of enhancing the visibility of certain features and consequently heightening the value of efforts, strategies, and successful handling of problematic situations.

As an example, contrasting the unfolding of a family evening when a parent struggles with impatience and yelling, with an evening when a parent makes an effort to talk calmly to the children, may heighten the visibility of self-control and its benefits. The conflicts and tears of three children for many hours can be very taxing. The difference between the energy expenditure to control oneself versus the energy required to deal with upset children, highlights the value of efforts to contain problem emotions, and intensifies feelings of satisfaction about successful regulation. The practice of contrasting is helpful in many segments of the journey and offers many therapeutic benefits since it:

- Exposes problems' distortions ("The panic always convinces you that you will die. How often have you actually died?")
- Highlights the effects of different choices ("If you had listened to the mad feelings, you would have been in trouble the whole day with many people, and since you listened to your patient side, how was the rest of your day?")
- Boosts people's appraisal of their abilities ("Depression tends to get people to dwell on problems for hours and on satisfying moments for just a few minutes. How long were you able to experience joy after the fun dinner with your friends?")
- Spotlights people's progress ("When we started, the distress made you consider harming yourself every evening, and now you fill this period of time by writing poems!")

Since much of the work with Bianca was discerning the interpretations of the insidious Eeyore program from her preferred self, a significant portion of the therapeutic conversation was now spent in contrasting. For instance, after the story of an interview, we contrasted how her day would have unfolded if she had allowed the Eeyore program to criticize everything she had said with what she actually did. She had successfully silenced the program, done her breathing exercise, and moved on to playing with her dog, reading, and resting. We also contrasted choices she made at work and how her new way of speaking up was shifting interactions. Bianca started reclaiming her life, feeling more confident, and describing her actions as being more proactive. Her partner had commented that she noticed the progress, that Bianca was back. As people at work became more respectful, she even decided to attend a social event, which she would have avoided a month earlier.

4. Embody Preferred Emotions

Most people describe in depth their physiological experiences of problems but not their embodiment of neutral and preferred affect. Becoming aware of one's embodied manifestation of a preferred self eventually allows one to intentionally enter preferred affect more easily via body positioning (Beaudoin, 2019; Ewing et al., 2017; Griffith & Griffith, 1994; Veenstra et al., 2015). Recent research shows that being happy makes us smile and also that smiling makes it easier to access the state of happiness (Söderkvist et al., 2018). Brain and body typically strive to be congruent (Beaudoin, 2017b). This does not mean that smiling alone will solve all problems but indicates that the body plays a role in intentionally facilitating access to preferred selves. The states of happiness, calm, determination, patience, and so on are all available physiologically in the brain and body at all times. It is access to these experiences, in certain contexts, that can be difficult to achieve. The more we know about the physiologically felt inner destination we wish to reach and its pathways, the easier it is to engage that version of ourselves. People tend to develop embodied patterns of affective expressions, which typically include facial muscles, shoulders, breathing patterns, abdominal tension, heart rate, sensations in the lower back, and connectedness (or absence thereof) to feelings in their hands and feet. Few people realize the extent to which their breathing can worsen problems. Fast chest breathing lowers levels of carbon dioxide in the lungs and can trigger fight-or-flight responses, mobilizing biochemicals and feelings of lightheadedness (Siegel et al., 2021). A client susceptible to anxiety can be empowered from knowing that simply breathing in such a way increases the vulnerability to a cascade of physiological reactions, leading to a panic attack. Every intense embodied aspect of a problem benefits from being addressed by a counterpart in the preferred experience, which will be discussed further in subsequent chapters. If a person's shoulders feel weighed down by sadness, an alternative embodied experience associated with the shoulders can be beneficial, to strengthen preferred emotions. Recognizing embodied patterns in problems and preferred experiences allows people to better prevent struggles and more easily connect to their preferred selves (Beaudoin, 2017b, 2019; Dunne, 2017; Ewing et al., 2017).

> Bianca was invited to notice the differences in her body when under the influence of the Eeyore program versus when she felt more like herself. She described the Eeyore program as creating tension in her forehead and eyes, a frown, a feeling of being small and insignificant. When her preferred self of confidence emerged, she noticed her spine elongating, shoulders opening up, head rocking back, facial muscles relaxing, and her eyes looking at people while talking. We determined that her eyes might be the headquarters of confidence. She could occupy more space, carry herself differently, and breathe more freely. People started noticing that she was more present and excited about projects.

5. Intensify the Preferred Self

Narrative conversations have historically aimed to help people move beyond experiences of problems and enable them to reconnect with a preferred version of themselves. Depending on the unique preferences of each individual, someone struggling with fears could be assisted in developing trust.

A person dealing with rage could be engaged in cultivating patience, and one with panic could be encouraged to develop calmness. All of these preferred experiences of the self can be brought to the forefront and sustained for some time by therapeutic conversations and a community of acknowledgment. However, from an intensity standpoint, it could be argued that problem emotions are ingrained more powerfully in the brain, and are more likely to be reactivated, than emerging experiences of self-confidence and calm, even if the latter are thickened with rich stories, histories, witnesses, and documents (Beaudoin, 2017a, 2017b, 2019). Enriching the preferred self with additional affective experiences can bolster their intensity and encoding, which increases their likelihood of being viable alternatives. A valuable practice to intensify the preferred self is to "line it" by asking: "If there was another emotion associated with confidence, what might it be?" This question is invariably met with a "hum . . . " as people shift inward to reflect and ponder. The answers are remarkably varied and often unpredictable in nature. A woman struggling with depression once exclaimed that another emotion she associated with calm was humor. Once identified, this newly identified emotion opened the door to fresh memories, forgotten stories of life, and new people who played an influential role and could be recruited in thickening the preferred self on an affective level. The new emotion does not have to be "positive"; it only needs to boost the intensity of the preferred state.

When Bianca was asked if another emotion was associated with being confident and proactive at work, she answered, "calmness." We explored situations where she embodied this state and she was able to set limits by calmly replying to her boss, "Please be patient," or firmly stating, "I won't be able to add this to my list today." Knowing all too well that confidence and calm may not be enough to set limits in a stressful, busy environment with a history of disrespect, I asked: "What else gave power to your confidence in the work situation you just described?" Bianca acknowledged some frustration at being taken for granted and underappreciated for so long. We explored the value of frustration, which she initially perceived as a "bad" thing, even though she could express it quite well when speaking up in unfair situations. The history of how frustration had been helpful in the past was discussed to enhance her comfort and trust in her ability to express it constructively. She felt the manager was now responding with apologies and respect for Bianca's pushbacks. Bianca felt empowered to continue "saying no," "keeping boundaries," "refusing to do unpaid overtime," and using her frustration to stand up for fairness, in ways she felt more comfortable with.

6. Develop a Flourishing Identity

Empowering people to overcome problems by bringing forth their preferred selves is a wonderful achievement and sometimes a realistic end to therapy. However, why stop there? Recent research has shown that happiness doesn't just happen, but rather has to be cultivated (Hanson, 2016). In our Western culture, most people have not been exposed to the prospect that there are many paths to well-being outside of the capitalistic model of buying material goods, a poor source of lasting joy. We have a responsibility to help people move beyond the stage of addressing problems in their lives to one where they can truly flourish. This can be accomplished with questions such as, *"Now that your life is better, if you could choose an emotion to cultivate, one that could come to represent who you wish to be in the world, what might it be?"* Many people would choose "happiness," which, given how commercialized this term has become, really benefits from being defined and narrowed down to something more specific and personal. People might then pick "contentment," "gratefulness," "compassion," "joy," or "love." This subject opens the door to a whole new line of conversational inquiries, such as: *"Tell me why you chose that emotion? People have different reasons to value this. When did you experience this in your life? Do you recall a specific example? What stood out about this experience? What difference did it make in your life to have tasted that? What would cultivating this emotion look like? Are there small moments every day that you could cherish more often?"* It can be helpful to zoom in on small daily moments, which can weave the tapestry of well-being in life and anchor the preferred self in a sustainable way (Beaudoin, 2004).

Practitioners can further support this process by asking: *"When you wake up in the morning, what is most pleasant to notice?" "Would it be possible to connect with kindness as you begin your day? How would that look and what would it feel like? When might you have done something like this? What effects did it have on your decisions and reactions to people?" "Where in your home do you most prefer to sit? Is there a chair or sofa that's sort of comfy?" "Is there something you'd want to appreciate more in your food?" "Is there a hand gesture you do more often when you are in the state of happiness?" "People often live their daily routine and forget to be content. Is there something that you wish to keep on noticing?"*

"People become who they practice to be" (Beaudoin, 2010; Beaudoin & Maki, 2020, p. xii), so as practitioners, let's actively encourage people to expand the time spent being their preferred selves, as it will progressively increase the ease of entering and maintaining these embodied states.

> Bianca reported that she really valued being kind and present. Observing her dog put a smile on her face. Being present and listening intently to her partner was important. Working out daily, doing yoga, painting, and taking time to do embroidery on her favorite comfy chair helped her remain anchored in her preferred self. At work, visiting a nice park near her office during lunch and looking at the trees out her window kept her priorities in the forefront of her mind.

7. Expand Beyond the Flourishing Self

Narrative therapy began with concerns about the influences of sociopolitical issues and social justice. Struggles were understood as arising from people's oppressive experiences or because of a mismatch between social expectations and personal preferences. Historically, our work as narrative practitioners has culminated with supporting clients to fulfill their version of a preferred self. However, what if we helped people move beyond a preferred self into a more expansive experience? In many collectivistic traditions, such as in Buddhist practice, well-being resides in a greater sense of connectedness (Post, 2005). In many collectivistic cultures, the purpose in life is to continue ancestors' values without taking up an individualistic posture and standing out as different. For narrative practices to remain congruent with an intention to free people from limiting discourses (such as individualism), requires an expansion of the preferred self to one much greater than being relationally connected to family, friends, and co-workers. Such work involves inviting clients, whenever possible and relevant, to consider their relationship to the greater good, and exploring whether they might have an interest in contributing to a particular cause. Such a step not only paves the way for a collective effort to better our planet but also, at the minimum, contributes to the client feeling like an agent of progress in our world. There is a significant amount of research that shows how people involved in volunteering, or contributing to something bigger than their own happiness, experience much more satisfaction in life (Hansen et al., 2018). These actions make life meaningful and give us a purpose. A Vietnamese woman once consulted Marie-Nathalie about a lingering depression and inability to find lasting happiness. She was happily married but the aging couple had decided long ago to not have children, as they both wanted to focus on their successful careers. She was now finding her life to be meaningless, in spite of all the comfort of her home and the luxurious trips they took every year. Externalizing the "blah feeling" and helping her identify moments of a contented preferred self were certainly steps in cultivating a more positive affect, but were not a satisfying outcome to therapy. Our work shifted in much more significant ways when we explored social causes that might matter to her. At first, there was none, but after much exploration of her life, she recalled having received compassionate care at Planned Parenthood when she had decided to terminate an unwanted pregnancy. The conversation shifted to her affective experience of this event and how grateful she had felt toward that agency. This made it possible to examine the embodied experience of gratefulness, intensify it, and spark a momentum to expend energy for this agency and give back in some meaningful ways. She felt a renewed surge of purpose in life and decided to not only contribute to the agency financially but also offer to physically be a volunteer.

While this type of work may not be possible with every client, we can still plant a seed for the idea of expanding meaning in life by supporting a variety of causes. For example:

- engaging in social justice work with the Black Lives Matter movement, supporting the LGBTQ community, eradicating poverty, and so on;
- working to avert the crisis in the natural world such as addressing climate change, supporting endangered animals, and engaging in wilderness preservation;
- involving oneself in organizations such as Planned Parenthood, homeless shelters, interpersonal violence shelters, and the like;
- supporting community causes such as working on gun control, engaging in hospice care, and participating in stopping human trafficking;
- participating in local community efforts such as cleaning parks, being an active recycler, and signing up with organizations like Big Brothers and Big Sisters; and
- targeting a type of person one would like to help, such as foster-care children, the elderly, or the disabled.

The intent in this section is to encourage clients to think beyond themselves and entertain the possibility of getting involved in prosocial actions.

Happiness, joy, and satisfying emotions in general tend to have an action potential "toward" doing something. Helpful questions to bring forth this theme include: "You've come such a long way and reclaimed your life from X! You now experience a lot more joy and peace, and I wonder if that gets you to look at the suffering in the world differently?" "Is there a person, a group of people, or something about nature that catches your attention more? What is it about this situation that particularly draws you in? Do you have a personal connection to this issue?" "If you were to contribute to this cause one day, what might you do? What would be the very first step of such an action? What would it feel like to do this? How would it enrich your own life? How might it shape the person you are becoming? As you grow older, how might you look back on this action?"

These questions are part of a wide repertoire of options that energize the idea of contributing to society and tasting the pride and satisfaction associated with altruistic gestures. The Buddhist emotion of *mudita*, feeling joy when seeing another experience joy, can also be invited into the conversation. This line of questioning is often generative and invites clients to notice children giggling in a park or dogs walking on the street with a wagging tail. It puts a smile on many people's faces. Again, these conversations are not necessarily a fit in all situations and the process is about co-developing clients' interests and not forcing anything. There are surprisingly more people, children and adults, than the reader might expect who are willing to partake in such an exploration and interested in developing a magnanimous self.

> Bianca, with a renewed confidence and connection to her value of fairness, decided to volunteer at an agency serving youth with disabilities. She found great joy in becoming more selfless and spreading kindness. By the end of our eight-week therapeutic journey, she had found a new job, and felt more connected than ever to the person she preferred to be in the world: loving and proactive.

All Journeys Come To an End

A few days prior to the last session, the U.S. Supreme Court reversed women's constitutional right to get an abortion. This briefly triggered the Eeyore program ("What's the point of anything if women don't even have rights over their bodies?") but Bianca was able to reset her emotional experience, read activists' responses instead of dwelling on the outrage, continue with important daily activities, which kept her afloat, and most importantly, she supported friends who were devastated by the Supreme Court reversal and made a small donation to local clinics, instead of isolating herself. These prosocial actions helped her move forward with her community and hold on to her preferred self instead of isolating in a dark emotional state.

The affective narrative map was immensely helpful in guiding Bianca through this journey of "surfing" through the waters of intense challenges and emotions.

When asked what had been most helpful during the therapeutic process, she shared the following: "*Seeing the depression as a neural network, calling it the Eeyore program, which was cute, and seeing it as separate from me.*" Her comment about calling the depression Eeyore stood out on a nonverbal affective level, as it was imbued with endearment and tenderness. We can wonder whether seeing Eeyore as cute in itself played a role in the affective turn toward being less hard on herself about her experience. The next day, Bianca sent an email sharing that in the moment, she forgot to comment on other aspects of the work:

> Some other things that I found very helpful were that you really helped me "slow down" the moments these depressive feelings came up, and it helped me better understand how these moments affected me on a physical level, which then only further reinforced them. You were very compassionate, which gave me the confidence to be vulnerable and really pick apart the insecurities. Our sessions also made me understand that I can turn negative feelings such as frustration and sadness into strength and confidence to stand up for myself, which helped immensely. Also, learning that I should form and focus on pockets of happiness during life is really effective in helping me deal with my depression related to global events that are out of my control.

Conclusion

This chapter proposed a conversation map to guide narrative conversations about emotions problematic to oneself or others. Externalization of emotions is discussed as an experience-near practice, which offers the advantage of facilitating the exploration of problems embedded in powerful visceral and physiological elements. Seven steps were examined to facilitate a shift away from a problem identity, with the last three expanding beyond foundational narrative practices to include embodied, flourishing, and global versions of the preferred self.

CHAPTER 3

Centered, Decentered, and Co-Centered Postures

Professional posture informs how practitioners navigate the most influential therapeutic factor: the therapist–client relationship. A practitioner can be equipped with the most artful questions, savvy conversation maps, and best intentions, but, without attention to a professional posture, may slip into reacting based on personal experiences or cultural specifications. A therapeutic relational posture provides a compass on how to handle unexpected events, influences the manner in which a practitioner will respond to clients, and shapes the interactional tone of the therapeutic relationship. This chapter will describe the evolution of therapeutic posture from centered to decentered in narrative therapy and propose a contemporary shift to co-centering to better represent the linguistic and felt experience involved in a narratively attuned therapeutic journey. The difference between these postures will initially be described using the story of Ella, who approached Marie-Nathalie for therapeutic help.

Ella had graduated from college with honors in June and had secured a job for the fall in environmental sciences in another city. During this period of time at home, she became increasingly worried about eating patterns she had developed and had tried to solve on her own throughout her time in college. She felt she was otherwise healthy, functioning well, not in any danger, and well supported by family and friends. At the first meeting with Marie-Nathalie, Ella shared that she had never opened up about these issues to anyone else, but had developed the habit of binge eating, overexercising, weighing herself, and counting calories. If she felt she had eaten too much, Ella would punish herself by starving the next day as her few attempts to purge had generally been unsuccessful.

After this summary, Ella anxiously leaned toward Marie-Nathalie and said: *"I've been so worried the past two years, I've resisted telling anyone about this . . . Do I . . . Do I . . . Do I have an eating disorder? I know these are really terrible problems . . . "*

As a practitioner, how would you handle this question?

Your chosen professional posture would shape your response. Let's first examine the posture of centering, its historical roots, limitations, and implications in clinical practice. We will then similarly examine decentering and co-centering and end the chapter with descriptions of co-centering practices illustrated by a transcript.

Centering

Historical Roots

Centering is likely familiar to readers, as this therapeutic posture focuses on expert knowledge to guide therapeutic interactions. This body of work guides practitioners to privilege theoretical knowledge, or their own perspectives, and the client is typically a more passive recipient of practitioners' interpretations. In practice, centering can involve issuing opinions about the problem, telling clients what is wrong and what needs to be done, sometimes with little consideration of other aspects of people's experiences.

With Ella, a practitioner taking a centered posture might answer, *"Yes, you have an eating disorder because you binge, purge, deprive yourself of food, and overexercise, all of which are classic symptoms of this disorder."* This centering posture has dominated the field of mental health since the early twentieth century, when Western culture moved toward what many influential writers call the modernist age. This was a period with many impressive discoveries in medicine, technology, and scientific innovation that immediately improved the quality of many people's lives. As Kenneth Gergen pointed out in his book *The Saturated Self* (1991), early adopters of modernism believed that systematic observation, measurement, and rationality could not only advance technology but also liberate the world from suffering. In the mental health field, observing and measuring became about developing a science focused on a deficit-based model (Gergen, 1990). The assumption was that if experts identified, studied, and measured people's shortcomings, they might be better able to help, just as locating the squeaky part of a machine allows us to fix it. The discipline of contemporary psychology was born out of this emerging modernist movement. By the 1970s, deficit-focused psychology was one of the most popular subjects to study in the United States, with its shortcomings not immediately visible.

The Challenges and Limitations of a Centered Posture

While Western science can make important mental health discoveries about the human condition and help mental health practitioners be accountable for what they do in the name of mental health, a loss of nuance and over-generalization can occur. For example, there is a risk that:

- Mental health practices simplify extraordinarily complex human beings into machine-like entities of isolated parts.
- A snapshot taken of people's worst moments, occurring at a certain time, place, and relational context, is mistaken for the totality of their lives.
- Only one dominant normative way is perceived as valid and "healthy."
- A way of being is idealized and decontextualized across very diverse sets of problems, situations, and people.
- One person (a mental health practitioner) is assumed to hold expert knowledge over another person's life without much consideration for what the latter brings to the conversation.

Take, for example, a practitioner in training who exclaims the following in a consultation meeting: "I just met with a new teen client and she shared that she hides 90% of her feelings from her parents! That's really bad, I've seen research on that! I need to help her express herself more!" This male graduate student is issuing a judgment that it's "bad" to not express feelings, which reflects his white-male cultural bias (the client was Japanese). He has very little information about the context in which the client is choosing this behavior (there was domestic violence and alcoholism at home) and he formulates a treatment plan rashly based on his own normative assumptions of how people should behave. The assessment is based upon his own personal journey and certain textbook training, which privileges self-expression. What's missing in this picture is the client's story, how she came to develop a survival strategy of limiting expression in an unsafe context, what skills she has developed in navigating a tricky home environment, how young people in her ethnic group handle adolescence, and what it is that she wants to improve in her life (in this case, her deteriorating relationship with a friend). The centering posture of the novice therapist, elevating his own ideas above the client's, supported by specific ideas about mental health, invisibilized crucial information in a way that most likely left the client feeling misunderstood, judged, or inadequate. Yet this young therapist had good intentions, was caring, and genuinely wanted to help the client. He had been trained to think about "truths" and dichotomous "healthy versus unhealthy traits" in his clients, devoid of contextual considerations, all in the name of helping others. He was very excited to have identified a problem that fit his training and about which he felt he could do something. Centering is often visible in how young people are treated in many settings including at home, at school, and in some therapists' offices, with little regard for their views and experiences.

In sum, the dangers of centering are many because it elevates the knowledge of one person over the life of another, with minimal information about and consideration of the latter. Centering is not always "bad" and there are circumstances in engineering, medicine, situations of abuse, or when directing a group, when a person has to take a leadership position or use scientific expertise to make an important decision by relying on their knowledge. Our view is that in therapeutic conversations, there are often great costs to centering and losing the richness of collaborative inquiry.

Effects on Clients Such as Ella

Answering Ella based on a few sentences of problem-focused information and confirming an eating disorder would center on textbook knowledge, and be oblivious to the many efforts and successes she had while battling the eating problem and body-image issues. It would provide a confirmatory expert clinical diagnosis, which would have been overwhelming to Ella, as she was terrified of this prospect. The diagnosis of a disorder seemed like an insurmountable problem to her. Receiving such a medical label would also lead down a "problem-solving" path and simultaneously leave her as a more passive actor in the conversation, waiting to hear what "should be done to cure her disorder." Her own voice of resilience and long-standing efforts in challenging the problem would be squashed or diminished. The therapeutic conversation would become more focused on the practitioner's knowledge of how a range of textbooks typically solve these issues, as opposed to being intrigued by the unique efforts and skills of this client in her own life.

The Turn to Decentering

Historical Roots

In the decentering posture, practitioners and clients collaborate as equals, and each contribute valuable expertise. Practitioners have expertise on the process of change and psychological understandings, and clients bring expertise in their life experiences, efforts, values, hopes, dreams, and community relationships. In practice, the practitioner asks helpful questions and withholds theoretical knowledge to leave the conversational space for clients to articulate their own thoughts, observations, and preferences. Decentering best describes the classical narrative therapy posture (and was originally spelled "de-centred"; White & Morgan, 2006). Marie-Nathalie, caught off guard by Ella asking intently if she had an eating disorder, and seeing how loaded this diagnostic seemed to be for her, attempted to remain decentered.

> **Marie-Nathalie:** *Well, what do you think?*
>
> **Ella (barely moving as she whispered):** *I really don't know, it looks like*

it is, that's why I'm here, I really need to know, please, what do YOU think?

The decentered posture is typically very respectful of the client's perspectives. In this situation, however, it didn't feel like it was honoring the client as intended and Marie-Nathalie found herself pondering the most helpful way to respond. There were many reasons to still maintain this posture, as visible in the historical review below.

In the postmodern era of counseling and therapy, it became evident that much was missing when the complexity of a life was reduced to a deficit-based diagnosis. Practitioners guided by the work of Michael White and David Epston became deeply suspicious of modernist theories and the impact of these forces on the delivery of mental health services. The mental health field in the Western world in the 1980s and even today is heavily driven by deficit-based approaches. Michael and David recognized that people were multifaceted in very complex ways and understood that clients know more about themselves and the details of everything they have lived. The narrative therapy community noticed that when clients' voices were centered, people felt respected, listened to, and cared for, and took bold steps to better their lives.

Michael suggested that the position that best fits with a philosophy of honoring people's knowledges is one where the therapist is "de-centred and influential" (White & Morgan, 2006). Being influential suggests that the therapist's questions affect the direction of the therapeutic conversation when selecting certain aspects of experience and giving these experiences salience, meaning, and attention. When narrative practitioners are "decentered and influential," they are present, attentive, and deeply involved in asking questions that will assist the client to connect with their unrecognized skills to navigate situations in accordance with their values. Decentering helps minimize the danger of the therapist delegitimizing the client's experience, especially when the client and practitioner come from very different backgrounds and power positions. Decentering is about valuing the knowledges of people of all ages, including the knowledge and voice of children.

The Challenges and Limitations of a Decentered Posture

When practiced thoughtfully, decentering is a very effective and honoring clinical posture. However, it is a difficult practice to teach, as most of us are strongly positioned by the problem-solving rhetoric associated with our training in modernist therapeutic approaches. Over many years of applying and teaching narrative therapy, we have been acutely aware of how many of our colleagues and new practitioners, and sometimes we ourselves, can slip out of the decentered posture. When not knowing what to do, when running out of time, when clients position us in the role of experts, or when undue pressure is imposed on us (for example, risk of divorce, hospitalization, life-threatening conditions, intense emotions, or violence), it is tempting to quickly deliver advice to clients who may be desperately seeking guidance. A decentered practitioner can also slip into centered clinical interactions when trying to "question a client out of a problem" or adopt a cheerleader posture with an enthusiastic rallying cry. Providing numerous forms of encouragement and affirmation to make changes that the client is ill-equipped to do in that moment is ineffective. This practice often fails to engage the client flooded with challenging emotions, who is in no state to onboard the advice of the most well intentioned.

People new to narrative practices can sometimes demand of themselves strict adherence to being decentered, while mistakenly censoring their own affective attunement to not impose their agendas on the conversation. Paradoxically, when the process of only asking questions dominates a unidirectional, staccato therapist-question–client-answer interactional style, it can inadvertently produce an expert flavor and misdirect the therapeutic flow. Ironically, this was not the therapeutic posture that Michael White and David Epston embodied in practice. Their communication style was much more dialogical, with a great degree of summarizing and checking in to ensure that a shared conversational experience occurred, and their affective presence was warm and caring.

Here is an example of how a practitioner new to narrative therapy can get so focused on decentering and the linguistic practice of externalizing that they can miss the most important emotional and bodily cues that a client is expressing. The narrative intern is sharing with Marie-

Nathalie her experience of working with a 10-year-old student in an elementary school.

> My client complains that she is bullied by a boy, and she gets in trouble for retaliating. The school perceives her as having an anger issue. When I walked out on the playground this morning, I noticed a group of students were trying to prevent a fight between my client and this boy. He had claimed she couldn't play football with them because she was a girl. I could see she was furious. She reluctantly conceded to not retaliate and they all agreed to just play. Within minutes of the game restarting, the boy managed to send a high-velocity ball to strike her back. She turned white with rage and just stood there, but then recess ended and the children ran to their classrooms. I went to see my client and was eager to discuss how she successfully contained her anger, so I asked her: "What is it that helped you control the anger? What did the anger want you to do that you didn't do? Who would be pleased to hear that?" The client refused to talk.

Why did the client refuse to talk?

The questions were classic narrative questions intending to highlight the unique outcome. They were decentered and focused on the client's skills.

What wasn't addressed was the client's emotional experience at that moment and her nonverbal responses, which led to the therapeutic interactions being not helpful and not influential. When Marie-Nathalie asked if the intern noticed anything about the client's nonverbal responses the intern said, "Oh! Yes! She was definitely fuming. Her hands were in a fist and her face tight."

> **Marie-Nathalie:** *What was dominating in her experience?*
> **The intern replied:** *The feeling of injustice.*
> **Marie-Nathalie:** *I wonder what it could look like if you acknowledged that you saw what happened and addressed the sense of injustice and the nonverbal responses. As an example, one could ask about what was going on for her. If it would be helpful if we walked for a few minutes?*

If the anger impulse wanted her to address the injustice, and if so, what came to her mind? Did she wish to talk to a school staff about this chronic situation? You could do it together, if she'd like.

Many well-meaning professionals, novice and experienced, fall into the misconception of using what seem to be perfect narrative questions at moments incongruent with the embodied emotional experience of the client, inadvertently leading to a disqualifying of a client's experience. Co-centering, discussed in the next section, incorporates multiple facets of experience: stories, events, efforts, emotions, and embodied nonverbal expressions.

Effects on Clients Such as Ella

In the scenario where Marie-Nathalie was caught off guard when Ella asked her if she had an eating disorder, engaging in a strict decentered position would focus mostly on the linguistic content of her communication. This posture, at that moment, would intend to minimize hierarchy but have the opposite effect of withholding information and effectively ignoring Ella's intense nonverbal demeanor.

From this interaction with Ella, another therapeutic posture was needed: one that would build on decentering from expert knowledge while also acknowledging the nonverbal dimensions of interactions.

A Call to Co-Centering

Co-centering is an intentional clinical practice where practitioners are attuned to clients' fluctuating affective states, in a way that facilitates mutually felt understanding and fine-tuned scaffolding of movement from problems to new possibilities of experience. Co-centering allows decentered practices to be influential, as it provides space for practitioners to honor the tradition of privileging clients' knowledge, while also integrating attention to affective, nonverbal, and embodied elements expressed by both therapist and client. When a practitioner is startled by an unexpected question, rather than just receiving the question at face value, the affective ramifications of the various choices are considered in responding to the client's problem and what this means for the practitioner–client relationship. Marie-Nathalie recounts:

> When Ella asked her question the second time, I paused, looked at her kind face, and noticed that she was anxiously holding her breath, leaning forward, not moving, and waiting eagerly for my answer. I also noticed the intensity of her gaze. This was a crucial meaningful moment for her, not just a casual question, something she's been wanting to know for a long time. Ella's pressing eyes as she leaned forward and stared at me were difficult to ignore.
>
> While in general I prefer to help clients find their own opinions on things, answering Ella's question seemed like it would reduce the negative emotion associated with the problem, increase hopefulness, and set the stage for this therapeutic relationship to be supportive. Not answering such a direct, pressing question could be experienced as disrespectful and demeaning, by privileging what I believed to be the "right" way of conducting therapy as opposed to what she, the client, deemed very important at that moment. I answered: "It looks like you have developed a habit that is unhelpful to you, like a skewed eating habit, and we can work on that." She sighed, leaned back relieved, and smiled: "Oh! I'm so happy. I was so worried I'd have an eating disorder. It sounded so horrible. OMG, a skewed eating habit. Surely I can deal with that. I feel so hopeful now, I'm glad I called you." I smiled too, sharing this moment of mutual relief and satisfaction that was strengthening the therapeutic connection. I proceeded: "Let's talk about what this skewed eating habit is doing to you."

Co-centering allowed the subsequent work to progress quickly, as it involved a complex blend of verbal and nonverbal input from therapist and client. Pauses, tone, speed of answering, trembling hands, flushed face, throat tightening, eyes looking at the ceiling, and affective presence—all convey crucial information about the unfolding experience. These aspects of experience are equally and sometimes more important to consider than the linguistic content shared. In some situations, this may mean intervening on three simultaneous levels, where a practitioner pays attention to the verbal exchanges, the emotions in the room, and physiological levels of activation in everyone present.

Historical Roots

An increasing collection of therapeutic work published by narrative therapy practitioners pays acute attention to the integration of emotion, body, and interactional effects of a sociocultural and sociopolitical landscape. These critical elements do not denigrate or diminish the established traditions of classical narrative practice. Griffith and Griffith (1994), writing nearly 30 years ago, spoke of the importance of therapists paying attention to the mind–body connection. Narrative therapy practitioners such as Beaudoin (2005, 2010, 2015, 2017b, 2019, 2020); Beaudoin and Duvall (2017); Beaudoin and Zimmerman (2011); Bird (2004); Carey (2017); Duvall and Maclennan (2017); Ewing et al. (2017); Hamkins (2014); Madigan, et al. (2018); L. Rosen, personal communication, May 8, 2018; Weingarten and Worthen (2017); Zimmerman (2018); and Tomm (2018) have made a strong case for strengthening narrative practice as it pertains to affect, language/culture, and the body.

Many narrative therapy authors now view the importance of working with the autonomic nervous system (ANS) when clients are affected by strong negative stimuli evoking a fight/flight/faint/freeze/appease reaction. Therapy practices are employed to help regulate the ANS by offering attuned communication, emotional balancing, response flexibility, and fear modulation, while also paying attention to input from the embodied senses, including the gut and heart (Beaudoin, 2017b; Ogden, 2021b). This is important because language provides a very incomplete rendition of experience, especially in high-intensity situations where our physiology is heightened, such as during trauma (Ogden et al., 2006).

According to van der Kolk (1998; personal communication, April 4, 2022), the linguistically based system of memory goes "offline" during sustained levels of stress, which can be caused by a physical or psychological threat. Levels of cortisol are shown to rise as fear increases, which has effects on the language regions in the brain. The ANS creates a hypervigilant response to the sensory cues in the environment. The nonverbal systems (visual, auditory, olfactory, and kinesthetic) are activated, and our attention becomes selective. Of course, this all occurs within a highly complex human system whose richness is lost in the attempts to language a fluid moment. Van der Kolk comments that we can be left with the remnants of the fear experience even once the threat is over, and sometimes without accompanying language to speak to it. Further, according to van der Kolk (2014):

> Even years later, traumatized people often have enormous difficulty telling other people what has happened to them. Their bodies experience terror, rage, and helplessness, but these feelings are impossible to articulate. . . . It is extremely difficult to organize one's traumatic experiences into a coherent account—a narrative with a beginning, a middle, and an end. (p. 43)

The Challenges and Limitations of a Co-Centered Posture

Despite enthusiasm among many practitioners regarding the confluence of postmodern-oriented therapies and attention to emotions, the body, and neuroscience, there is disquiet among a few narrative therapy scholars. Some authors are concerned that practitioners might become overly consumed by conceptualizations of physiology, slip back into simplifying views of experience, become oblivious to sociocultural forces, and lose the richness of human context (Denborough, 2019; Sacks, 2010). Our hope is that practitioners can attend to physiology with critical intention, while still remaining anchored in narrative therapy's values and practices. Giving the body greater attention in therapy does not mean abandoning the importance of context but is rather a way to disrupt Cartesian dualism and better support our clients (Duffy, 2012; Monk & Zamani, 2019).

We believe this vision is in line with the original work of Michael White, who was fully attuned in therapeutic conversations; and David Epston, who always exhibited a buoyant, enthusiastic posture, demonstrating a compelling and infectious hope for positive clinical outcomes for his clients. His exuberant presence and unrelenting faith in his clients' resiliency consistently helped desperate people face almost insurmountable odds because of life-threatening challenges like anorexia, childhood asthma, and highly dangerous suicidal ideation. David never flinched from being completely dedicated to supporting his clients' aspirations to stay alive and thrive when feelings of impending doom, hopelessness, and emptiness were overwhelming. Seldom is David's affective posture ever written about when people reflect upon his clinical giftedness. Instead, attention is almost exclusively drawn to his creative questions and verbal mastery in therapeutic interactions. Yet, if a person with a cold demeanor asked the same questions as David, the effects would be significantly different. The absence of attention to affective and nonverbal dimensions has misled a whole generation of practitioners to perceive narrative therapy as a textually based and "cognitive" approach, appropriate only with verbal clients. In reality, the dignifying and respectful aspects of narrative practices can be immensely helpful, even with children struggling with selective mutism or autism, by virtue of attending to their nonverbal experiences and preferred versions of self.

Effects on Clients Such as Ella

Immediately after getting an answer, Ella's body language relaxed and reflected a demeanor of comfort in discussing her concerns. She was engaged, attentive, and interested in our conversation. Ella was eager and empowered to address the problem, which she did in a short amount of time.

Clinical Application and Practices

Co-centering applies neuroaffective studies to tease out how practitioners and clients' emotions can be used to harness regulation potential. The practice involves tracking interactions to ensure that clients' emotional state is appropriately responded to and not neglected or intensified because of practitioners' own affective activation. This issue is also common between children and adults, when the latter's reactions increase the child's problematic emotions, creating an escalating loop of dysregulation. As an example, an intern was once called to intervene with a six-year-old child overcome by anger, threatening to hurt other children, and flipping chairs in a school office. She noticed that he didn't seem to care, hear, or listen to the upset adults' verbal requests to stop. The intern proceeded to calm the relational space nonverbally by sitting on the ground, humming softly, and drawing on a paper. Pretty quickly, the child approached her with curiosity. As soon as she looked at him and tried to talk, he seemed compelled to slip back into anger, so she decided to read a storybook out loud, and felt the child huddle nearby to see the pictures. Once the child's body was calmer, a conversation would be more productive. The intern shared with Marie-Nathalie that having a word such as "co-centering" to label what she was attempting to do had been very valuable, as it gave her confidence that she was actually intervening therapeutically by simply embodying a calm and trusting presence that would influence the child's emotions and behaviors.

When we teach co-centering practices and encourage our trainees to be aware of their sensations, many report discovering with surprise that their body was tenser than expected with a client, or that they were breathing from the chest, because of lingering anxiety from other issues in their lives such as running late or missing a deadline. When a mindful body scan identifies tension, many breathing practices can help settle and ready practitioners in preparation to meet clients (Beaudoin & Maki, 2020). This is important because when practitioners become overly captured by problems and have to regulate their own intense emotions arising from the sympathetic nervous system, they are biologically less available to support clients. Practitioners become at risk of *joining* in the pain, or irresponsibly *inverting* the relationship and requiring clients to either take care of them or withhold sharing painful experiences to protect the practitioner (see Table 3.1). In general, the emotional intensity of the practitioner's experience should be finely modulated so that their parasympathetic nervous system remains available to support and focus on the client. When both clients and practitioners are co-centered in a similarly low affective intensity, and captured by the conversation, they can be in "flow," a brain state of complete engagement in a collaborative conversation with little awareness of anything else and with time passing quickly (Csikszentmihalyi, 2000). When clients are dysregulated and overwhelmed by emotions, practitioners experience a greater wave of compassion, a brain state where the pain and reward centers of the brain are activated simultaneously, allowing therapists to feel the pain of clients through mirror neurons, but also feel calm, connected, trusted, and deeply united as human beings (Germer, 2014; Rizzolatti et al., 1999; Wallace, 2011).

	Practitioner regulated	**Practitioner not regulated**
Client regulated	Co-centering in flow	Inverting roles
Client not regulated	Co-centering in compassion	Joining in the pain

TABLE 3.1 **Practitioners are encouraged to pay attention to both their own and the client's affective embodied states to ensure they are providing professional support and fostering emotion regulation of the relational dyad.**

One of the key elements of co-centering between practitioner and client is the practice of attunement. Siegel (2010) describes attunement as a person's ability to sense the inner world of another person. When a therapist remains in a state of attunement, calm, and compassion, this increases the likelihood that the client will be able to access that affective state within themselves. This close tracking of affective practices requires an emotional attunement with ourselves and with our clients.

Bird (2004) states that the process of discovering clients' meaning in the present moment includes "*the attention to thoughts, feelings, sensations, visions, body responses, smells, the said, the partially said, the struggle for words, the emotional quality of the words spoken, the look, the presence, the absence and much more*" (p. 35). To fully engage a client who is experiencing strong emotion requires the skills of an empathic, attuned practitioner engaged in emotional resonance.

This is also well described by Hamkins (2014):

As a psychiatrist, when I meet with patients, I try to attend carefully to the emotions that are arising in them and to the stream of emotions that are arising in me in resonance with them. What do I see and hear? What do I feel in my solar plexus, my chest, my face? Are tears rising in me, anger, fear, tenderness, playfulness, joy? When I can feel those feelings and observe that I am feeling those feelings, it is calming and clarifying to me, and, often, moving. . . . I can convey my awareness and acceptance of those emotions to the patient in a myriad of ways, in my demeanor, the expression on my face, the tone of my voice, and in what I say. When I succeed in my emotional validation . . . patients communicate by becoming more relaxed, more forthcoming, more self-accepting, and more hopeful. (p. 27)

Attunement is experienced as an authentic sense of connection, as "feeling felt" by the other person (Siegel, 1999). It requires presence and attention so that the right brain of the therapist can feel the right brain of the client (Schore, 2014, 2019). The research on mirror neurons has revealed that human beings have an ability to feel and sense in the moment what another is experiencing (Iacoboni, 2009; Johnston et al., 2013; Rizzolatti et al., 1999).

In the clinical example below, we show the importance of being co-centered and keenly attuned to the verbal and nonverbal messages exhibited by both practitioners and clients.

Clara

On the phone, Clara shares being a mother of four children, seeking help for a depression that is sapping all her energy. She is struggling with getting out of bed, taking care of her home, and doing activities she previously loved. She is consumed by thoughts going around in her mind all day about how she has failed as a mother, since three of her children have struggles. One suffers from low self-confidence, another dropped out of college, another hangs out with the wrong crowd and does drugs, and the last one is doing well. Her first child was born when she was 17 years old; she dropped out of school to work. She wishes for a better life for her children.

Right before the first video session with Clara, Marie-Nathalie engages in her usual grounding practice, which helps her transition from her own life, or previous meeting, to being fully available and attentive to what her client shared.

Marie-Nathalie shares: In a minute or less, I mindfully engage in a three-step process that I call triple awareness, which involves slowly broadening awareness from self, to space, to person(s). This practice requires checking what's going on in my body to make sure it is relaxed; then expanding awareness to the room around, including space, furniture, light; and then eventually welcoming the client with an awareness of their state of being. Being able to address another person's suffering responsibly requires a professional presence that does not bring additional tensions into the therapeutic space. This triple awareness provides a more solid foundation for co-centering.

> Clara is welcomed into the therapeutic space and is invited to share what's going well in her life and recent satisfying moments in life. She reports very few enjoyable activities other than social media and trying to take care of her home, children, and husband, whom she loves dearly.

While paying attention to the linguistic content of Clara's answers, I am also aware, in the background, of her body breathing, and of my intention to remain a nonreactive presence to whatever will be shared. I take in her slumped shoulders, slow monotone cadence, a very low energy level, and downcast eyes. This is the emotional canvas or affective landscape from which the pace and content of narrative questions emerge. My awareness fluctuates between intentionally *sensing* both of our embodied experiences, mindfully *recognizing* what is unfolding, and thoughtfully *scaffolding* a therapeutic process. Attention to these three levels of awareness allows me to offer a therapeutic "presence," defined by Pat Ogden (2021, p. 225) as: "a participatory state of 'being' rather than observing, of engagement with rather than awareness of an object or even noticing the engagement itself. . . . Presence is a felt sense of merging with each fleeting moment and participating completely," which leads to resonance.

Clara talks about being a failure as a mom. Her agreement with her husband has been that he'd earn the family's income and she'd raise the children. She says, "He did well and I did poorly." She has given parenting every second of her day all these years but failed. She dwells on her "poor decisions" all the time, what she should have done instead, and shares, "I have regrets and thoughts turning around in my mind all the time, night and day."

Clara is crying softly, with just a few tears silently trickling down from the corner of her eyes. Her facial expression is tired, sorrowful, and embarrassed. I sense that Clara is at the border of her WOT and soften my tone of voice, since prosody has a direct impact on the limbic system and people's emotional experience. I find myself shifting into a more pronounced compassionate stance. I can relate as a mother to the intensity of a parent's desire to support her children. This nonverbal demeanor is automatically expressed through eyes, facial expression, leaning forward. I offer a statement to demarginalize her experience and express that I have no intention to criticize her.

> **Marie-Nathalie:** *In my professional and personal experience as a parent myself, I know that mothers try really hard to do what is best for their children. Everyone I've encountered wishes they could take something back.*

Clara nods in agreement and seems less embarrassed, but still sorrowful. It's time to invite perspective through an externalized verbal exploration of the problem.

> **Marie-Nathalie:** *These thoughts going around in your mind, how would you qualify them?*
>
> **Clara (thoughtfully):** *Well . . . they make me feel like I did everything wrong. I was not good enough. Recently, I read a book about the problems caused by "helicopter moms" (mothers who always save their children from hardships) and I think that depicts me. I drove my daughter's*

*science fair project to school because she forgot it on the day it was due.
I allowed my kids to drop out of after-school activities they didn't like
instead of forcing them to stick with it. Now they have less skills than
other kids who were forced into music and extra math.*

Marie-Nathalie: *So there's a not-good-enough-feeling (NGEF) that criticizes
you for a lot of things you did as a mother, even when you were helpful
to your children and listened to their opinions about their preferences?*

Clara: *Yes, I know it would have been better to let them fail and learn from
their mistakes.*

Clara is more animated and fully engaged. I co-center in a state of flow and
respectful curiosity; time passes quickly. The NGEF positions Clara as being
a "helicopter mom," a contemporary and overused way mothers are pathologized for being caring. This idea benefits from deconstruction.

Marie-Nathalie: *The NGEF and the "helicopter mom theory" make you
think it would be better if they learned from mistakes. Is it possible
that listening to this theory and letting them fail could have made
things worse?*

Clara (thinking): *Hum . . . I hadn't thought of that . . . I guess they
wouldn't have learned the value of helping . . .*

Clara's nonverbal responses are now shifting. The sorrow has dissipated,
and she seems intrigued by the conversation. A lighter mood is palpable, yet
there is a felt sense of uncertainty as to whether this is significant enough
to rejoice or not. Clara is making eye contact and seems interested; this
nonverbal information encourages me to proceed.

Marie-Nathalie: *What would your children have learned from a mother
who is not helping them succeed? Would your relation to them be different now, or would they be different people?*

Clara (thinking): *Hum . . . They might not reach out to me for help any-
more . . . that would be sad . . . Hum, those are good points, I'd
feel worse.*

> **Marie-Nathalie:** *So, they reach out to you for help and do they sometimes help others?*
> **Clara (lighting up slightly):** *Yes, actually, they are really helpful to others.*
> **Marie-Nathalie:** *Is that a skill that you value?*

Clara considers her parenting outside of the purview of failure as a mother. Had Clara not been engaged enough by the conversation and indicated on a nonverbal level that she valued "helpfulness," I would have moved on to something else. After discussing a few examples, Clara shares that acknowledging her children's skills is helpful and worth remembering. However, there is one decision she deeply regrets—changing her son's school. This, she reports, is the biggest mistake of her parenting, and the NGEF haunts her about all the implications of *her* "bad decision," since he thereafter became bullied. I sense loneliness and isolation, a hesitation to talk about someone else.

> **Marie-Nathalie:** *So, the NGEF is making you regret that change of school and focus on your son's loss of friends and bullying experiences. (Very softly, communicating nonverbally with compassion that she has no intention of blaming him.) Is it okay for me to ask how your husband participated in this decision to change your son's school?*
> **Clara (after a pause):** *He heard my going back and forth about it.*

This sentence could be interpreted verbally that he was supportive. However, the nonverbal response was one of silence, thinking, looking to the ceiling, debating how she would answer this, and responding very slowly. This hesitation lets Marie-Nathalie know that the conversation ought to proceed carefully; the nonverbal expression feels incongruent with the verbal statement of having been listened to and supported. In these situations, the practice of acknowledging good intentions can help to reconfirm safety.

> **Marie-Nathalie:** *He heard your back-and-forth about it. Would you say he had good intentions to support you?*

Clara (tearful but with less hesitation): *Yes, he had good intentions to support me, but his focus was on his work.*

Marie-Nathalie: *So, he had good intentions but his focus was on his work like many men in this culture? (Nods.) If his focus was on his work, how did it affect his listening and the support you experienced?*

Attention to the body created an opening for sociopolitical considerations of gender dynamics and division of labor.

Clara: *He never said much. He was not really engaged in the conversations. He said it was up to me. He didn't seem to care as much, I guess, since it was my job.*

Marie-Nathalie: *So, your husband, like many men in this culture, left parenting up to you; does that mean you were fairly isolated with big decisions?*

Tracking the affective responses aids in identifying isolation, which many women feel when positioned as responsible for all matters related to the social and emotional welfare of family members.

Clara (crying): *Yes.*

Marie-Nathalie circles back to the externalized problem as she invites Clara at a deeper level to evaluate the effects of the problem.

Marie-Nathalie: *The NGEF gives the impression those decisions were entirely problematic, and then makes them all about you "failing," but is the NGEF being oblivious to positive effects of your parenting, and factors outside of your control such as isolation, and other people's influence, which also contributed to these events? (Nods.) I wonder what other factors contributed to your children's journey?*

Clara (thinking): *Well . . . I guess each of my children has a disposition . . . their own interest and ways of doing things . . . hum . . . . They're also influenced by their peers and their teachers . . .*

As Clara is slowly generating this list and getting perspective, she seems to grow more settled. All along, Marie-Nathalie has noticed moments that seem to appease Clara, and she can compose a summary contrasting what seemed nonverbally and verbally meaningful to her. Most importantly, Marie-Nathalie can highlight what stood out as supporting the embodied experience of a preferred self. The session ends with examining briefly how confidence feels in her body and connecting this experience to other moments in her life and to relationships.

What Co-Centering Is Not

There are knowledges and perspectives that therapists have accrued that can be beneficial for clients to hear. Making an occasional statement is considered different from giving advice or making compliments. While we are advocating for practitioners to occasionally share community knowledge, we are committed to still mostly asking questions, using clients' language, and constantly checking that we are maintaining a decentered and co-centered approach; otherwise the therapeutic conversation can be derailed (Beaudoin & Estes, 2021). Questions still account for about 90% of practitioners' communications. The main reasons to make a brief statement instead of asking a question include

- revealing something about oneself, without taking the focus away from the client, to increase safety or connection (e.g., "I am a parent too");
- demarginalizing someone's experience (e.g., "Many people are struggling with the isolating effects of this pandemic");
- sharing sympathy without joining a problem (e.g., "I'm sorry there is so much sorrow right now"); and
- introducing information outside of the zone of proximal development that clients would likely never discover on their own (e.g., "Emotions are like glue in the brain").

Conclusion

In conversations, as stated by Siegel (2012, p. 84), "*a story is created by both teller and listener.*" If the nature of our profession is to assist people, then it would make sense for practitioners to use their professional knowledge to "*structure contexts for people's skills to become more richly described*" (White, 1994).

Working from a co-centered therapeutic posture allows decentered practices to be influential. The combination of these postures involves adjusting therapeutic interactions based on clients' verbal and nonverbal expressions. Practitioners will generally experience a low intensity of their own affective reactions, and pay attention to potential effects on the problem, the preferred self, and the relationship, as they match or not the affective valence of their clients' experiences. Co-centered therapeutic work involves asking attuned questions, responding to non-verbal embodied affective expressions, and occasionally including therapists' sharing of knowledge to support clients' trajectory toward preferred identities. This balance is also done in a way that is well discussed in the mindfulness and compassion literature and is helpful in facilitating emotion regulation. In the next chapter, we will discuss a version of co-centering using ideas from IPNB.

Neutralizing Intense Problematic Emotions With Ideas From Interpersonal Neurobiology

Interpersonal neurobiology (IPNB; Siegel, 1999, 2021) offers interesting concepts that can help with intense problematic emotions and restore our ability to move forward with preferred-identity development. There are many overlapping premises between narrative therapy ideas and IPNB, as visible in Daniel Siegel's following comment:

> We . . . experience many selves or self-states that are enduring patterns of subjective experience, perspective, and agency filled with particular memories, emotional tendencies and narrative processes that make meaning out of those experiences. This multitude of selves in turn shapes the layers of identity we have; and that in turn shapes our experiences of belonging. (Siegel, 2021, p. 21)

In a nutshell, IPNB acknowledges that the brain is neuroplastic, constantly changing, and that people construct identity narratives based on their relationships, their life experiences, and the cultural contexts in which they evolve (Siegel et al., 2021). Experience shapes the brain and the brain shapes experiences (Siegel, 1999). In particular, IPNB offers possibilities of bettering our work with regard to understanding emotion regulation and well-being, associated with differentiation, linkage, and integration (Siegel, 1999, 2010, 2012, 2021).

Differentiation refers to each part of a whole being able to function in an optimal way, while also contributing to a cohesive, harmonious, bigger system, which incorporates information from many other areas. Linkage connects all these unique areas into a functional whole. "Integration entails differentiating and linking in which the linkage does not destroy the differentiation: Integration is more like a fruit salad than a smoothie" (Siegel, 2021, p. 12). In therapeutic conversations, integration involves the consolidation of left and right hemispheric processes, as well as bottom-up and top-down information (Siegel et al., 2021), and generally leads to a coherent life story. A person would, for example, experience a regulated emotion (mostly right hemisphere), which would be analyzed and labeled (mostly left hemisphere), felt in the body (bottom up), and storied in the neocortex (top down). Since research on brain hemispheric differences shows that some people operate in the opposite way, and that both hemispheres can be involved in many experiences, we invite readers to think more in terms of processing styles and functional nuances, rather than fixed dichotomous biological descriptions (Morton, 2013; Siegel, 2012). When one segment of this process goes into overdrive or is blocked, or the system cannot integrate, people's well-being is compromised, and they struggle with regulating emotions, make suboptimal decisions, or feel stuck in their lives.

In this chapter, we share clinical practices in each of these four dimensions. Some of these concepts may be familiar to narrative practitioners although presented in a new light, and others are novel, inspired by fresh ideas from IPNB. We are not advocating that the practices described below benefit every client, or that they should be implemented in any particular order. They are conversational knowledges held in "our back pockets" that can become part of a wide repertoire of ideas, help people reclaim their preferred identity, and diffuse intense problematic emotions.

1. Addressing Affective Experiences and Their Meanings: Tapping Into Right-Hemisphere Processing

The right side of the brain tends to be associated with metaphors, emotions, sensations, imagination, intuition, creativity, relationship, and attunement (McGilchrist, 2009; Siegel, 2012). A therapeutic journey involving intense emotions typically starts and ends with right-hemispheric processing because of its key role in meaning making (Badenoch, 2021; Schore, 2014, 2019). Intense problem emotions can unexpectedly spill out in a therapeutic space, as happened in Marie-Nathalie's first session with the client in the story below, and knowledge of the right hemisphere can help us determine how to best respond.

Amir, a very soft-spoken and shy 29-year-old of Middle Eastern descent, was smiling and polite in the waiting room before his first therapy appointment. As soon as the office door was closed behind him, without even having uttered a sentence, he suddenly shifted emotionally and collapsed on the sofa, sobbing tears. His emotions were so intense that he couldn't speak and struggled to breathe. I uttered a soft supportive sound and gently offered him the box of tissues, even if it was within reach for him, as this gesture expressed a caring intent. Not knowing this client, except for a brief, pleasant phone conversation where he expressed wanting to improve work relationships, there was not much I could scaffold verbally. Drawing on IPNB knowledge, I was aware that my own emotional choice at that moment would have a significant physiological effect on his experience. I felt filled with compassion toward him and grounded myself nonverbally. Connecting with inner peace in my own body and co-centering contributed emotional stability to our relational dyad. I tried to gently normalize his experience so the physical space wouldn't be filled with awkwardness. I did so while remaining tuned to his nonverbal response: *"It's okay to cry, some things are hard to talk about . . . (more sobbing) . . . and you don't have to talk about them today . . . (more sobbing) . . . I'm here for you, for whatever feels helpful to you . . . (less sobbing) . . . and you've already taken a step in addressing this problem by being here today . . . (less sobbing) . . . Let's try to breathe together for a few minutes, inhaling slowly and exhaling slowly at the same time. Inhale . . . Exhale . . . Feel the sofa supporting you and the safety of this room. Inhale the calm in the room all the way to your toes and exhale the sadness."* By doing this, I engaged in what we have defined as co-centering, which overlaps with right-brain-to-right-brain regulation in IPNB.

A. Right-Brain-to-Right-Brain Regulation

The right brain is heavily involved with the experience of intense emotions in most people and luckily is also very sensitive to the felt experience of another caring person available to regulate the dyad's joint affective level (Ogden, 2021; Schore, 2014, 2019; Siegel et al., 2021). If a person is overwhelmed by an intense emotion and is sharing it with a listener anchored in compassion, kindness, and trust, the client's neural firing will progressively internalize the other person's calmer state and shift to regulation (Cozolino, 2016; Schore, 2019). This is made possible by the existence of mirror neurons, which provide each person with a felt sense of what another is experiencing, an impressive physiological ability involved in attunement (Iacoboni, 2009). The presence of a calm and compassionate listener also keeps the social engagement system functional (ventral branch of the vagus nerve) in a way that supports felt connection, safety, and ultimately regulation (Porges, 2011; Siegel et al., 2021). When there is an outpouring of emotions limiting verbal interactions, there are still many possibilities of helping, depending on what is appropriate in a culture and specific context of work, by using distance between people ("Would you like me to sit closer?"), gentle touch ("Would it help if I placed my hand over your hand, or my foot beside yours?"), breath ("Let's inhale slowly from the lower belly together"), sounds ("I'll play a recording of ocean sounds and you can consider synchronizing your breath with the waves"), senses ("Try to feel the cushiness of the carpet under your feet"), physical space ("Notice how this room is keeping both of us safe"), time ("Let's anchor ourselves in the present, just here and now"), weights ("Would the heavy weighted blanket right there be comforting?"), and kinesthetic movements ("How about we both stand up and reach toward the ceiling?"). These practices overlap with bottom-up work discussed later. With Amir, only gentle breath work was used and he progressively settled into a calmer state.

B. Lining Distress With Agency

In order to widen the WOT, expressions of suffering can be interwoven with experiences of agency to highlight clients' capabilities. As discussed in Chapter 2, this is a back-and-forth dance of eliciting descriptions that may trigger a manageable level of problem emotions, while returning to regulating strategies in ways that expand a person's comfort levels.

Not wanting Amir to further spiral into a highly agitated state, and not knowing much about his life, it was more therapeutic to explore his experiences of his preferred self, and come back to the sadness later.

> **Marie-Nathalie:** *Let's put hardships on hold for a few minutes and talk about other things, then we'll get back to it, is that okay? (Meek smile and nod.) What was your most relaxing moment this past week?*
>
> **Amir (smiling gently, in a soft voice):** *That's a good question. Hum . . . I was most relaxed when . . . I was building a new remote-control airplane.*
>
> **Marie-Nathalie (intrigued):** *Building a remote-control airplane? Tell me about it; how do you do that and what makes it relaxing?*

Amir becomes more animated as he talks about feeling skilled in building model airplanes, which took a lot of attention to details, concentration, creativity, and contrasted with not feeling valued or accepted at work. We externalize the sadness and how it got him to criticize himself to the point of avoiding contact with coworkers.

As he became more relaxed and gained perspective on the problem, the externalizing conversation progressed swiftly. By the end of the hour, sadness was fully externalized and I had become the very first person he openly came out to as being gay, a subject scorned and taboo with his very close, but extremely religious, Iranian parents. Since he was born and grew up in the United States, his views differed from his family's on many issues. He struggled with the weight of the secrecy, which made him feel like a fraud. The combination of terror and desire to come out had led to the intense emotions at the beginning of our session. His coming out in the last few minutes of the meeting was made possible by the co-centering, the right-brain-to-right-brain connection, and the compassionate conversational space of seeing him as a valuable person, separate from the problem. He seemed so relieved, he left looking taller. I was honored by his trust and pleased he felt so much better.

C. Identifying Meaningful and Intense Affective Counter-States

Clients usually share stories of feeling defeated, discouraged, incompetent, worthless, angry, or worried about their ability to handle a situation or fit in a group. They are ascribing meaning to the challenges of their lives in such a way that their sense of competence appears insignificant and the hardships overwhelming. Amir felt inadequate because of the sociocultural constructions around homosexuality, which may have contributed to his low-energy, shy style of interacting. He was ascribing meaning to these aspects of his experience and felt unlovable. The first meeting was a step in addressing this construction by providing him with a different relational experience. In a later session, we could directly deconstruct the discourses behind these beliefs (mostly a left-hemisphere process), and also examine various experiences of feeling worthy, with reauthoring conversations (see White, 2007, 2011; White & Epston, 1990). In this early phase of therapy, I decided to address the intense emotions spilling uncomfortably in his life by exploring potential counter-states, that is, ways of being that contradict and neutralize the problem experience (Beaudoin & Zimmerman, 2011). Since sadness involved a "pulling away" action potential, I was interested in emotions eliciting a "moving toward" action potential. In my clinical experience, two groups of emotions stand out as having a significant action potential that physiologically mobilizes motivation and power in human beings: love and anger.

The experience of love and all its multiple variations, such as compassion, kindness, patience, gratefulness, and so on, is associated with a different heart-rate variability (HRV; Childre & Martin, 2000), which engenders a special pattern of electrical firing in the brain and the production of hormones such as oxytocin (a bonding and relaxing biochemical) and dopamine, associated with well-being (Kerr et al., 2019). Conversations eliciting experiences of love can be highly effective in facilitating a movement toward preferred actions. Eliciting memories associated with loving, protecting, contributing, creating, sustaining, supporting, mentoring, teaching, healing, leading, and so on provide great momentum in therapeutic conversations.

Anger is well known to increase physical strength and fearlessness due to its associated increase in adrenaline (Davis, 2021). Anger can mobilize actions and move crowds of protestors to engage in destructive acts when perceiving injustices. The Fairness Across the World module of the 2018 Gallup Poll study of 65,856 people across 60 countries revealed that fairness is an issue that concerns most people across a wide spectrum of differences. Much of the world reports that income inequalities should be reduced (Almås, Cappelen, Sørensen, & Tungodden, 2020), but there are striking differences in how people view fairness between developed and developing countries. Most of these differences can be accounted for by understanding how people make sense of unfairness. In the West, there is a greater focus on individual worth and merit, which makes it a powerful personal motivator. In other countries, it may be more frequently explained by luck, hard work, religion, or by viewing the privileged as selfish (Almås, Cappelen, & Tungodden, 2020). Tapping into people's sense of justice and fairness can energize clients to take action in their own and others' lives in many communities of the world.

Amir seemed eager and motivated in the next session. He had joined a gay group online and had really enjoyed their first meeting. He felt uplifted and now really wanted to talk about work. In the past five years, the sadness had gotten him to stay away from coworkers, not ask questions even when he didn't understand, and never speak in a staff meeting. As a result, he had recently been assigned something he didn't want to do, and shouldn't have to do, and he felt depressed about it.

> **Amir (deflated):** *I can't believe my manager allowed this other guy to pass on this boring task to me, I've been so sad about that, and it got in the way of me sleeping last night. I couldn't stop thinking about it.*

Marie-Nathalie: *What did the sadness make you think about over and over again?*

Amir (on the verge of tears): *Why isn't she standing up for me, that's her job as a manager, that's what I'd do if I was a manager.*

Marie-Nathalie: *So the sadness is making you preoccupied by this situation and you have some ideas about the role of a manager?*

Amir: *Yes, a good manager should support employees, help them with their projects, and encourage them to find a balance between different priorities.*

Marie-Nathalie: *What does it mean about her that she doesn't do that?*

Amir (thinking): *Hum, I always wonder if she likes me or not but what it means about her . . . hum . . . maybe that she's stressed . . . and also it might be hard for her to stand up to this guy.*

Marie-Nathalie: *So, people have a hard time standing up to this guy? (Nods.) Does this lead to chronic unfairness?*

Amir (resentful): *Yeah, it's often unfair; he always gets his way, I'm not sure why, he's such a jerk and can be so entitled.*

Marie-Nathalie (noticing the resentment): *Does this unfairness make you tempted to say or do something?*

Amir (resentful): *Yes, I should say something, I feel so resentful. This task shouldn't be assigned to me, it's not in my project, it'll take a lot of time and it means I have to do overtime or sacrifice my own project to do it.*

The conversation continued and Amir examined how the resentment helped him feel more confident, find words to verbalize his concerns, and embody his conviction, and how he was able to express himself in proactive ways in the past. The state of resentment about unfairness creates a powerful counter-state with a forward action potential, which can better neutralize the sadness and render it less paralyzing. With more time, this conversation could have also been followed with a discussion about someone who may have appreciated (or loved) his confidence and impulse to protest unfairness.

2. Reengaging the Power of Logic When It's Derailed by Problems: Tapping Into Left-Hemisphere Processing

A significant body of research has concluded that in most people, the left hemisphere of the brain tends to be associated with functions related to problem analysis, sequential thought processing, logical reflection, ability to work with numeracy, analytical thinking, predictions, and, interestingly, the state of happiness (Iturria-Medina et al., 2011; McGilchrist, 2009; Siegel, 2012). Intense troublesome emotions tend to hijack the brain's left hemisphere and skew mental activity in many ways. In our clinical practice, we have found that the exploration of two specific tendencies is particularly helpful to addressing intense emotions: the certainty trap and focusing poles.

The certainty trap refers to feeling convinced that one's thinking is completely accurate even when it's not (Burton, 2009). One's emotional conviction that a problematic belief is true can be intense enough to lead people down the path of taking extreme actions, such as attempting suicide or hurting others. The certainty trap, or veracity trap, can wreak havoc in relationships when it gets people to ascribe malevolent intentions to others. Educators and parents may interpret children's behaviors through the lens of control ("He's trying to manipulate me, I know it"). Couples in a stressed relationship can ascribe to their partner an intention of hurtfulness ("I know for sure, she did it on purpose"). The problem belief can endure, even in the face of contradictory information, as people assume that their problem view is more a representation of the truth and that the exceptions are meaningless or random occurrences. Inviting empathy and care in a therapeutic conversation may not be effective until the certainty trap is exposed as an effect of the problem ("Sadness convinces you that nobody likes you. Might there be any evidence that this is not always true?").

In the absence of a better term, we conceptualize "focusing poles" as the skewed thinking of under- and overfocusing on certain aspects of a situation. Biologically, this is due to the change in bioelectrical firing in the brain that will instantaneously mobilize all resources to address real or perceived threats, and temporarily restricts attention on the arousing detail (Hill, 2021; Porges, 2011). The preoccupation with an element of the problem, mentally repeated over and over, increasingly reinforces itself with every strong affective activation in the brain. This narrow focus in itself limits possibilities of uncovering solutions, perspectives, or other aspects of experience that could solve the problem. We have noticed that the regulation of intense problem emotions is more likely to occur if the over- and underfocusing bias is recognized. Questions can be asked such as, "When sadness gets you to become convinced that you are worthless, might it be over- or underfocusing on something?"

The brain's tendency to get stuck in the certainty trap and focusing poles can be addressed by engaging the left hemisphere in mental activities that can reset perspectives using externalizing, numeral questions, and speculation.

A. Externalizing

Externalizing problems refers to the linguistic choice of speaking about problems as separate from people's identity (White & Epston, 1990). This practice conveys that people do not choose to have problems, which often result from the interaction between self and context, and that a person is much more than their problem. In IPNB terms, externalizing provides a shift in perspective, which reorganizes neural firing in the brain by increasing the number and kind of circuits available to a client to understand their experience and observe the problem's influence. It is also an act of differentiation, where the problem state is observed as being distinct from other, more preferred states. The linkage and therapeutic gain arising from differentiation will occur when this left-brain observation can be paired with a right-brain experience. Externalizing conveniently taps into a few left-hemispheric processes: labeling, observing, understanding, analyzing, sequencing, and gaining perspective.

B. Numeral Questions

Numeral questions involve quantifying an experience in a perspective-inducing way, which typically recruits left-hemisphere processing. The most well-known numeral questions involve scaling, such as, "On a scale of 1 to 10, how intense was the shame?" Or "On a scale of 1 to 10, how much sadness did you experience, and what did you do to prevent it from becoming a 10?" While these questions can be very helpful, there are many other ways to activate numerical analytic activity, and the eight categories of affective activity markers discussed in Chapter 1 offer many possibilities to practitioners (see Appendix 1). Numeral questions trigger a different experience of problems, preferred selves, and possibilities. More specifically, they enhance opportunities to discredit the certainty trap, expose skewed focusing, heighten the clarity of relational patterns, help simplify complex problems, and make intangible experiences concrete. Numeral responses can move conversations beyond the known and familiar linguistic descriptions to a level of conceptualization clients have never articulated before.

C. Speculation

Engaging clients in speculation about the future is a left-brain activity involving evaluation. This practice was introduced by Michael White (1989) and the questions typically involve a "What if . . . " formulation. For example: "The depression makes you feel hopeless right now, but *what if* there was another way to solve this suffering aside from hurting yourself; would you be interested in exploring it?"

With Amir, once sensations of sadness emerged, the sadness convinced him that his life was one big loss. This drove him to dwell not only on current experiences of missing out on intimate-partner relationships but also on imagined losses. The dialogue below demonstrates speculation as well as the use of numeral questions and externalizing, which helped to reengage Amir's logical thinking.

> **Amir:** *The sadness made me cry so much this week, thinking of my grandmother.*
> **Marie-Nathalie:** *What did the sadness get you to think about?*
> **Amir (tearful):** *It's just that I love her so much, I imagine how horrible it will be when she dies; she has a health issue and the doctors give her another five years at the most.*

Marie-Nathalie: *So the sadness gets you to live her death ahead of time?*

Amir: *Yes, it makes me practice so I'll be better prepared when it happens . . .*

Marie-Nathalie: *So the sadness makes you think you'll be better prepared and that this is a helpful practice? (Nods.) Let's examine that idea. What percentage of the future does the sadness actually know for certain?*

Amir (interested): *Well, that she'll die but not much else.*

Marie-Nathalie: *So sadness doesn't know much about the future but it is getting you to live ahead of time one version of many possible scenarios. What percentage of this movie is sadness actually making up?*

Amir: *Probably a lot . . . It gets me to imagine the scene, the people there, how I'll dress, how lonely I'll feel . . .*

Marie-Nathalie: *So it gets you to imagine even the visual elements of the scene? (Nods.) Let's put an actual number, between 0% and 100%, on how much of this scene is imagined, with 100% being a completely fabricated and probably not reliable prediction.*

Amir (thinking): *Hum . . . probably over 95% is completely fabricated.*

Marie-Nathalie (kindly and slowly): *So the sadness is tricking you into fully living a 95% imaginary scenario of a painful future, . . . and in the meantime, is it making you miss out on 100% of the present time's reality?*

Amir (smiling): *That is so true! I should call her more often instead of crying.*

Marie-Nathalie: *So calling her more often, like how often?*

Amir: *Well maybe three to four times per week. That's probably the number of evenings I spend crying over her death.*

Marie-Nathalie: *Let's play with those numbers, let's say 3.5/week × 52 weeks/year × 5 years = 910. So the sadness could make you live a completely imaginary version of her death 910 times instead of once, and you're proposing to enjoy her presence instead, by calling her more often. What difference will it make if you do that? Is calling her and spending time with her more in line with how you wish to live?*

Amir (laughing): *Yeah, actually I never thought of it this way!*

Marie-Nathalie: *Are we also discovering something about sadness? I wonder if it gets you to overfocus on an imaginary loss, and underfocus on a real presence?*

Amir: *Yeah . . . that feels accurate . . . . Sadness gets me to overfocus on a loss and be completely unaware of the imaginary part of these scenarios and the time I'm wasting. I really want to remember this conversation. I should just make more good things happen and focus on her being alive right now!*

Marie-Nathalie: *Making more good things happen and focusing on her being alive? What would that look like?*

Amir (motivated): *I should talk to her and more people, spend less time with the sadness.*

Marie-Nathalie: *So talking to her and other people more, and spending less time with sadness. When was the last time you did that and enjoyed it?*

Amir: *Last week, I joined the connection program at my company. They draw our names randomly to lunch with people from other departments and I met a coworker I liked. It felt good to talk and share.*

Marie-Nathalie: *Can you give me an example of a minute when you were being the person you prefer to be during that lunch?*

Amir (smiling): *Yeah, I was laughing about his story, and asking questions. I was just relaxed and present, not in my head. He eventually invited me to join a big group of people going to the Renaissance Fair this weekend.*

The conversations ends with accruing more details about the unfolding of the preferred story that was being coauthored.

3. The Five "T"s of Embodied Affect Deactivation: Addressing Bottom-up Experiences

"Bottom-up" experiences refer to the sensory information collected in the body and sent upward to the brain (Siegel, 2012). As mentioned earlier, if a problem involves a specific body part, the preferred self also needs to mobilize that specific body part to ensure the stability of the progress (Beaudoin, 2017b). The five embodied practices below offer examples of working with bottom-up processes. The first one is well known to narrative practitioners but the others are derived from IPNB.

A. Tend to Sensations Associated With Unique Outcomes

Unique-outcome questions create opportunities to examine moments at the border of the WOT (Beaudoin & Zimmerman, 2011) when clients have been able to shift their emotional experience without necessarily being aware of how exactly they did it. Clients feel empowered knowing they've already been able to manage problem moments and need only to refine existing skills.

With Amir, the problems of both sadness and nervousness about speaking up silenced him and choked his throat. Reauthoring questions needed to carefully discover throat sensations associated with his preferred self.

> **Marie-Nathalie:** *In the example you just shared when you were feeling relaxed and present, how did your throat feel?*
>
> **Amir:** *It felt fine . . . it's hard to describe. Hum . . . let me think . . . . It felt normal, like there was space there, and air could get through my vocal cords to make sounds.*
>
> **Marie-Nathalie:** *Your throat felt like air could get through and make sounds, so did the sound of your voice change?*
>
> **Amir (realizing):** *Yes, actually, my voice was softer, lower, and probably more quiet . . .*
>
> **Marie-Nathalie:** *Your voice was softer, lower, more quiet; would any visual image represent that?*
>
> **Amir (smiling):** *I was like a ninja who's sneaking around the emotion and calmly doing what he wants!*

We continued to name these embodied changes and elaborate on the visual representation (aesthetic sense), since awareness of these sensations and the use of metaphors can later facilitate access to this preferred state.

B. Transform the Construction

As described in Chapter 1, we adhere to the view that there is no unique physiological activation in the brain or body for each specific emotion (Barrett, 2017). This lack of specificity in activation has the disadvantage of a wide variety of meaningless moments being interpreted by the problem story, which eventually reduces the range and granularity of affective experiences. For example, people might assume they have a depression relapse when they are physiologically slowed down by the beginning of influenza, a poor night's sleep, hunger, tiredness, watching discouraging media, or feeling bored. On the other hand, this lack of specificity opens the door to questioning the interpretation of experience and relabeling it in more neutral or productive ways with questions such as: *"Are we sure it was a sadness relapse that hit you when you came back to work Monday, or could it have been the common disappointment of a great weekend coming to an end?"* In Chapter 1, we referred to this therapeutic process as delinking sensations of discomfort from problem interpretations.

C. Transfer the Activation

Since embodied experiences lack specificity, a number of emotions activate the body in similar ways. For instance, it is sometimes possible to slightly adjust an expression to transfer its activation to another experience, with questions such as: *"What would it look like if you were to transfer the nervous energy inside of you before a meeting into an outward excitement of meeting new people? Could that be helpful? Can you think of a time you might have done something similar?"*

D. Teach Mindfulness or Movement

The crafting of artful questions dominates most narrative therapy practices, as the intent is to help clients discern their experiences and reconnect with their skills, values, and preferred identities. Occasionally, teaching may be necessary to facilitate the discovery of helpful tools the client may never encounter otherwise, such as mindfulness meditation (Germer, 2014; Kabat-Zinn, 1990, 2003, 2005; Salzberg, 2015; Winston, 2019).

As mentioned in Chapter 1, most clients' mental activity dwells in what is called the default state, where the mind wanders freely between inner chatter (easily problem saturated) and external attention such as listening to others (Wallace, 2007). During such mental activity, specific regions of the brain are activated, such as the medial prefrontal cortex and posterior cingulate cortex (mPFC and PCC; Raichle et al., 2001). In contrast, mindfulness meditation is associated with a unique pattern of neural activation called the experiential network, which requires instruction and offers the benefits of inner peace, mental stability, and a reduction of emotional engagement (Brewer et al., 2011; Chun et al., 2011; Farb et al., 2007; Mason et al., 2007). The process involves directing attention to sensory information that is present-time focused and, ideally, pausing involuntary thinking (Kornfield, 1993; Salzberg, 2021; Smalley & Winston, 2010; Wallace, 2007). This is further discussed in Chapter 8. Many forms of mindfulness exist, and I (MNB) have found that practices most relevant to clinical work focus on interoception and body-scan awareness, or breath work (*pranayama*). Breath work offers many advantages, as it modifies a person's physiological and biochemical state almost immediately (Goleman & Davidson, 2017). This can be immensely useful just before an examination, athletic event, performance, high-conflict conversation, or any high-stress situation, such as an important interview. Breath work is also appealing to clients who are eager to shift quickly out of distressing bottom-up physiological states. Breathing practices are easier to implement when the exercises include an intriguing dimension where the curiosity networks of the brain are engaged, making it more feasible to forgo thinking about a problem (Beaudoin & Maclennan, 2021; Beaudoin & Maki, 2020). While it is beyond the scope of this book to detail breathing exercises, readers may be interested to know that breathing can be divided into four segments (inhale, pause, exhale, pause) and that by varying each one of these steps we can develop breathing practices targeting different emotional states (Beaudoin, in press). For enduring structural rewiring to occur in the brain, and for certain structures to actually increase in thickness and connectivity (Goleman & Davidson, 2017), people need to practice daily, which is more easily accomplished by joining a formal class such as a mindfulness-based stress-reduction program, originally designed by Jon Kabat-Zinn (1990, 2003, 2005). Moving the body can also help dissolve troublesome sensations and facilitate entry into preferred physiological states of being (Ogden, 2021). These can involve conventional yoga, simple gestures, postures, or walking, which can all change a person's experience of their embodied activation (Beaudoin, 2019; Griffith & Griffith, 1994; McGonigal, 2021; van der Kolk, 2014). Mindful movements are safer for people who experience trauma, as they reduce the likelihood of the quiet mind being flooded by flashbacks, or resurfacing sensations associated with disturbing events (van der Kolk, 2014).

> **Marie-Nathalie:** *Amir, I know you've been practicing the breathing exercise every night before falling asleep and it's been helpful. Are you interested in a next step? (Nods and smiles.) Since you are feeling really confident right now, can you take a walk around the office for two minutes, making sure to walk confidently, and notice how you hold your body, shoulders, head, and gaze differently? Also, take notice of the size of your stride, if there's a bounce in your footstep, how your foot hits the ground, how your arms move and how you breathe. Try to breathe in the confidence and intensify it in your body.*

E. Transition to a Bridge

In some situations, shifting from the physiological activation of a problematic emotion that is immobilizing to a freer preferred state can be difficult to do and may benefit from an in-between transition state. Practitioners can guide clients into a two-step process, where an experiential bridge is initiated to reset the body physiologically, followed by a preferred embodied emotion, previously articulated either from personal life, therapeutic conversations, or mindfulness training. With Amir, this process was suggested when his manager was considering him for a desirable promotion, which required interviews with upper management and triggered the old problem in spite of many weeks of being his preferred self. Sadness was threatening to immobilize him again in a low-energy state, where he imagined stuttering, failing the interview, and being stuck in his current position forever, so I asked: *"You've mentioned that sadness is trying to immobilize and 'mummify' you again by dwelling on the scene of walking into the interview room in a sheepish way. I wonder if we can find something that can help you connect to confidence right before going into that interview room, like a transition state for your body. It could be doing jumping jacks in your office to increase oxygen in your brain, an invigorating breathing exercise, drinking cold water, or listening to upbeat music . . . . Does this idea feel like it could be helpful?" (Enthusiastically nods.) "What might be most appealing to you? After that reset of your body, it might be easier to reengage with being outspoken. Would you like to try it?"*

4. Stories That "Hijack the Hijacking": Tapping Into Top-Down Processes

The combination of a logical sequencing of facts (mostly left brain) and their associated meanings (mostly right brain) creates a top-down narrative that guides people's decisions and actions in everyday life (Siegel, 2012). The top-down stories create an attentional net in which certain aspects of experience get caught while others slip away without our even noticing, leading to a belief that only what is observed matters. Since life is rife with a vast amount of information and sensations, only what is deemed personally relevant is attended to, easily leading to a closed feedback loop, stagnating with redundant problem-centered information.

Narrative conversations provide fresh ways of activating the neocortex and harnessing this part of the brain's capacity to story events, so that new possibilities of meaning arise. With Amir, the reauthoring progressively became about preferring to be a social and outgoing person. It became important to emotionally thicken this story, so it would take precedence over the previously intense problem experience that had prevailed for so long.

Thickening a preferred story involves foundational narrative practices, such as uncovering its past, connecting to values, recruiting an audience, documenting, and collecting examples of unique-outcome moments (Epston, 2008; White, 2007; White & Epston, 1990). These practices are all necessary to counterbalance the power of problems, which typically stand on a foundation of select events, memories, and witnesses. To effectively intensify this preferred identity, so it has a fair likelihood of neurally becoming a viable option in the face of duress, a series of additional practices inspired by positive psychology and mindfulness can be added:

A. Grafting: This practice was inspired by the gardening process of attaching a desirable but fragile fruit-tree branch to the strong roots of another variety so that the two become permanently united. Inspired by this metaphor, I've (MNB) experimented with finding a *powerful* experience (which may appear unrelated) and then extracting from it stories that could reinforce the preferred self. This practice ties again into the use of action potential and could include questions such as: "What emotion gives power to your ability to speak up?" Followed by: "Where does this emotion come from? Can you tell me its history in your life and who inspires it?" This crisscrossing of strands of seemingly different branches of preferred identities can pave the way for the establishment of an integrated self.

B. Granularizing: As discussed in Chapter 1, granularizing adds a *variety* of descriptions of emotions and preferred identities, as reflected in the following questions: "What other positive emotions might be associated with this experience of being outgoing and social? Who in your life helps bring forward this emotion in a way that you like? Can you tell me a story about this person?"

C. Embodying: Questions focusing on embodying experiences mobilize the bottom-up system and, in practice, are interwoven into the top-down storying. Here I wish to incorporate stories of *influential people's* embodied expressions. For example: "When you are walking with confidence, does that remind you of someone you've respected?"

In our work together, Amir developed a preferred story of being outgoing, enjoying humor, talking with people, and being more comfortable with his gay identity. While this account showed progress, there was a concern that sadness was neurally wired in much stronger ways than his preferred self, and would be activated in much faster, more intense, and longer-lasting ways. This issue of intensity is evident in fMRI studies, which have revealed activation of up to 35 areas of the brain in states of sadness, compared to only an average of nine with happiness (Vytal & Hamann, 2010). While the number of activated areas does not entirely account for experience, preferred stories benefit from having as much affective and embodied reinforcement as possible. In my work with Amir, I had elicited from him many examples of preferred-self moments, as well as helped him list successful strategies to address his problems. We had found significant family members or friends in Amir's life who could bear witness to the preferred changes he was making. We discussed the relief of coming out to his grandmother as gay, and he reflected on the significance of his being able to share parts of his life that had been previously hidden. However, there was a need to reinforce Amir's ability to hold on to his sense of himself as fun, loving, and outgoing in the face of sadness's attempts to occasionally reoccupy his life. Here is a set of interactions that used the practice of grafting to interconnect other powerful emotions with his preferred sense of self.

> **Marie-Nathalie:** *When sadness snuck up on you yesterday and wanted you to curl up and cry in bed after the stressful workday, you managed it by "going for a walk and refusing to go down that hole." Can we examine that moment when you transitioned from sadness's invitation to cry in bed, to taking control of your body and leading it toward the door for a walk? What emotion might have helped you do that, this time?*
>
> **Amir:** *I'm fed up with this sadness. I lost so much time and opportunities, I don't want to do that anymore no matter what is going on, but it's still hard to pull myself away sometimes.*
>
> **Marie-Nathalie:** *So being fed up because you lost so much time and opportunities, and you can do it (encouraging modulation), but it's sometimes still hard to pull away. Would you say you used a similar strategy to what we've discussed the last few times? (Nods.) Okay, so let's explore something new; what's another really powerful emotion that has mobilized you to do hard things in your life?*
>
> **Amir (thinking):** *Oh! I've done a few hard things in my life . . . . Hum . . . . Now that I think of it, some of the hardest things I've done were . . .*

hum . . . let me think . . . . Oh! I know! I've done hard things out of a sense of duty.

Marie-Nathalie: *Sense of duty? Can you share an example?*

Amir shares a story of saving someone he didn't like when he was in the army. We then examined other moments when there was an internal pull to do or not do something, even tracing it back to childhood and not wanting to do a school assignment and yet completing the task out of duty. While there is no English word that conveys the emotions experienced in that state, acting out of duty was definitely a felt affective state for Amir. It was associated with feeling honorable and tied to his religion. He had learned it from his father, who was a very responsible man and whom he admired. Amir felt proud to share these accounts. These stories were all new in our therapeutic journey and could be interwoven in the stance against the hegemony of sadness.

> **Marie-Nathalie:** *I wonder if this powerful sense of duty, its connection to your father, and the pride it engenders, can play a role in limiting the influence of sadness in your life?*
>
> **Amir (excitedly):** *For sure! I'm realizing that I have a duty to be there for my grandma, there's only the two of us in this area, and I can't allow myself to wallow in the small sad events of my day.*
>
> **Marie-Nathalie:** *Would you say that the sense of duty makes you a person who is attentive to others, while the sadness typically gets people to overfocus on themselves (it does that to everyone)?*
>
> **Amir:** *That's a good point, it does make me self-centered, always analyzing what everyone said to me or how they looked at me . . . which is not at all the kind of person I want to be.*
>
> **Marie-Nathalie:** *So sadness makes you overfocused on yourself, while you've historically been someone who has a strong sense of duty, and likes to support and even save others. You're now reconnecting with that, along with becoming outgoing, more talkative, and open about yourself. How can that sense of duty help when an immobilizing wave of sadness creeps up on you?*

Amir (excitedly): *It sure will, I can remember I've controlled other waves of not listening to my impulses in the past and done the right thing instead; that's more like me! I have a duty to overcome wasting time, mulling on myself because of sadness, and maybe do something for someone else who's not feeling great; that is going to be more rewarding, more useful to others, while sadness is not useful to anyone, not even myself.*

Marie-Nathalie: *Remembering that sense of duty to others will be more useful to your grandma than the sadness, and more rewarding to you. What difference will it make in how you feel?*

Amir: *I'll feel so much more proud of myself and deserving of respect!*

The conversations moved to following the lead of different stories associated with these new emotions and eventually extracting the embodied experience of "sense of duty," "pride," and "deserving," as explained in the previous section on bottom-up work. The preferred story increasingly becomes laden with many complex layers of affective experiences crisscrossing many aspects of preferred identity and relational experiences. It eventually expanded into trusting other people's love enough for him to be more open, be able to thrive, and gain joy from contributing to others' lives.

Marie-Nathalie: *By the way, is your grandmother noticing a difference between how you talked before versus now?*

Amir: *Oh! Yes! She commented on my energy level and confidence. She gave me a big hug when I came out to her and shared that she always knew but didn't dare to ask. She was the one crying, grateful that I opened up to her before she dies.*

Marie-Nathalie: *So, she gave you a hug and was grateful! Does that seem very different from the scenario that sadness had placed in your mind? (Smiles vigorously and nods.) What was that like for you?*

Amir: *It was a huge relief and now I love her even more! I can also talk to her more.*

Marie-Nathalie: *What is becoming increasingly visible about who you are?*

Amir: *Well, that I'm gay but also that I really like talking with people, sharing, being open, and laughing with them. I guess I'm more social than*

I thought, and people are more accepting than the sadness made me imagine, even at work.

Conclusion

A problem identity can be understood as a seemingly logical conclusion that the left brain makes about a subset of affective experiences in the right brain, which is intertwined with bodily sensations (bottom up) and meaning (top-down storying). Understanding each quadrant of integration proposed by IPNB helps us better address the biological hijacking of problems and tailor our practice to best support clients. Neutralizing intense problem emotions directly can be a worthy pause in our narrative journey, as it can then allow the work to progress swiftly and be more sustainable. These practices can be immensely helpful when assisting people to reclaim their lives in the aftermath of trauma.

CHAPTER 5

Working With Traumatic Experiences: Bodies, Stories, and Identities

A traumatic experience can be understood as arising from a significant event that defies a person's ability to ensure their feelings of safety or sense of integrity. Such an event can occur once, as in a severe accident or witnessing a disturbing event happening to others, or can be repetitive, as in war and child abuse. The body is typically mobilized into a complex set of physiological reactions involving intense affective experiences that can lead to states of hypo- or hyperarousal (Kearney & Lanius, 2022). States of hypoarousal are often associated with reduced movement, numbness, disconnection, shutdown, freezing, or fainting; while hyperarousal usually leads to increased sensations, hypervigilance, reactivity, panicking, actions of protest such as fighting, fleeing, crying, or intensely expressing distress. These states occur outside of the window of tolerance (WOT) explained in Chapter 2. Embodied work will be the focus of our writing here, as the application of classic narrative practices to work with traumatic experiences has been described at length elsewhere (Beaudoin, 2005; Carey, 2017; Carey et al., 2009; Denborough, 2006; Durrant & White, 1990; Duvall & Beres, 2011; Duvall, 2019; Vermeire, 2023; White, 1989, 2004b, 2006, 2007).

A therapist, nonverbally co-centered with the client's affective experience, can verbally engage in practices that revive stories of agency. Since no one tolerates suffering passively (White, 2004b), a significant dimension of our role is to highlight actions taken to survive the event and bring forth a sense of resiliency. Given the intensity of traumatic events, people's mental and physical resources are typically mobilized to target the imminent danger, leading to incomplete and problem-saturated accounts. Stories of traumatic experiences tend to be particularly oblivious to a portion of the micro- and macro-heroic acts taken to minimize suffering. Highlighting agency progressively "thaws" the problem story so that nuances, movements, possibilities, new memories, choices, and valuable perspectives progressively emerge.

> Just as fish can swim through rough waters but not ice, people can move through trauma but not frozen stories. (MNB)

This chapter describes helpful practices to heighten experiences of agency and address the embodied effects of trauma. We will first delineate the difference between conversations that elevate clients' abilities and those that can be retraumatizing. These ideas will then be exemplified by two stories. The first involves an enduring disconnection from the body after a life-threatening medical situation (hypoarousal). The second addresses intense emotions associated with implicit affect from a preverbal trauma (hyperarousal).

Retraumatizing Versus Retelling

In general, discussing efforts to protect integrity is the safest and most helpful conversational path to take, along with how far clients have come in handling the effects of the trauma. Attending to people's present-time abilities and accomplishments keeps the focus moving forward with agency instead of pulling them back into the struggles of the past. While most narrative work concentrates on the future and preferred stories, there are a number of instances when clients wish to share details about traumatic events. They may benefit from revisiting scenes to deactivate crippling embodied issues of dissociation or overwhelming moments of flashbacks, nightmares, or panic. In some instances, reprocessing the trauma using narrative practices integrated with EMDR may be necessary, as discussed in Chapter 8.

When it seems beneficial to revisit portions of past traumatic experi-

Identity-story elements	Retraumatizing	Reauthoring
Content	Mostly on past traumatic events	Mostly on past efforts to protect integrity and present-time agency
Main protagonists	Clients are viewed as more passive and the traumatic event or person committing violence is centered	Clients are viewed as active and exert self-protective efforts
Sequence in time	Based on the chronological unfolding of the traumatic event	Focused on the linking of self- sustaining actions
Emotions	Powerlessness, despair, numbness, disconnection	Hope, determination, agency
Implicit affect	Reactivated and energized neurally	Acknowledged, labeled, processed, stored explicitly
Embodiment	Often disregarded or pain focused	Includes sensory and kinesthetic competency
Outcome	Sense of self feels more damaged	Sense of self renewed, enriched
Sustainability	Struggles may continue to arise	Resilient preferred identity emerges
Values	Attended minimally or not considered	Reintegrated in a continuous sense of self over time

TABLE 5.1 **Therapeutic conversations about trauma can foster agency and avoid retraumatization when practitioners pay careful attention to the conversational elements listed above.**

ences, considerations listed in Table 5.1 can reduce the risk of retraumatizing. In particular, the retelling is more likely to be helpful if clients are positioned as active agents, who engage in self-protective efforts aligned with values held before, during, and after the disturbing event.

These narrative connections provide a precious sense of autobiographical continuity over time (White, 2004b) and shift the focus from what happened to the client, to what the client did in response to what happened (Beaudoin, 2005; Carey et al., 2009). Importantly, these patterns of action-reaction have repercussions on the body, as will be discussed below. It is crucial to avoid a retraumatizing context where our clients would relive powerlessness without any gain in regulation (Levine, 2015). We wish to not only avoid unnecessary suffering but also prevent the preferred identity from being recaptured by a problem-saturated narrative. When this occurs, an earlier traumatic memory can be infused with another layer of powerlessness from the present time. A memory is not a videotape but, rather, a reconstruction of lived experience in which different neural networks fire together to reconstitute an image, just as a puzzle is reconstructed with many pieces (Ecker et al., 2012). A practitioner witnessing powerlessness without intervening could harmfully reencode a traumatic absence of support. In comparison, stopping the retelling to insert moments of regulation could be transformative and progressively shift the reconstructed memory. In other words, since "memory is the way past events affect future function" (Siegel, 2012, p. 46), the encoding of an agency-promoting interaction about the challenging situation will directly affect future recall of the experience.

Listening for Stories of Agency

Double listening is the practice of attending to problem descriptions while also keeping an antenna out for subtle moments of agency (White, 2006). It involves an attuned awareness to the fact that for each instance of fear or suffering intensification, there is often a renewed effort to counteract the problem (White, 2004b). This can take the form of mentally focusing on knowing this will end soon, or disconnecting altogether from bodily sensations. The terminology of "affective double listening" was introduced to explicitly move beyond verbal expressions and encompass attention to embodied sensations and physiological manifestations (Beaudoin, 2020). Three general scenarios involving the WOT are possible.

1. The client is managing the painful emotions and telling the story within their WOT. The person is gaining comfort in sharing an organized sequence of events perhaps for the first time, and the co-centered therapist anchored in a caring stance of affective double listening can inquire about moments of regulation, efforts, and agency.

2. The client can become hyperaroused, with emotions spilling outside of the WOT. Practitioners can actively use the IPNB-inspired practices from Chapter 4, facilitate regulation by pausing and doing a breathing practice together (simultaneously), and focus on clients' efforts to help themselves. This can realign the narration with the client being a primary protagonist of the story, responding heroically to the situation. The conversation weaves threats of dysregulation with awareness of successful regulation, over and over again, thereby widening the window of tolerance.

3. While attempting to share the story, the client can be heading toward a hypoaroused state of powerlessness and freeze, and it may be necessary to pause the narration to reset the emotional experience closer to the WOT. This involves reconnecting with an outward focus on present-time safety, inviting synchronized movement with the practitioner to prevent the physical disconnection (e.g., "Let's press the floor"), and sensory awareness of the room with its walls, floor, sofa, and so on. It can also include a zooming-out process, where the client is invited to view the scene, present or past, from a distant viewpoint such as being in a cloud above, or watching a screen where a small segment of the situation is unfolding. Present-time embodied sensations are kept dominating the forefront of the client's awareness while involvement with challenging scene, if necessary to examine, is limited to a visually-contained space.

Story 1: Surviving a Terminal Illness

Stella, a 30-year-old, single woman working as a pharmacist, sought therapy with Marie-Nathalie for lingering shame associated with her fight with cancer.

> **Stella (crying discreetly):** *Battling cervical cancer was horrible. Even if it happened five years ago, it still ruins my life and makes me feel so ashamed . . . . That's why I called you. I've never really talked about it to anyone.*
>
> **Marie-Nathalie (slowly, softly):** *Battling that cancer still feels like it's impacting your life. It triggered shame, and now you'd like to solve this and talk about it . . . . How did the cancer affect you, and what helped?*
>
> **Stella (crying less):** *My cousin was so helpful; he held my hand, and I could feel his concern mixed with a determination to fight this. I wasn't alone. My heart was racing so much I thought it would burst. After the moment of shock and panic and shame, I immediately went into planning mode. I asked questions about the surgery, my likelihood of surviving, potential complications, and if I could still have children.*
>
> **Marie-Nathalie:** *Your cousin was there to support you, and even though your heart was racing and there was some panic, something inside of you went into planning mode and you started asking questions. Can you describe what that planning mode felt like inside, and what you might call this side of you?*
>
> **Stella:** *It's the scientist in me; I think rationally about what needs to be done and I become very focused.*

At this point, we are scratching the surface of the traumatic event and highlighting agency to bring forth a preferred narrative and consolidate regulation. We now know that her cousin's presence and hand were helpful, and her "scientist side" contained some of the suffering. Having clearly articulated and established this, we can later revisit more precisely what was happening in her body, allowing for a growing integration of affective embodied sensations while staying within the borders of the WOT. The process could be likened to weaving a state of integration. The elements include integrating the story of challenge *lined* with agency, the affective experience of overwhelm lined with regulation, and the embodied sensations of panic-racing heart lined, for now, with rational planning. These elements can later be described in more embodied terms. This will be especially important because the client eventually shared a complete disconnect from any sensations in her abdomen, avoiding touching, feeling, washing, and looking at this area, even when shopping or dressing at home in front of a mirror.

Such a first session would invariably end with a brief summary of her overcoming the hardship, battling shame, and recognizing moments of agency. If appropriate, I like to add: "We've talked about the many complex effects of this experience. I wonder if it might also have changed you in ways that you like." Or "Is there something about you that you value and that you discovered in this journey?" The timing of this question matters greatly. It can be asked only when the client feels that they have already surmounted a portion of the traumatic event, or when the event happened a long time ago. Research has shown that posttraumatic growth can occur on many levels, such as in a deeper appreciation for life, one's relationships, sense of personal strength, openness to embracing opportunities, and wisdom (Plews-Ogan et al., 2019). Stella thoughtfully replied: "Hum . . . I've never thought about that, I'd like to think about it."

As mentioned in Chapter 4, interpersonal neurobiologists (such as Siegel, 2021) have proposed that well-being is associated with the integration of left/right and bottom-up/top-down neural processes, and this framework is very helpful in trauma work. Shifting her embodied and affective experience into an integrated preferred narrative was the next step.

> **Marie-Nathalie:** *Last time, you shared how you overcame cancer and its surgery with your scientist mind and the support of your family, but there was still some shame left. I also encouraged you to consider taking a brief moment to observe sensations in your belly, when you felt ready to do so. Did you have thoughts, feelings, or sensations after our conversation?*

My intent in inviting her to glance at that area of her body was to consider whether there was another problem such as resentment, or if it was shame. I encouraged her to do it on her own, trusting that, based on her history and regulation skills so far, she was not at risk of slipping completely into hypoarousal. She also seemed a very private person, culturally unaccustomed to public displays of discomfort. I would not have encouraged a woman who had endured rape and struggled with a freeze response to explore this on her own, to avoid any risk of retraumatizing. A person who reports moments of complete hypoarousal benefits from "regulation protections," that is, the nurturing presence of a co-centered practitioner who carefully plans the process of revisiting a small portion of the traumatic experience, only if it is evidently beneficial, and will keep the client anchored in the present time, safe, and functioning. If the client was visibly slipping toward hypoarousal, the practitioner would invite gentle movements to keep the body connected to linguistic capabilities and a sense of being together in the here and now.

Stella stayed in her WOT and answered: "*I thought about it for a long time and, as you suggested, I took a few minutes to feel that area. It was quite numb at first; then I noticed the heaviness and shame again.*"

I asked what helped her manage the sensations of numbness and heaviness, exploring the subject in safe increments, and she replied:

Stella: *I know I can feel things and move on, I've done it before.*

Marie-Nathalie: *You know that about yourself. Does it mean you can trust yourself?*

Stella (pause): *Hum . . . actually, that's interesting! Yes, I can trust myself that if I have something to do or a deadline, I can take a walk or spend some time with my dog and I'll be fine after.*

Marie-Nathalie: *So, trusting yourself, walking or spending time with your dog. Has this trust in yourself grown because of the event?*

Stella (thinking): *Hum . . . . That's possible. I never thought of that.*

Marie-Nathalie: *Are there other words that would describe what you've gained?*

Stella (rolling head back, thinking): *I've learned to value life. Life is special; most problems are minor things. It also showed me that I have strength, and I can live a good life even if there is shame.*

The conversation here is weaving

- a sense of loss because of the traumatic event, with an experience of gaining a sense of strength and a value of life;
- a story of feeling fearful, with the scientist in her managing the event; and
- sensations of discomfort, with trusting herself to end those sensations at will.

This preferred-self foundation, coupled with a recognition of her ability to manage, makes it safer to deconstruct the crux of the problem: the lingering shame.

Cultural Deconstruction

Marie-Nathalie: *What meaning does shame give to having cervical cancer?*

Stella: *It means my reproductive system went wrong.*

Marie-Nathalie: *Does having something go wrong with your reproductive system mean something about a person in your culture?*

Stella: *Why yes, it's associated with a core function of women. In my culture, it means the woman is deficient. Not being able to have kids has a stigma. I don't believe in that, of course, and I'm completely fine with adopting a child, but I haven't accepted any dating invitations, even from a wonderful persistent man I like, because I can't imagine he'll still be interested in me once he finds out I can't have children.*

Marie-Nathalie: *So, the shame is making the decision ahead of time, for you and him, focusing on reproduction only, and making you imagine his response? (Nods.) This shame is based on cultural beliefs that give the impression a woman is deficient if she can't have kids. You said you don't believe in that. What do you believe?*

Stella: *I believe it happens randomly to people. I didn't do anything wrong (I double-checked that with a few doctors). It's unfortunate . . . because overcoming this does take strength.*

Marie-Nathalie: *So, cancer happens randomly, and overcoming it takes strength. What do you think gives value to a person?*

Stella: *It's how they lead their lives, the kind of people they are, and hopefully they care for someone or something . . . make themselves useful and contribute to something . . . I guess their values. That's how my parents raised me; they're just glad that I survived, but if I married someone, my in-laws would be very unlikely to think this way.*

Marie-Nathalie (slowly repeats her answer, writes the statements down, and adds): *So shame's views are very different from your own? (Nods.) Shame gives more importance to the reproductive system than to the strength it took to overcome cancer and the kind of person you value being? (Nods.)*

Shame is partially deconstructed and externalized, but no action potential was elicited. Stella has perspective and can separate it from identity, but no emotional momentum to counter shame is produced. I try externalizing more intensely by continuing the summary in a way that emphasizes shame as the source of the problem.

Marie-Nathalie (slowly, and listing on a paper for visual effect): *Shame gets you to feel insufficient and worthless. Shame gets you to feel not good enough. Shame gets you to worry about people and try to please. Shame gets in the way of shopping or relaxing with a massage. Shame gets in the way of dating. Shame imagines ahead of time what another person will give value to. Shame gets you to avoid and disconnect from that part of your body. The voice of shame comes from the outside of you, the culture, and it's fencing off areas of life. But your family and you do not agree with the belief that cancer is shameful. Does that sound accurate?*

Stella (sadly): *Yes, we don't agree with shame. But the culture's voice is inside of me, and even if I don't like it, I feel it strongly.*

Externalizing and deconstructing are helpful when an action potential to do something about the problem is triggered. In this situation, the externalization seems to create an increasing amount of sadness and resignation, which is sometimes found when people have been enculturated for many years to accept the status quo whether they like it or not (as is common for women raised in some patriarchal cultures). The present-time deconstruction and externalization is not enough to mobilize an intrinsic motivation to silence the powerful voice of shame. In fact, it may just increase it, since Stella might feel ashamed of her inability to free herself from it. I decide to address this issue by finding a preferred experience that could be more intense physiologically than shame. We start by finding a moment of success (unique outcome) at silencing shame and she shares forgiving herself for not changing her dog's water.

> **Marie-Nathalie:** *So yesterday you were able to let that go instead of feeling guilt and shame. Who were you being when you gave yourself a break?*
>
> **Stella:** *I guess I was more . . . hum . . . forgiving . . . more . . . flexible. I just let it go.*
>
> **Marie-Nathalie:** *What effects did it have when you were forgiving and flexible? Did it free up time and energy?*
>
> **Stella:** *Yeah, it did. It felt lighter. I wish I could be like that more often, kinder toward myself. I'm always nice and friendly with everyone else but me.*

While being nice, kind, and lighter provides an entry to a preferred identity, it is unlikely to be strong enough to neutralize the intensity of her disconnection from her abdomen and lifelong cultural meaning of shame. The preferred self will benefit from embodied affective practices that intensify the emotional power of this preferred self. In Chapter 4, we discussed embodiment and possibilities of bridging from one experience to another using a two-step process of mindfulness. A special version of such an exercise will be introduced in this situation.

Back to Affective Embodied Dimension

Marie-Nathalie: *You value being kind, friendly, nice, forgiving, flexible; and you are like that when shame is not in the way. You also mentioned your body feeling lighter. Can you go back to that moment when you "just let go" and describe the sensations in your body a little more?*

Stella (thinking): *Hum . . . it was like . . . I was less dense, less heavy, less ashamed, maybe more able to move and play lightly with Anika, my dog. (Smiling.) She loves it when I'm like that.*

Marie-Nathalie: *Lighter, less dense, less heavy, and more able to move and play with Anika. Would you be interested in doing an experiment to intensify that side of you? (Nods.)*

Marie-Nathalie invites Stella to join her in a state of embodied relaxation with eyes closed (if that feels comfortable) and connect to the rhythm of the breath. After about 30 seconds, Marie-Nathalie progressively encourages Stella to feel the love for her dog, Anika: *Slowly inhale, and imagine increasing the intensity of this love . . . . Locate the headquarters of this feeling in your body . . . . Notice its epicenter . . . its borders . . . . And now, imagine that it is a comforting liquid . . . . Notice its comfortable temperature . . . . Allow it to slowly spread . . . . Feel it seep soothingly into other areas of your body . . . very slowly . . . . This liquid is slowly, gently, lovingly infiltrating all areas of the body . . . arms . . . head . . . abdomen . . . legs . . . feet . . .*

Liquid metaphors can alter people's experiences of themselves. Creative studies have revealed that washing one's hands or face can contribute to reducing guilt and self-judgment, even vicariously (Xu et al., 2014). Here, Stella is invited to expand her love for her dog to her entire body using the sensory mediums of a liquid combined with a temperature of her choice. While not enough to resolve all the issues, this sensory imagery can facilitate new interoceptive possibilities.

After a few moments of enjoying this experiment, Stella is invited to open her eyes and share the experience.

Stella (takes a deep breath and smiles): *That was amazing! I was overtaken by kindness and love for my dog; then I realized this ability was in* *myself, that I was also a source, not just Anika. The love was radiating from my chest, and I tried to let the liquid flow into my belly. It didn't happen right away, though; there was like . . . a . . . a dam. I hesitated, but I felt so relaxed, so full of love and connected, that I decided to let a drop pass and then a little more . . . the liquid made it easier. Wow, that was strange.*

Marie-Nathalie: *What was strange?*

Stella: *Actually feeling something down there, as if it was a part of me; I guess it is a part of me, and then seeing myself as a whole, including that area. It makes me want to cry . . . (Stella moves one hand to cover her face and places the other tentatively on her belly, and starts trembling) . . . and I'm shaking. It's weird . . . and scary.*

Marie-Nathalie (gently giving the tissue box): *It's okay to shake and cry. It's a common way the body releases trauma. It's your body letting go of what happened and shifting after being disconnected for so long. Let's take a slow deep breath together and send fresh air down into the belly area . . . . Can you welcome this experience as helpful and allow your body to move freely? (Smiles and nods, breathing deeply, tears still streaming softly.) You can gently stroke your belly, too; it is a part of you. Notice the subtle shifts. (Another deep breath.) How are the sensations changing?*

Trembling has been described as a common way to release traumatic experiences in all mammals (Levine, 2010). Most mammals, such as dogs or bears, will shake after a fall or scary situation. Stroking and tapping the body have also emerged as ways to modify the electrical signal the brain is receiving from that region of the body (König et al., 2019). It alters the production of stress hormones and changes one's awareness of body homeostasis as registered by the insula (Church et al., 2014; Bach et al., 2019). As Stella settles in the aftermath of this exercise, she progressively seems more relaxed and exclaims, "*I feel more whole now, less caved in the middle of my body. The shame seems so pointless, I did what I could to survive, it wasn't my fault, and this event doesn't have to define me. I should love my belly. It's been through so much. There's no reason to love my dog more than myself.*" As our time comes to an end, I encourage Stella to walk around the block and enjoy these sensations before driving away.

Memory consolidation of new perspectives takes a while to settle and needs some reverberating time to become biochemically translated into lasting neural changes. Research has found that this process is active for about two hours after a therapy session (Nader & Einarsson, 2010). There are many great benefits to encouraging a client to muse, walk, or take a bath after a session so that the brain can just focus on the task of integration of this new experience.

Over the subsequent weeks, the clinical work took a dramatic turn. It moved to thickening her embodied preferred identity as a kind and whole person and becoming confident. The intense love she experienced for her dog was turned inward to help her recover from the shame and develop a flourishing preferred self.

Upon the last meeting, Marie-Nathalie asked Stella if this love and kindness might extend to doing something for others in the world. She replied that she would like to, but needed to think about it. A few months later, Marie-Nathalie received a heartwarming email from Stella. She had traveled to another city to spend the holidays with her parents. During that time, she came across a homeless man with a dog who evidently had a significant tumor. Stella's heart was immediately touched and she proceeded to offer to pay for the dog to be evaluated by a veterinarian, receive the surgery to remove the cancerous lump, and get medical follow-ups during the recovery period. Helping this otherwise healthy dog, the only companion to this homeless elder, turned out to be extremely meaningful to her and filled her with joy. She had discovered her magnanimous self and a cause to which her heart could be devoted.

Story 2: Working With Implicit Affect

While Stella was keenly aware that her struggles were linked to the traumatic experience with cancer, many clients seek help for intense emotions not realizing their ties to affect from the past. Siegel (1999, 2012) divides affect into two types: explicit and implicit. Explicit affect, mostly stored in the hippocampus, is associated with intentionally retrievable memories of events taking place at a specific time and place, such as the memory of a wedding. In contrast, implicit affect is a raw, nonverbal affective experience that was unprocessed and stored in suboptimal ways, generally in the amygdala and the body during a traumatic event, and usually encoded as sensations. Implicit affect tends to be reactivated by insidious triggers in present-time life, sometimes minuscule influences of the past that inflate a person's emotions or, in some situations, color much of daily life experience. "We act, feel, and imagine without recognition of the influence of past experience on our present reality" (Siegel, 2012, p. 52). When implicit affect chronically infiltrates daily life, the past becomes the eternal present and, by extension, the only future imaginable (Badenoch, 2011). Recognition of implicit affect is not sufficient to free people from its influence. The process of freeing a person from implicit affect involves a movement from non-languaged experiences stored in the limbic system (mainly amygdala) and dominating the right hemisphere, to an emotion that is articulated explicitly, recognized, understood with left-hemisphere processes, then deactivated physiologically, stored more effectively, and ultimately replaced by another coexisting, preferred, and present-time state (Siegel et al., 2021). This process is illustrated below with the story of Mr. E.

Mr. E.

At the first session, Mr. E. presented as a friendly, attentive, and engaging 28-year-old man, proud of his career, well connected with family and friends. He was deeply in love with a girlfriend who lived in Europe and talked with her every day. After 10 minutes of hearing details about what was going well in his life, I asked what was troubling him. His expression darkened, his eyes became watery, and a gripping feeling of death densely filled the room. *"Despair,"* he said, *"paralyzing, hopeless despair every day."* Mr. E. leaned forward as a broken man and slowly recounted his story. He had happily graduated from college, feeling free and confident, but was unable to find a job. Over the subsequent months, his emotional state slowly deteriorated from worrying about finding work to worrying about what would happen if he had no money, no insurance, and poor health. He ended up with a pink-eye infection and paid for medical treatment out of pocket. Since then, he had become obsessed with the idea that he had health concerns and was always checking his eyes. This was deeply distressing at night when he was alone in the bedroom of his tiny studio.

The narrative process of focusing mostly on skills, actions taken, and identity is immensely helpful to many clients, but when there is implicit affect, additional practices are beneficial. Implicit affect is experienced as intense and unpredictable and acts as an invisible rip current on people's affective experience. The emotions of this high-functioning young man were so intense and unusual that I immediately wondered about the presence of implicit affect. I tried to locate it the usual way by following three simple steps that I have used successfully with countless other clients: (1) describe the embodied sensations experienced during moments of affective intensity; (2) explore what the experience means; and (3) recall other times when a similar emotional experience took place. If embodied sensations and meanings are effectively engaged in the session, this retrieval of past events becomes facilitated by state-dependent recall, a process by which the brain easily remembers events encoded in similar affective states (Lang et al., 2001). Once the original event is recalled and connected in embodied ways to its affective elements, the implicit affect can progressively be transformed into explicit affect, processed, and stored in the hippocampus, where it will intrude less into present-time experience (Badenoch, 2011).

> **Marie-Nathalie:** *How does this despair feel in your body?*
>
> **Mr. E. (going inward):** *It's immense as a black hole that sucks me in; it's bottomless, shapeless, dark; nothing else exists. I become small, hopeless, a crying mess.*
>
> **Marie-Nathalie (slowly repeats the description and adds):** *What does it mean to you when you start feeling that way?*
>
> **Mr. E.:** *It means I will die. There's a certainty that there is something wrong with my health and I will die. It's so intense that I even fainted once when I thought I was feeling a lump under my arm and thought it was*

cancer. I'm always looking to find out what is wrong with my health, it's an inescapable gut feeling.

This is another sign that there may be implicit affect and trauma in his past. The gut is highly involved in detecting dangers; it contains over 100 million neurons (a little more than a hamster's brain!), which is why it is called the enteric nervous system (Furness, 2006). It is able to learn, remember, and attend to certain types of information (Mayer, 2011). In utero, it forms from the same embryonic tissue as the central nervous system. Contrary to popular belief, most of the communication between gut and brain involves the gut informing the brain of a danger about perceived stressors (90% of the nerve fibers are "afferent," or go to the brain; and only 10% of the fibers are "efferent," or relay the brain's information to the gut; Hadhazy, 2010). The gut is also where 80% of our immune system lies, and where most of our serotonin (a mood-stabilizing neurotransmitter) is produced. People who have endured trauma often have digestive and gut-related issues, from the enteric system having been too intensely or frequently mobilized in a way that eventually skewed its functioning (van der Kolk, 2014).

Marie-Nathalie: *An inescapable gut feeling, a certainty that you will die. Do you remember feeling this in your body at another time in your life?*

Mr. E.: *No, it really started when I was depressed from not finding a job. My mood was just going downward, and I was concerned about not having health insurance; it's so expensive to get medical care. Doctors have told me I'm hypochondriac. It's true that I'm paranoiac about my health. I see that but knowing that doesn't help me.*

Marie-Nathalie: *So, it started when you were depressed from not finding a job; then it morphed into despair and a feeling of certainty that you are dying of something. Have you ever been close to someone struggling with a terminal illness, like a close friend or family member who passed away?*

Mr. E.: *No, I am lucky that all my family members, and close friends from college, are still alive. Most of them don't know of my struggles and still think I'm the guy I was then.*

Marie-Nathalie: *How would they describe you?*

Mr. E.: *As a good person with strong values, caring, kind, hard-working, confident, positive.*

The conversation ends with a summary and a "brain map." A brain map is a simple sketch of a head containing a thick path, temporarily representing the problem neural network, and a thinner path representing the preferred self. Key words summarizing the influence of these two (or more) "programs" are included. The intent of therapeutic work will be to reverse the intensity of these programs, where preferred selves will become dominant ways of being. Clients usually request a copy of the sketch and appreciate the concrete illustration (for examples, see Beaudoin, 2010, 2014, 2019). Mr. E. said that he felt clearly better thinking of the despair as a program in his mind and took a photograph of the brain map. I added:

> *Since you become who you practice to be, whenever you feel the despair program starting, I'd like to invite you to stop it, and think about what the confident part of you might reply. Also, can you just check with your mom and dad to confirm that you weren't exposed to someone passing away when you were a child?*

Uncovering Implicit Affect

Mr. E. comes to our scheduled session, pleased that he was able to control some moments of despair during the day by remembering that it was a mental program and by focusing on other things; however, he was unsuccessful at night, when it felt very real and paralyzing.

Marie-Nathalie: *Let's start by examining the specifics of those moments of control, and then we can talk about the nights. By the way, did you get a chance to ask your mom and dad about knowing someone who passed away?*

Mr. E.: *Oh, yeah! I almost forgot. As it turns out, my dad shared that my biological mother died when I was one year old. one always thought she died at the time of my birth. I'm really close to the mother who actually* *raised me, so I never think of my biological mother. I only know she was devastated by her diagnosis of terminal illness and died really young. My father doesn't like talking about this period, but he said that for the last six months of her life, my biological mother used to stare into my eyes intently and talk to me a lot. At the very end, he said, she would isolate herself with me in my room, crying for hours every night, but I don't have any memory of this; so, I can't imagine it would play a role in my problem.*

Marie-Nathalie (slowly): *So, you had a biological mother who was dying and spent a lot of time crying with you during your first year of life . . . What would it mean if . . . it did play a role?*

Mr. E. (hesitating and with disbelief): *That would be weird . . . to think that someone I don't care about and have no memory of would affect my life . . . . Is that possible?*

The implicit affect was now uncovered but not in the usual embodied way that facilitates felt recognition and languaging. It was important to check the client's interpretation of this discovery, as he could have had a secondary affective reaction such as, "Yuck, I can't believe I have in me this stranger's experience of dying," which would have added another layer of problem. Luckily, Mr. E. didn't have that reaction, and the concept of implicit affect was explained as below.

> **Marie-Nathalie (gently):** *Even if you have no recollection, the intense distress of caregivers affects babies, and their experience can become stored as what is called "implicit affect." You can look it up: It is essentially the nonverbal encoding of sensations and emotions during intense experiences. Since they are stored in an unusual way in the brain, they pop up in life when reactivated by a trigger. Anything similar to feeling down, discouraged, having regrets, worrying about health issues, hyperfocusing on your eyes, could have triggered the implicit affect. (Slowly and softly) What would it mean if the despair and certainty of dying did not belong to your life, if it was the imprint of someone else's experience?*
>
> **Mr. E. (stunned):** *I don't know . . . . It makes the despair seem more*

> *irrational. But then who knows? I might have an illness too and die*
> *young just as she did. If this is implicit affect, as you said, will it affect*
> *me for the rest of my life?*
>
> **Marie-Nathalie:** *No, we can definitely work on that. You've already taken*
> *steps to address it. In fact, is it okay if I ask you about those moments*
> *when you controlled it?*

The session continues in classic narrative ways, examining the details of moments of efforts, minute by minute, how he stopped the despair, put on music instead, shifted to looking at documentaries and not letting himself dwell on health worries. In particular, we explored the embodied experience of his preferred self—being confident and positive—and we identified a person who inspired him along those lines (his neighbor when he was growing up), and bolstered the intensity of those ways of being by collecting more evidence and descriptors.

Narrative Progress, Implicit Stuckness

Mr. E. felt emboldened by the discovery that the despair was not his. He read about implicit affect and was able to brush off the experience more frequently during the day. We collected many more instances of being positive and confident, and granularized the experience by elaborating on descriptors: satisfied, inspired, proud, accomplished. Walking meditations were recommended and helped him cultivate a sense of positivity. Going to bed at night and trying to fall asleep remained much harder to control, and he described his experience as follows:

> Darkness, silence, loneliness, nothingness, eyes, regrets, anguish, desperation . . . gripping despair, fear of dying . . . crying, curled up, small, powerless in bed . . . falling asleep only when exhausted late into the night.

The cognitive knowledge that a problem is irrational, unjustified, or unwanted is helpful but usually not enough to completely modify overwhelming embodied sensations. We had successfully externalized despair, challenged the certainty trap, recognized the overfocusing on health, separated his identity from the problem, changed the story, intensified the preferred self, and connected his identity relationally to his neighbor and to his values. We were trying to "de-story" the implicit affect from his identity and leave room for new possibilities. But how can we free a client who, every night for many months, can slip into an intense paralyzing despair vicariously encoded in a preverbal period from a dying mother? Something extra needed to be done specifically to address the biological freight train of implicit activation.

Changing the Body

Trauma specialist Peter Levine (2010) has written extensively on the importance of completing movements that the body was inclined to make but that were blocked at the time of the traumatic experience. If this was to be helpful in Mr. E.'s situation, I wondered what movement a one-year-old baby could possibly wish to do when cradled by a gazing, despairing mother. When asked if there was a possibility of doing some exercise in the evening or when despair approached, Mr. E. welcomed the suggestion and mentioned that he had been thinking of joining a gym near his home and wanted to take that step. I encouraged him to try different forms of exercise, such as biking and running, wondering if a movement accelerating his heart rate might hijack the racing heart of fear and alter the embodied sensations.

At the following meeting, Mr. E. enthusiastically shared that he had joined the gym and gone whenever the despair was creeping up on him. He tried many different exercise stations and, strangely, felt very soothed by the rowing machine.

> **Marie-Nathalie:** *What is it like for you to be on this rowing machine?*
>
> **Mr. E.:** *I don't know. I like that sensation of pushing away.*
>
> **Marie-Nathalie:** *What do you feel in your body when you're pushing away?*
>
> **Mr. E.:** *I'm not sure, it's satisfying. I feel strong, powerful, in control. I love it!*
>
> **Marie-Nathalie:** *Can you give me a specific example of a moment when the rowing machine helped you shift out of the despair?*

Mr. E.: *Yeah, actually, last night. I had an upsetting phone call with my aunt, in the gym's parking lot, then went straight to the rowing machine. I could feel the despair lurking inside of me, but I put all my might into rowing. There's something funny about looking at myself too.*

Marie-Nathalie: *Looking at yourself?*

Mr. E.: *Yeah, the machine faces a wall on which there's a big mirror, so you can see everything happening in the gym. But I tend to just look at my own face and eyes, getting closer and farther away as I row, and become sort of hypnotized (laugh). I don't know: it's weird but it works. I feel different after.*

Marie-Nathalie: *How do you feel after?*

Mr. E.: *Like more myself . . . grounded in reality.*

Marie-Nathalie: *Grounded in reality? Do life problems and the despair feel different after rowing?*

Mr. E.: *Yes, things are less of a big deal. I can look at the despair as an abyss, I know where it is; I know it's dangerous for me to go there; but I can walk beside it and not fall into its darkness; my body feels tall and strong.*

The foundational pieces of the affective embodied work with Mr. E. were now in place. Moving the body (kinesthetic), involving the eyes, and feeling powerful when despair arose, coupled with shifting the implicit affect into a clear explicit affect, freed him to develop a preferred sense of self. We created another brain map, this time highlighting the progress.

Changing the Context

As confidence emerged more frequently, it became important to create a home environment that would support its expansion and further dissolve ties to the evening despair. His sensory experience of the space through exteroception needed to be readjusted.

Marie-Nathalie: *If the confidence and satisfaction you experience during the day, and during rowing, inspired you to change something about your bedroom or evening environment, what might that be?*

Mr. E.: *Hum, I guess I could decorate the room. I left it bare.*

Marie-Nathalie: *So, decorating it. And how might you do that to reduce the likelihood of despair?*

Mr. E.: *Maybe I can put colorful images on the wall, photos of my girlfriend and family.*

The conversation continued to explore ways of changing the evening sequence and the environment for falling asleep. Mr. E. progressively elaborated a plan to include listening to classical music, installing a night lamp, sticking fluorescent stars on his ceiling, displaying photos, moving furniture around, sleeping on the opposite side of his bed, and reminding himself of everything he was grateful for as he attempted to fall asleep. Over the subsequent weeks, progress finally became more stable. He fell asleep more easily and woke up with positive energy for the day.

Freedom to Narrate the Flourishing Identity

The rest of the work, as we reduced the frequency of our meetings, involved sustaining and developing the preferred identity, nuancing the strategies in different settings, continuing to articulate moments of success, and, most importantly, developing a vast repertoire of sustainable life-enhancing emotions that allowed him to flourish in life. Over the next few months, every month, we solidified frequency, intensity, duration, recovery period, and metaphors of well-being.

At our last meeting, Mr. E. had happily decided to move to Europe to live in Switzerland with his girlfriend. He felt he could invest in a future without living in fear of imminent death. Integration was achieved. He had languaged the implicit affect associated with the fear of dying and despair and turned it into explicit affect. He experienced bottom-up sensations of feeling his body being athletic, full of life, capable, and healthy. He had a top-down personal narrative that allowed him to freely cultivate preferred embodied experiences of being confident, kind, loyal, and very funny. He discovered that his sense of humor delighted everyone everywhere and felt emboldened to contribute laughter in his professional and personal communities. Mr. E. was discovering *mudita*, as discussed in Chapter 2, and it contributed to his ability to flourish.

Conclusion

In sum, this chapter reviewed embodied work with clients who have faced traumas that impact their relationship with their emotions and body. Discussing traumatic experience can be retraumatizing if the same aspects of the story are repeated over and over again while the client remains powerless and efforts to survive are invisibilized. Cautiously reviewing traumatic events can be helpful when the story has not been told coherently before and when implicit affect is derailing present experiences. Throughout this work, the focus is on facilitating dignifying understandings and integration of experiences, where the main protagonist-hero is the client. Many embodied practices are key in helping people transition from being stuck in overwhelming chronic emotions to enjoying a state of freedom and fully living the preferred version of themselves.

CHAPTER 6

Working With the Five Primary Senses: Unexpected Solutions

Have you ever stopped to marvel at the complexity of the human body? How we walk upright, or run on two legs? How eyes discern a bird in a tree, and sound waves are translated into mental concepts? Just imagine the sheer amount of energy that goes into our heart pumping without ever stopping for a break for our entire lives. Think about how our lungs transform oxygen 15 to 30 times per minute into usable fuel, and how our brain coordinates the action of billions of cells! Our body is the home in which we live, the vehicle in which we travel, and the interface between inner experiences and the outside world. No body, no experience, no life. As discussed earlier in this book, the body can influence emotions, just as emotions can influence the body. Working without the body is like working with a black-and-white picture of an experience instead of its colored version (Beaudoin, 2019). When a significant amount of crucial information is lacking, our ability to offer the best possible therapeutic services may be limited.

This chapter explores the world of the senses and the value of exteroception, which provides rich material to deconstruct problems and promote the development of preferred selves. Information from most senses arrives in the middle of the brain, above the brain stem, and in the thalamus, which relays neural data to different cortical regions. Researchers have observed a 40-times-per-second sweep, where information seems to travel from the back to the front of the brain to relay information to the different hemispheres and the prefrontal cortex, where a conscious state of awareness of self is concocted (Baars, 2019). The frequency and speed at which sensory information shapes experiences of ourselves can be used to support the emergence of flourishing identities.

We will now review unique benefits of including sensory information, describe micropractices, and share five stories illustrating this clinical work.

Benefits of Working with Sensory Information

If feeling hot is the very first manifestation of a cascade of physiological activations leading to an unwanted emotional outburst, being aware of this sensation and changing its course right away can help people avoid the worst of a problem. Since the body and its senses play an integral role in problematic patterns of emotional activation, leaving a key body part or sensory information unquestioned by therapeutic conversations leaves clients vulnerable to being physiologically hijacked by the speedy onset of intense emotional reactions. Clients who attempt to manage a problem emotion at an activation level of 7 on a 1-to-10 scale, when it turns into fury and clouds their thinking, are less likely to regulate their emotional state as quickly as they might have if they had recognized it earlier on. An intense problem emotion triggers dozens of biochemical reactions in the body, which pick up speed just like a freight train, and it is easier to stop the momentum when it is just starting than when it reaches its full speed. Such a blind spot in therapeutic conversations weakens the likelihood of early successes, and endangers the sustainability of progress. Including sensory information in our work therefore offers several advantages. It can

- provide valuable information about problems,
- increase the likelihood of early regulation,
- offer powerful pivotal moments,
- create bridges to transition from one affective state to another, and
- strengthen embodied preferred experiences of self on a neural level.

Micropractices

Umwelt

Most people tend to assume that others have similar sensory experiences as themselves, even when living beings are from a different species. As an example, many people deny their dogs the experience of sniffing on walks, not understanding the importance of olfaction in a canine's world. They reduce walks to simply exercising; a more valued activity in human minds, not realizing that animal studies reveal clear differences in dog's measures of well-being when their daily walks allow them to enjoy smells (Horowitz, 2010; Horowitz & Frank, 2020). For humans, who tend to be more visually oriented, the equivalent would be if parents took their children out blindfolded every time they left their home. The late German biologist Jakob von Uexküll (Ostachuk, 2019), known to have influenced many French philosophers, including Foucault, proposed a concept to heighten our awareness of sensory differences: *umwelt*. Umwelt refers to the unique experience of a living organism's interaction with the world from their point of view, that is, what has relevance, salience, and meaning, and how they live it (Kull, 2010). This concept can be immensely helpful for practitioners and help us cultivate a stance of "not-knowing" (Anderson, 2012; Anderson & Goolishian, 1992), not only with verbal understandings and meanings but also with regard to nonverbal, sensory, and embodied dimensions of life. This stance is akin to that of anthropologists who are trying to understand meaning and worldviews, rather than missionaries or experts imposing their interpretations. General questions can be asked, such as, "Walk me through a day that you've appreciated; what is it like to be you, to live in your body, your environment; what stands out when you look at places or people; what do you tend to notice when you're driving? What kind of music is appealing to you?" Having a better sense of someone's umwelt increases our likelihood of understanding the many complex biopsychosocial facets of a problem and adds granularity to possibilities of preferred identities.

Stage

If you as a practitioner were asked to play the role of your client in a film, would you know how to walk, talk, sit, move, eat, stare, listen, and hesitate like the client?

This microchain of unfolding gestures can often reveal crucial information and inspire many important questions. With children, this can involve the practitioner attempting to recreate a scene and play the role of the young client, who is placed in the position of correcting the therapist-actor, about words said and which part of the body is moving first. In a situation of chronic conflict, the practitioner can ask: "*So when you and Timmy were playing with Legos, did you sit side by side? I'm trying to imagine the scene, did you have a mound of blocks in front of you? Were you giggling loudly? And then what happened exactly during that minute when things started going in an upsetting direction; did you both reach for the same piece of Lego? Did the mad feelings get the two of you in a tug-of-war? Do mad feelings get you to look at your friend as an enemy and make your hands tempted to demolish his construction? Let's pretend you are Timmy, and I am you. Tell me how the mad feelings are changing my face. Would it be like this?*" Examining the scene frame by frame primes the child's memory to recall details otherwise inaccessible, and helps to uncover important transitions toward or away from the problem. The child correcting the adult's rendition of the unfolding scene also adds playfulness and perspective for all involved.

Sensory Information

Each sense affects the brain in different ways and at different speeds. A little knowledge of all the senses' physiological effects can sometimes be immensely helpful. Sensory information goes from the eyes, ears, skin, and taste buds to the thalamus, which then distributes the information to different areas of the brain for processing and responses. The only sense to bypass this triage is the sense of olfaction. Smells go directly to the amygdala and can trigger instant emotional reactions. Each sense activates biochemical and bioelectrical stimulations in the body and can be recruited to soothe a client or strengthen a preferred self. For instance, a weighted blanket on a distressed child who has endured medical trauma can increase the production of serotonin and can be very calming; eliciting such haptic sensations may even be the only path to regulation in some circumstances (Beaudoin & Maclennan, 2020).

Under intense problematic emotions, many experiences are more extreme and sensory information can be either ignored or heightened. Identifying what dominates a client's awareness can provide a key to transforming the experience. The five stories below will exemplify the usefulness of considering sensory information.

Clinical Stories Using Micropractices With the Five Senses

Sounds

A sound is a physical force that enters the ear as a vibrating wave and can affect the brain in complex ways (Reybrouck et al., 2021). The right hemisphere activates more for rhythms, harmony, and non-speech-related sounds; the left tends to react more to intensity; and both are involved in reacting to aspects of human speech (Hwang et al., 2005). Sounds are well known to affect people's emotions and actions (Campbell & Doman, 2012). The sound of a baby crying is distressing for many, while hearing classical piano can facilitate relaxation and rehabilitation in hospitals (Vik et al., 2018). Many studies show that upbeat music can lift a crowd's spirits, and favorite tunes generally enhance athletic training and performance (Reynolds, 2010). Even the heart rate is different if doing a task to the sound of music versus doing the same exercise without music, and some research suggests that we consume less oxygen doing an activity with music than without (Campbell & Doman, 2012). As will be discussed in Chapter 7, sounds and rhythms have been used as healing practices in many First Nations for centuries. In therapeutic settings, practitioners' voice, pace, and pitch have also been found to alter the firing of the amygdala, since one of the "first signals that safety of social engagement is compromised is tension around the larynx, heard as tension in the voice" (Ogden, 2021, p. 318). Given how sounds profoundly affect people's embodied experiences, it is sometimes important to explore their presence or absence in our clients' experiences of problems, as exemplified in the work with Aisha.

Aisha, an underprivileged woman in her late 20s, was referred to therapy by her doctor for postpartum depression. Her voice was slow and tired on the phone as she explained that it had started after giving birth to her second child 3 months earlier. She just didn't have the energy to give quality care to her baby and toddler, chores at home were piling up, and she even avoided spending time with her husband and family members, all of whom she loved deeply. She requested to meet Marie-Nathalie through video calls to avoid the demands of driving. Having to carefully consider energy expenditure also applied to skipping grocery shopping and social events, a source of friction with her husband. At our first session, Aisha explained that after a smooth birthing process through the night at the community hospital, she was discharged to go back home with her baby to . . . the childcare center she directed in her small rental apartment. She had hired someone to cover for her during her absence but had to resume caring for nine young children, including four who were still in diapers. Since then, Aisha had remained exhausted, and unable to care for her own or customers' children in the same quality way she used to provide. Moreover, her cousin sometimes came to help, but also sometimes to just drop off her own three children while she ran errands. Overwhelm got Aisha to cry in the evenings and be unable to do the massive kitchen cleanup of the day. She wished she could spend more time bonding with her own children, rather than caring for all the others, but she felt trapped financially, and the deep heaviness associated with this stuckness was palpable on a nonverbal level.

Overwhelm was externalized and its effects examined, but there was also a very real physiological issue and Aisha had rejected her doctor's recommendation of a medical leave. Among other things, overwhelm got her to think: "I can't do this, I'm so exhausted . . . but I have no choice, I can't afford to not work." Aisha recognized that she was taking on more than she could handle but overwhelm made it hard to say no to people she desperately needed help from, like her cousin, her husband, and her mother, who was also struggling with Lupus and needed assistance. Refusing her husband's requests was particularly hard as it triggered huge fights in the evening, which increased her exhaustion and sleep deprivation. Aisha described: "*Every day, I wake up with dread.*" When asked to elaborate, she replied, "*Either I won't be able to deal with the children, or on weekends, I won't have any energy for my husband's family outings. Sometimes during the day, I am so exhausted that I feel very close to passing out.*" We examined the ramifications of this statement, and explored whether it was possible to communicate her struggles to her family, to be better supported during this time, and to check up with her doctor. Since the risk of passing out seemed to occur more frequently during the day-care hours, we explored that further, and I eventually asked about senses.

> **Marie-Nathalie:** *In those moments, is it possible that one of your senses gets heightened, like smells, sights, or sounds?*
>
> **Aisha:** *Sounds.*
>
> **Marie-Nathalie:** *Sounds?*
>
> **Aisha:** *All the children crying, playing with noisy toys, babbling, yelling, talking to me, asking me something, calling me from across the room, whining . . .*
>
> **Marie-Nathalie:** *How do these sounds affect you more specifically?*
>
> **Aisha:** *It just feels like a huge, loud tsunami wave that takes over me, I can't stand it.*
>
> **Marie-Nathalie:** *So the children's sounds contribute to the overwhelm, and does overwhelm also make you notice them more?*
>
> **Aisha:** *Yes, I think that's right, it's as if there are moments when the sounds are magnified and take all the space in my mind. It becomes so loud and overbearing that I can only run out of the room and hide in the bathroom.*
>
> **Marie-Nathalie:** *So children's sounds are around you all day, and in those moments, overwhelm focuses on and magnifies these sounds to a level of unbearable intensity that makes you leave the room? (Nods.) Right after you leave the room, how do you reduce the overwhelm?*
>
> **Aisha:** *I open the water faucet to drown all the sounds and sit on the floor for a few minutes.*

We explored whether she'd tried other ways of preventing or dealing with the overwhelm, and she hadn't. We then discussed the preceding signs of overwhelm building up, which often involved her breathing pattern becoming shallower, her heart accelerating, her throat tightening up, and the rise of overwhelm, "*I just can't do this, but I have to.*"

> **Marie-Nathalie:** *I understand the feeling of "having to work," and I wonder if it might be possible to have moments of rest and quiet, when you could step outside of children's sounds, while someone else took care of the children, even briefly? Or, would it be possible to plan for moments of playing gentle music or relaxing sounds that would reduce the overwhelm for some portion of the day?*
>
> **Aisha:** *That would be wonderful, I never tried that.*

Having identified and addressed the primary sensory information, we shifted our focus to finding instances when she had seriously considered hiring lunch help and refused her cousin's children. Those initiatives were explored further, allowing Aisha to articulate her thought process, how she expressed herself firmly in the past, what it took to engage in those actions, and the potential effects on her babies if being firm reduced the overwhelm. Mindfulness was introduced in the last segment of the first meeting, since talking more than 30 minutes was exhausting. She really enjoyed the peacefulness of the mindfulness and listening to her breath.

At our second meeting, Aisha was still exceedingly tired but she had practiced meditation every day and loved it. She had also explained the overwhelm to her husband, refused her cousin's extra children one day, and requested help during lunchtimes. When asked if she had thought of the link between sounds and overwhelm, Aisha replied that after our meeting she had started vacuum cleaning her apartment many times during the day to drown the sounds of children. This stood out. Therapeutic conversations halted the usual narrative progression to further explore her relationship to sounds.

> **Marie-Nathalie:** *What do you like about the vacuum sound?*
>
> **Aisha:** *It's constant.*

Marie-Nathalie: *Have you always been affected by sounds? (Nods.) What are your favorite sounds?*

Aisha: *The ocean.*

Marie-Nathalie: *When was the last time you were by the ocean?*

Aisha: *A year ago.*

Marie-Nathalie: *What effects did ocean sounds have on you then?*

Aisha: *I was more present, like myself.*

Marie-Nathalie: *Can you recall the details of that trip to the ocean? (Nods.) Can you describe how your body felt when you were present, like yourself, and listening to the ocean sounds?*

Aisha: *I was relaxed, I could actually feel my body, my arms and legs, as opposed to the cloud I feel now.*

Marie-Nathalie: *You were relaxed and could feel your body, arms, and legs, unlike now. How did being in this state and hearing ocean sounds tweak your view of life and problems?*

Aisha: *Things were less of a big deal.*

Marie-Nathalie: *If ocean sounds could be heard these days, how might they affect the overwhelm?*

Aisha: *They might reduce it.*

Marie-Nathalie: *What might you see differently?*

Aisha: *It's okay to say no and reduce my hours.*

Marie-Nathalie: *Would there be a way of bringing ocean sounds into your life now?*

Aisha: *Yes, maybe I can put on a recording a few times per day, instead of vacuum cleaning.*

Marie-Nathalie: *Are there other sounds that could help?*

Aisha: *I like singing.*

Marie-Nathalie: *Singing and I wonder if humming can help too?*

Aisha: *That's a great idea!*

I suggested humming, as it has been found to reduce anxiety by virtue of its effects on the vagus nerve and heart-rate variability (Sujan et al., 2015).

For the third session, Aisha decided to come in person. She felt slightly better, and her posture was significantly straighter. The daily ocean-sound moments, and the helper over lunch, allowed her to nap. She also spoke with more confidence to her family, and they supported her request to rest more often. Her vitality was slightly improving. The day prior to our meeting, she had come to an important realization, right after five minutes of ocean-sounds listening: "*Maybe I've done childcare services long enough, I could take a break; my husband, babies, and I can move in with my parents, and I'll just find another type of job later.*" That idea seemed to lift her spirits, and she was seeing possibilities in her life. Being firm and refusing people's requests had also allowed her to focus on quality giving instead of quantity. She had a burgeoning sense of freedom, confidence, and hopefulness that things could be better.

Therapy wrapped up the next session when she had notified all her customers of the childcare business closure. We examined the positive effects associated with this life change, her growing confidence and calm presence with her children. We also did a mindfulness meditation specifically on cultivating positive states with a tiny heart-rate variability feedback device, which provides a gentle sound when people experience a positive emotion. Aisha really liked the experience of these rewarding sounds.

Narrative sessions typically end with summaries organizing information discussed in the session, and clients are encouraged to share what they are taking away. This was not ideal with Aisha, given her extraordinary level of fatigue and tendency to answer briefly, especially toward the end of sessions. So she was handed a small chime to gently tap whenever she wanted to convey a desire to remember a specific idea, and Marie-Nathalie then wrote it on a paper for her. The pleasant chime sound helped her communicate her feedback, and also more strongly encode key reauthoring sentences she wished to remember, without talking.

Pleasant sounds are often used as rewards in biofeedback sessions, as they activate the dopamine reward circuit of the brain. This practice also works well with children, as it transforms the summary into a music-making game that they typically enjoy. They therefore keenly pay attention, especially if the practitioner starts the summary with an acknowledging sentence such as: "Timmy likes to be a kind person!" Clients can also be invited to audio-record practitioners' end-of-session summaries on their phones, and relisten at a later time, which will support memory consolidation.

Smells

A number of scholars attribute the limited use of our sense of olfaction in English-speaking countries to the fact that there are very few words available to describe odors (Majid & Burenhult, 2014). When researchers travel to hunter-gatherer communities such as the Jahai people in the tropical rainforest of Malaysia, for example, they discover a wide repertoire of words to describe smells, as many as we have for colors (Majid & Kruspe, 2018). People can, in fact, discern up to 10,000 odors, sometimes within 110 milliseconds (Blumenrath, 2020). The brain organ processing smells (olfactory bulb) is located right beside the limbic system, involved in intense problematic emotions and reactions to threat. Neutral smells detected in anxious states such as traumatic experiences can become encoded as aversive, paving the way for people to thereafter be activated negatively by everyday-life odors (Krusemark et al., 2013). Smells can have lasting effects on thoughts, emotions, actions, and brain activation, even after they have faded away (Carlson et al., 2020). Given the extensive connections between olfactory processing and a wide range of emotional learnings, opportunities to involve this sense in therapeutic conversations are worth exploring.

Audrey, 28, struggled with being single. Every morning, as soon as she opened her eyes, she grabbed her phone to see if anyone had contacted her or liked her posts on social media. This led to starting most days disappointed and hating her life. She drove to the store where she worked, kept to herself, then came back home to watch a movie or visit dating websites. At the first session, Marie-Nathalie externalized hating and how it got her to focus only on certain interactions with people ("likes" of her posts) at the expense of other aspects of her life, and how it led to living in a state of *waiting* to find a partner. This was in contrast to creating her own contentment and savoring the privileges already in her life.

On her birthday, and before our second session, her mother offered Audrey a massage, which she thoroughly enjoyed. Leaving with a body completely relaxed, Audrey surprised herself by feeling calmer, grounded, and without the usual ache in the pit of her stomach from hating everything. Surprised, she went for a walk and admired the nature around her, perfectly comfortable with herself, and grateful for some aspects of her life. At the next therapy session, Audrey was invited to describe what stood out in the experience of the massage. After sharing how it felt good and soothing to her body, she suddenly remembered the smell. She had loved the scent of the lotion used by this therapist, which she described as "flowery, foresty, but not too strong, subtle and gentle." She had not washed the shirt she wore right after the massage, to keep the soothing scent. We wondered about the potential effects of purchasing this lotion, and using it as a sensory "bridge" to her preferred self. This idea engaged Audrey immensely. The scent offered an experiential tool to more easily access a different embodied state. It reminded her that well-being didn't have to depend on gaining something external, like a partner, but could be cultivated as an inner state.

As Audrey settled into her new routine of starting her day with a shower followed by the lotion, making her bed so she'd accomplish something early on, morning yoga, breakfast, and talking on the phone to her best friend while walking to work, it became easier to focus on what she appreciated in her life. We traced the history of this preferred self, its connection to her high school friend-group's fun experiments with different perfumes, and how it widened her abilities to approach coworkers for lunch and participate in after-work activities. She eventually decided that she wanted to cut her long hair as a symbol of starting a new life with less "weight on her shoulders." We discussed the possibility of giving the cut hair to Locks of Love, a charity organization that provides custom-made hair prosthetics to underprivileged children facing loss of hair because of serious medical issues. She loved the idea.

While the scent alone was not enough to change the problem experience, it jump-started possibilities of connecting with a satisfying experience of herself on an embodied emotional level and opened the door to unexpected reauthoring possibilities. The work supported the emergence of a magnanimous self, and eventually reconnected her to multiple facets of her identity.

Taste

Tasting and sharing food connects people of all ages in many communities. Children have a keen sense of taste, with an average of 10,000 taste buds, which makes them more reactive to liking or not liking certain foods, while this number may drop to below 5,000 as we age (Parker, 2007). Tasting is an art and a science, as beautifully depicted in the movie *The Hundred-Foot Journey*, where an immigrant Indian family starts a restaurant across the street from a fancy French restaurant. Eating certain foods connects us to memories of childhood and many important experiences, such as being nurtured by caregivers or soothing ourselves (Wein, 2015). The association between taste and emotions is interesting in that some languages, such as Chinese and English, occasionally use taste descriptors to talk about an emotion, such as affectionately calling someone "sweetie pie" or acknowledging that an event leaves a "bitter taste in one's mouth" (Zhou & Tse, 2020).

It is believed that the detection of sweetness in food can affect mood and relational behaviors (Meier, & al., 2012; Ren, & al., 2015), and vice versa. Variations in emotions affect our perception of flavors in such a way that positive emotions can enhance perception of sweetness, and negative emotions (such as losing a hockey game) increase the perception of sourness (cited in Noel & Dando, 2015). Because of the powerful impact of the sense of taste in our life, it can be helpful to include it in our reauthoring work when relevant. Many clients really enjoy this process, and it adds humor and sensory material to the experience of the preferred self, as illustrated below.

Ranita was an elder from India struggling with overgiving when taking care of her husband and three adult children. This often led to exhaustion and health concerns, given her battle with fibromyalgia. She consulted Marie-Nathalie a few weeks before the Thanksgiving holiday, knowing all too well that overgiving would get her to plan everything perfectly for the dinner, focus on serving others, and overdo it, which meant that, once again, she would be in pain and bedridden for the second round of celebrations taking place during the December holidays shortly after. Her family encouraged her to seek therapy, as they were worried about the toll of stress on her health. She had rejected all their efforts to help prepare any holiday events. We started by mapping the effects of overgiving. It led her to clean the house thoroughly, plan a several-course meal weeks in advance, shop for unusual ingredients, lavishly decorate the table, plan a surprise dessert, choose a background music ahead of time, and so forth. During dinner, overgiving got her to keep an eye on people's glasses and make sure they were never empty for too long, notice whether everyone ate everything on their plate, offer refills, and anxiously pay attention to whether the meal was seasoned enough or needed extra spices. Overgiving even got her to overdo it when she was invited for dinner at friends' homes, as she would often initiate clearing the table and doing the dishes. Ranita had not invented overgiving. She had been raised in such a way by her parents, who themselves were encircled by a patriarchal culture expecting women to serve, especially around meals. Given how important it was culturally for her to care for others, the map of effects became interesting for Ranita when we examined the effects of this behavior on others: *Does overgiving allow for a relaxed atmosphere where everyone is just enjoying their meal, or does it lead to others trying to prevent you from doing too much? Does the overgiving allow you and them to actually immerse yourselves in savoring the exquisite meals you prepared, or is everyone preoccupied by worries, you about them and them about you? Does overgiving contribute enjoyment to the evening and make it more successful, or does it tend to take away?* Ranita was stunned to realize that overgiving got in the way of everyone tasting their delicious meal. This created an emotional reaction, an action potential to do something about the problem, which provided an opportunity for change.

Eventually, we explored moments of freedom from overgiving and Ranita realized that when she allowed herself to trust that everything would be fine, and attentively tasted her own food, she became less preoccupied by others' well-being, and everything became more enjoyable for everyone. Being present became more valued than overdoing. When asked for a food metaphor that would best describe the distinction between being present and overdoing, she shared the following: "*Overgiving is like putting chunky sugar on a cake, it's very visible, and it's too sweet. Being present is like putting baker's sugar on the cake, it's more subtle, delicate, and gourmet, there's just the right amount when you taste it!*" Since eating food was such an important experience in her life, associating a tasting metaphor with her preferred self thickened its experience in a meaningful and embodied way.

Analogies to food can be used with people whose presenting problem has nothing to do with cooking. The transformative power of tasting is also used in mindfulness training, such as with the attentive tasting of a raisin exercise (Kabat-Zinn, 1990) or in groups helping children discover mindful states by tasting a mystery food and finding the special sweet-tasting spot on their tongue (Beaudoin & Maki, 2020).

Touch

Our bodies are covered with nerves sensing tactile information in the skin, sending signals to the brain at a speed of up to 400 feet per second. Most people will register touching something within 0.01 second. Skin is the largest organ, measuring about 18 square feet (about the size of a twin bed) in an average human, with a thickness varying from 0.5 mm (eyelids) to 5 mm (soles of feet; Parker, 2007). Sensory information from the skin can be recruited to support therapeutic intentions, as illustrated with Adele.

Adele, a Jewish middle-aged woman, sought therapy with Marie-Nathalie for what she called an anxious energy, doubting herself, and feeling insecure, which interfered with her marriage. She reported that her husband always complained that she behaved like a child, and he wished that she was more responsible, outspoken, and assertive. After asking for a few examples, it became clear that he was fairly emotionally abusive.

Adele was encouraged to discuss couples therapy with her husband. He declined, saying all the problems were her fault, that they had already tried twice, and that therapists had repeatedly encouraged her to be more "assertive," with no success. Adele really wanted to pursue individual therapy, so the nervous energy (NE) was quickly externalized, and examples discussed. NE typically occurred when she got home from her housecleaning job and started walking on eggshells, trying to please him to avoid his wrath. Whenever blaming rants started, NE made Adele fearful and unable to think clearly, so she tolerated the lectures silently. Time seemed to slow down. NE made her body feel small, shaky, fragile, overwhelmed by a racing heart and shallow breath, disconnected from her arms and legs. She felt as if the relative size of her body grew smaller, while he seemed to grow taller and bigger. NE also raised the pitch of her voice if she attempted to talk. As I mentally engaged in staging the unfolding scene in my mind, I wondered what it would be like if Adele brought back her legs and arms into her awareness and, in particular, if she could stand and feel the unmovable surface of the floor beneath her, or touch a solid object nearby unaffected by hurtful words. Since she preferred to not say anything in those moments, she could focus on *touching* something and become one with its stillness.

In the therapy session, we spent a few minutes breathing together and feeling the floor beneath our feet and inhaling the unwavering stillness of the furniture around us. Adele really liked that experience. By the next session, she had used this strategy three times and felt much less emotionally and physically demolished during and after conflicts with her husband.

Stabilizing her emotional experience by physically touching solid surfaces around her had opened the door to observing the incidents more clearly. While NE previously had her think, "He's right, I messed up again, why can't I ever do anything right," she became able to calmly examine the actual content of what he said. Over time, she was able to see the patterns and how he always repeated the same thing: "If you were smart, you would have done X." Her newly found ability to not get demolished by those incidents reduced her fear of these episodes and the NE, which increased the therapeutic possibilities of broadening her perspective on what triggered the conflicts, the patterns of interaction between them, each of their contributions, and how to modify at least her side of these patterns to protect her well-being. She started mentally replying to his attacks and saw all his contradictions and inconsistencies. She didn't wish to fight back, as he thoroughly enjoyed a "good fight" and she didn't. She skillfully started avoiding unpleasant interactions by speaking to him more boldly outside of conflicts, pointing out his responsibilities, and taking the dog for a walk when he was irritable.

This eventually led to a reduction of his power to influence her sense of self-worth and led to more respect for her opinion. Ultimately, using her sense of touch and first stabilizing her body allowed her to more easily access preferred ways of being. This practice didn't entirely solve the problems, but it made them more manageable, and gave her a newfound voice to advocate for couples therapy.

Oxytocin is well known to be associated with bonding and relaxing and is in fact triggered by a wide range of low-intensity haptic (tactile) contacts (Kerr et al., 2019). This hormone decreases cortisol, heart rate, and blood pressure; it facilitates the regulation of emotions, and is associated with the production of dopamine. All of these effects have been observed when people have a loving moment with a pet (Beetz et al., 2011; Odendaal, & Meintjes, 2003). Marie-Nathalie's work with an emergency room doctor, who struggled with a fear of mistakes and insomnia, was accelerated when he was encouraged to take a silent moment before bedtime, to be present with and stroke his cat, in the dark. This effectively shifted his physiology to a more sleep-conducive state. Slowing down the body in the evenings resolved the insomnia quickly, while addressing the fear verbally took a few more therapeutic conversations.

Sight

The visual cortex is one of the largest sensory processing areas in the brain and significantly affects people's experiences, choices, and stories. Along with birds of prey, humans have one of the most precise and sharp visual capabilities in the animal kingdom (Caves et al., 2018), allowing us to read small letters on a page and notice intricate details in facial expressions. More than 80% of the sensory information sent to the brain is visual (Jensen, 2008). Visual information such as the weather, the colors of a sunset, or the glare in someone's eyes may seem insignificant at first, but can be powerfully encoded with an event and transform the course of therapeutic conversations. Tiny visual details can be associated with implicit or explicit affect and become the key that opens the door to a complex memory. As mentioned earlier, memories are not videotapes but, rather, puzzle-like reconstructions involving the firing of different groups of neurons. Just as doing the border of a jigsaw puzzle facilitates placing its middle pieces, recreating the physical location and visual details of a scene facilitates retrieval of the inner felt process a person was experiencing at the time (Beaudoin & Zimmerman, 2011). As an example, a client remembered a moment of breaking free from a group of boys bullying him as a child, and the only thing he recalled at first was the gray overcast of the day, not what allowed his escape and bravery. Another client had locked eyes with his father as he was dying and thereafter struggled with panic attacks whenever he made contact with someone's eyes with remotely similar features. It was working on the implicit affect associated with eyes combined with narrative practices that eventually freed the client. Eyes are heavily involved in traumatic experiences because of their rapid connection to the periaqueductal gray, a structure in the midbrain involved in blocking pain and modulating responses in threatening situations (Kearney & Lanius, 2022). This will be further explored in Chapter 8. Sight can be discussed in therapeutic conversations in a large number of ways and is sometimes key in overcoming problems, as in the story below.

Nick was a kind, friendly middle-aged man, originally from Vietnam. He worked in the tech industry, had important responsibilities, which he enjoyed greatly, and was highly successful. He was very appreciated, moving up rapidly in his company, and working was taking up most of his life. But Nick had a dark secret. When he left work at 8 p.m., and got on the highway to drive home, he was overcome by rage, which got him to drive exceedingly dangerously, speeding, zigzagging, racing, swearing at other drivers, teaching them a lesson, and cutting them off sharply. The week prior to scheduling the therapy appointment with Marie-Nathalie, rage had terrified him, as he nearly caused a deadly accident. The next day, he eagerly hoped his bad habit would be eliminated . . . but it wasn't. He was completely overcome by road rage again, and realized to his horror that he just could not control it.

Rage has an enormous action potential in the brain, especially when encoded repetitively, while good intentions and kindness alone are unlikely to neutralize the neural intensity of a well-established problem emotion. Nick was ashamed to discuss this behavior, and scared it represented a multiple-personality disorder of some kind. He felt it did not fit at all with the kind of person he preferred and was socially known to be, yet it seemed insurmountable. Full of sorrow, he shook his head and said, *"I've become a monster."*

As a first step, we explored his preferred self. As I co-centered on how deeply important it was for him to be a "decent human being," I felt myself being touched by his gentle, polite manners and co-centered with his sorrow. We externalized rage, mapped its effects, and, in particular, examined how it felt in his body. Nick described it as an explosive fire, a volcano that erupted in his chest and face when he got in his car after work. A part of him even looked forward to living this intense energy and treating other drivers poorly. Nick shared that while rage was there he felt free, powerful, and passionate; but when he got home, he felt his actions were outrageous, wrong, and scary.

There were two turning points in the brief clinical work. The first involved working with his eyes and exploring what he saw when he had been scared of creating an accident and decided to stop the behavior the week prior. It took some poking around in his memory of the frightening scene until he finally realized that, for a fleeting moment, his eyes had locked on the terrified face of an elder. I asked him to describe the face, and then what effects this sight had on him. He replied: *"It was like a slap in the face. I was raised to pay respect to elders. When I saw that I almost caused this person's death, I felt very ashamed; this wasn't like me at all to do such things . . ."*

As the conversation unfolded, connecting Nick to his values and preferred ways of being, we realized that rage was getting him to overfocus on annoying cars in his way and treat them as annoying "objects," such as those in video games.

There is some evidence that anger and rage tend to be at their peak intensity when something or someone is perceived as a danger *or* as blocking something we intensely desire (Martin, 2021). The experience of feeling blocked often gives a surge of energy, a powerful forward action potential. Foundational narrative practices such as externalizing often benefit from this momentum, since the externalized aspect of experience becomes positioned *in the way* of people's preferences. Since Nick's rage focused on other drivers being in the way, therapeutic work needed to reduce the power of his rage and increase the intensity of his preferred self in those moments.

Making an effort to notice people's face in some situations can reengage areas of the brain around connectedness, which go offline in states of intense anger. Studies show that it is much easier for people to engage in harmful behaviors when they do not see another's face, or when their own identity is either transformed or hidden (Krahe, 2020). Allowing the brain to register the eyes of another and actually seeing their facial expression can alter the self-sustaining loop of objectifying and feeling disconnected, so I asked: *"The rage is making you see annoying cars. What would it be like to actually see real people with 'invisible' constraints?"* The concept of "invisibles" was created to help children imagine what was influencing other people's behaviors. It became hugely popular in schools, beyond expectations, and greatly increased students' abilities to experience empathy (Beaudoin, 2010, 2014; Beaudoin et al., 2016). This concept is also helpful with adults.

Nick really liked the idea of seeing people, not just cars, and also imagining their "invisibles," like why someone was slow, in a hurry, or a poor driver, or other aspects of their lives. In particular, he wished to remember that these were fathers, mothers, daughters and sons, maybe neighbors and friends. This idea engaged him greatly, as he shared growing up in a community where people were seen based on their relationships to one another rather than as individuals. This connection to his collectivistic culture, the concrete strategy to use his eyes to actually see people in cars, imagine their "invisibles" and relationships to others, really helped contain the rage and helped him drive in a safer manner . . . but it didn't completely erase it. Something else contributed to the physiological intensity of the rage and had the power to overturn his best intentions.

We then examined whether anything in the unfolding of his days contributed to his body accumulating pent-up agitation. Initially, Nick couldn't find anything; he loved his job. When asked to describe a day, he shared that he often skipped lunch, never took breaks, and sometimes felt irritated toward his coworkers if they interrupted him with questions. We wondered if his body became out of balance during the day, and if eating lunch, socializing more, taking a walk afterward, leaving slightly earlier, doing some exercise, and relating to stress differently might help to keep him anchored in the person he preferred to be. This made the final difference in our journey.

Ultimately, the combination of taking care of his body throughout the day, reconnecting with his values, and *seeing* people rather than objectifying them helped put an end to the problem. Rage became seen as the obstacle in the way of his remaining connected to his family values, mobilizing action potential against it.

Inviting people to see another's eyes and facial expressions is a very helpful practice in many situations and, in particular, with parents. When parents are very angry, they often perceive their child in an objectifying way, as an "annoying thing" in their lives that needs to learn a lesson. Helping them notice how they look at their child differently when they are parenting with care versus anger often yields meaningful realizations. There are many other practices that engage our affinity for visual information, such as photographs, metaphors, drawing, brain maps, and other documents.

Conclusion

It is undeniable that we all live in a body. Acknowledging the role of senses in problematic and preferred experiences of self can propel therapeutic effectiveness forward. In the next chapter, we will acknowledge how senses and embodied expressions have long been used for healing purposes in many ethnic groups of the world.

CHAPTER 7

The Importance of Collectivist Practices

We have noticed in the mental health field in some North American con-texts a strong pull toward embracing more holistic approaches to mental health well-being, informed by many Indigenous and contemplative cul-tures. Now more than ever before, we as mental health practitioners are paying attention to mind–body connections alongside the linguistic and cognitive characteristics so long emphasized in Western health-delivery systems. This trend has now been going on for several decades in North America and is the first sign of efforts to decolonize mental health services in the West. Decolonization is focused upon providing those who are not served by the dominant psychiatric models in the West with rights to men-tal health services that are delivered on the clients' own terms (e.g., Good-man et al., 2015; Gorski & Goodman, 2015; polanco, 2013; Shin, 2015; Tate et al., 2015).

In this book we want to be careful about not exacerbating a Western global trademarking of narrative therapy. We see instead the practice of narrative therapy as constantly unfolding and maintaining its transforma-tive edge as it responds to both the recognition and application of diverse Indigenous knowledges on the one hand and the contributions of Western discoveries and their evolution of knowledge and practice on the other. This chapter pays attention to many of the Indigenous communities' gifts of heal-ing pertaining to the mind–body connections, and explores the meanings made of these practices by contemporary neuroscience and the study of affect to advance the practice of therapeutic work.

Relational Flow

Ancient ways of knowing, developed within diverse contexts across time, have long known the significance of attending to what the interpersonal neurobiologist and psychiatrist Daniel Siegel (2023) calls the relational flow of energy that is shared between people and their natural habitats. He describes this relational energy flow as being historically downplayed in medicine and science, as the focus has tended to emphasize what he calls the embodied flow, which occurs within the skin-encased body and brain. The embodied flow is important to understand in ways that have been articulated in some of the clinical work laid out in this book. The connection between the relational flow of energy and the embodied flow is best illustrated by what Siegel describes as how the right side of the brain cortex sees the context and relational connections, which fits with many Indigenous perspectives that attend to the relationships among the parts. The left side of the human cortex focuses on the attention on individual parts and this part of the brain has often received more attention, as we have overly valued the mental construction of a closed, separated view of reality rather than the perceptual right side of the human cortex. He states, *"The wide perspective of our right mode lends a distinct but equally important way of perceiving aspects of reality. A broad, systems view . . . enables us to perceive patterns and systems"* (p. 13).

Prior to the 21st century, much of modern psychology placed little value on addressing the mind–body connection in promoting mental health and emotional well-being. If people received healing or improvements in their mental health through engaging in different kinds of mind–body practices, this was often put down to the placebo effects of ritualistic quackery or hocus-pocus. However, the Western sciences are discovering that all along, there are sound neurobiological explanations for why many ancient collectivist mind–body practices have been so effective over the centuries.

In Western contexts, mental health has been exclusively focused on the dominance of a brain ruling the body from the head. However, in recent research there is a widely recognized understanding that the human body effectively has brain cells, neurons with the ability to learn, spread in different areas of the body, namely in the gut, heart, and brain. Damasio (2018), a neuroscientist, comments that our bodies are essentially driven by the subcortical regions of the body, meaning that the head brain is in service of neurological activity going on in the heart and gut. Neurological research shows that understanding the role of our heart and gut in shaping our emotional and mental well-being allows us to see that our whole body is involved in constructing our thinking, feeling, and actions (Siegel, 2023).

Modernist psychology, as a discipline, not so very long ago would have pooh-poohed the idea of a mental health practitioner or Indigenous healer saying to a troubled and confused client, *"Listen to your heart to hear what it is saying"* and *"Concentrate on what your gut is telling you."* From a neurobiological perspective, Siegel (2023) suggests that humans should draw more upon our sensory systems provided by our heart and gut brain when needing to make decisions and address challenges. Trusting the sensory systems of the heart and gut in providing guidance to people is a practice familiar to many contemplative cultures in the world.

Engaging With Us and Them

As we know, in those first milliseconds of the counselor–client interaction, often unconsciously the client is determining how psychologically safe this series of personal interactions is going to be. Attention is paid to the greeting, to facial expressions, noting how people are dressed, noticing skin color, gender, sex, age, all to determine: Is the counselor an Us or a Them? Of course, all of these same processes are going on nonconsciously for the counselor in deciding if this person is "my people."

It is a serious problem when families in dire need of mental health services find seeking help from mainstream health-care providers potentially threatening and even psychologically dangerous because of the mismatch of expectations and cultural traditions around sharing vulnerability and emotion. Myers (2007) suggests that human beings draw upon risk intuition, which assesses threat in our environment. He says our brains do not have to work as hard to assess threats when we see others whom we regard as most like us. Lieberman (2013), a neuroscientist, said that when there are threats to our social bonds, *"the brain responds in much the same way it responds to physical pain"* (p. 40). Research by Lewis et al. (2000) shows that the heart rate, blood pressure, and mood are synchronized with others around us, and those who are emotionally influential can impact others' mood, even without any words being spoken.

Lewis et al. (2000) noted that we regulate or dysregulate with others, and this out-of-conscious awareness occurs at a deep biochemical level. As was discussed in Chapters 3 and 4, when the collective physiology becomes synchronized, emotional resonance occurs. This is the biological experience of feeling an "Us-ness." When we are part of a cooperative group, we feel safe. Lewis et al. (2000) state that our brains rapidly process displays of emotion in our environment often nonconsciously, and show a proclivity to being drawn to others who are most like us.

Maori Threads and Contemporary Counseling Practice

One example of an Indigenous community that has focused on the centrality of the relational flow and mind–body connections over hundreds of years is the Maori people. The second author of this text, Gerald Monk, was raised in a small town in Aotearoa/New Zealand surrounded by a predominantly Maori population and was exposed to teachers such as Rangimarie (Rose) Turuki Pere (1991), who translated the ancient teachings of the tribal groups Ngati Ruapani, Tuhoe Potiki, and Ngati Kahungunu for educators, physicians, and mental health practitioners. With the Indigenous Maori from Aotearoa/New Zealand, there are two important qualities or characteristics that are adopted by successful practitioners to reach people seeking mental health services and emotional and spiritual well-being. One is the expression of *aroha*, which involves the demonstration of empathy and compassion, and *manaakitanga*, which is the expression of kindness, respect, generosity, and support to look after others. The manaakitanga enhances *mauri* (spark or essence of life) of all involved. The demonstration of aroha and manaakitanga builds mutual trust and respect between practitioner and client. Robinson et al. (2020), writing about the importance of how Maori healers interact with others, stated that it is essential to demonstrate "he ngakau aroha (a heart of love)" when developing relationships with clients to communicate care, kindness, compassion, consideration for others, and empathy. These are qualities that we do our best to demonstrate with the people we work with who are suffering. When we are doing in-person counseling, if we are in a position to do so, we want to create a space that feels welcoming and hospitable. If the physical environment can be well lit with natural light, it makes for a welcoming space. We might have tasty snacks available in the waiting room. Clients might help themselves to tea or coffee or we might make a pot of tea to serve them as we begin to talk about difficult things. We want people to be comfortable. We are thoughtful of the images we project in our counseling rooms. We are mindful of the art we hang on the walls, the ornaments that we display that say something about us, and we hope that what we display is not offensive to the people we are about to have an intimate conversation with.

The demonstration of manaakitanga (kindness and respect) is critical to building bridges between the practitioner and the client(s). When Gerald conducted therapy in Aotearoa/New Zealand with Maori, he would typically greet people with a *hongi*. The *hongi*, which is also defined as the *ha* (breath of life), is performed by one person pressing their forehead and nose on the forehead and nose of another person, demonstrating a shared human connection.

When meeting with our clients in person the first nonverbal exchanges are important. Some of us like to shake people's hands to make that physical connection before beginning an intimate dialogue. In the last chapter, on senses, we discussed the importance of human touch and the sensory environment to therapeutic engagement. These practices are in complete alignment with the value narrative therapists place on the practice of attunement and the reaching for an authentic sense of connection with clients, as discussed with co-centering in Chapter 3.

Of course, when working in telehealth now, we are not in a position to touch the other or even respond to a client-initiated hug after a harrowing session. While some of our clients and some therapists now prefer video telehealth for ease of access to services and to reduce the chances of getting sick or catching the latest virus, it is not optimal to lose out on being physically present in the same physical space, as we believe human contact optimizes the relational flow.

When in a telehealth session, we can get closer to the camera on the video screen, and can project our warmth on our faces and use a quiet, soothing voice tone in an effort to comfort the other. We can use hand signals to express our care and make use of the emoji tools that young clients are so used to trading back and forth with their young friends. More than ever, we are looking for nonverbal cues, tracking the facial muscles and zeroing in on the upper body if we can see that on our video screen. Shoulder positioning of the client, the rising and falling of their breath, the color pigment change, and all the cues we take from voice tone assist us to attend to relational flow and attunement.

Bridging Diverse Forms of Emotional Engagement Arising in Collectivist and Individualist Contexts

Narrative therapy practitioners who honor the theory and practice as laid out by Michael White and David Epston understand the importance of the sociocultural landscape when working with diverse communities to assist those struggling with mental health challenges and relational distress. As we know, counseling and therapy in the West can be characterized by the display of strong verbal and emotional expressions between practitioner and client, and thus counseling therapy tends to match the display of Western middle-class norms. It is not surprising, then, that families raised in collectivist communities, who are not expected to show emotional vulnerability with strangers or even show strong emotion with family members, struggle to engage with Western mental health services, as therapy is viewed as an alien activity. This is well-illustrated in the story below.

Adriana, a 10-year-old, has been sitting largely alone in her classroom for six weeks now since the first day of elementary school. She is new to the school. She is not interacting with other children at all, including in the recess and lunch breaks. The teachers are worried about her. Despite their best effort to engage Adriana, she puts her head down or shakes her head no or yes to simple requests or seems to ignore most questions altogether. One teacher recommended that Adriana get assessed by the school psychologist for autism and selective mutism.

What the teachers are unaware of is that Adriana is a relatively new immigrant to the United States from Guatemala. She does not have official documentation that allow her to be legally living in the United States. She was separated from her older sister at the U.S.–Mexico border, as the human traffickers, or *coyotes*, directed them to be split up to ensure they wouldn't be caught. Adriana was kept in a small concrete-block room in Tijuana before being smuggled across the border in a *coyote*'s car—driven by a woman she had never met before. There were multiple traumatic events that happened to Adriana and her older sister both before leaving Guatemala and on arriving in the United States. Adriana and her sister are living with a second set of relatives, after it didn't work out with the first set of relatives. That is why she is at her second school in six months. Her current school is largely white and middle class. The English as a Second Language (ESL) resources at the school are not well developed. None of her teachers speak Spanish.

As we fill in more context it becomes obvious why Adriana does not engage. Adriana is terrified of attending this school. She doesn't understand 90% of what the teachers are saying. She does not have the ESL resources she needs. She is expected to demonstrate middle-class English and be open and outgoing with her emotional expressions, as other students are encouraged to do. The vast majority of her classmates do not speak Spanish. Besides, she was taught by her family in Guatemala to keep her mouth shut and to not speak up in the family. Even her extended family in San Diego reinforce the expected emotional expressions of a 10-year-old child to be quiet until spoken to. All of her extended family constantly remind her of the dangers of talking to strangers, who could alert the immigration police. For Adriana, these teachers are strangers and so are the classmates. Not surprisingly, on top of all these profoundly difficult circumstances, she is living through the trauma of what she has recently been subjected to. Frightening memories flood her mind whenever she is not distracted. It is easy to pathologize and categorize others when trauma is present. The struggle to understand and speak a second language is daunting for anyone, and when fear and anxiety are close to being intolerable it makes sense to shut down. The additive challenges of adjusting to different ideas about emotional expression and managing rapidly changing living circumstances only add to the long list of distressing situations.

For Adriana to thrive, she needs somebody in the school to understand what she is going through. She would benefit from a counselor who speaks her language, understands the effects of separation and trauma, facilitates connections, and understands the political realities of being undocumented in a border city with different cultural expectations about emotional expression. A safe relationship with someone who can co-center with her embodied experience, speak her language, and view problems and preferences from a biopsychosocial lens would be the first step of a therapeutic journey, as it often is for people.

How we were raised as children gives us guidance to determining what are socially appropriate emotional responses to make in different circumstances. F. Rothbaum et al. (2000) observed that many Japanese children were encouraged to keep hostile feelings to themselves. Children are taught that expressing hostile or angry feelings is completely inappropriate, as doing so could threaten the very fabric of strong familial relationships. Japanese children also learned that the promotion of assertiveness and being autonomous is uncultivated and immature. The cultures we are exposed to give us information on how we express ourselves when experiencing distress and suffering. Keller (2022), reflecting upon many parenting styles in collectivist cultures, noted that a child is often viewed as an apprentice who needs to be inducted into the community through direction and instruction. Children's outward displays of sadness, hurt, or anger are often deemed inappropriate in communal contexts, and harmonious behavior is expected in the family and community settings. Iliana Lopez Yañez (2022), reflecting on the importance of managing her emotions in her collectivist Mexican culture, made the following statement:

I truly believe that if you had a quarter for every Mexican child that has heard their parent say "Deja de llorar o te voy a dar una razón para que llores" ("Stop crying or I'll give you a reason to cry") . . . you would have quite a bit of change in your pocket. When the implicit instruction is that you shouldn't outwardly express positive or negative emotions, the alternative becomes to experience them only on the inside. Talking about emotions becomes taboo. (pp. 9–10)

In stark contrast, Mullen and Yi (1995) reported on research that showed how many middle-class Western mothers engage their children to talk about thoughts, feelings, past experiences, and other people's feelings and thoughts. Understanding different perspectives of social–emotional expression is critically important—especially when members of an extended-family household have different ideas of emotional care.

Take, for example, a situation where some members of the family, who are acculturated into middle-class Euro-American cultural norms of emotional expression, end up in a relational conflict with non-acculturated family members engaging emotionally in alignment with collectivist norms of emotional display, and vice versa. It is then easy to understand why there can be significant relational distress when one part of the family feels that the other part of the family is violating their emotional norms and can end up pathologizing the other. Narrative therapists are tasked with deconstructing these wider macrolevel cultural clashes, which enables them to more skillfully help family members address the microlevel mental health struggles that can ensue.

The story of Mimo is an example of a clash of a relational style of communication and emotional expression under one roof. Mimo was raised as a Muslim and when she was a small child fled with her family from civil war in Somalia and moved to the United States. Shortly after their arrival Mimo's mother was worried about Mimo losing faith, losing her modesty, and getting caught up with drugs and alcohol and becoming Americanized. Mimo was figuring out how to live two lifestyles. At home she was required to follow the house rules and be respectful. Respect meant being quiet, not drawing attention to herself, and being obedient—not challenging elders, and doing what was expected. What was going on at home ended up in stark contrast to life at school and with her friends. Outside the house she was encouraged to express her opinions and feelings and live emotionally, as modeled by Oprah Winfrey on television. She read white teen-adventure novels that again modeled an emotional style that involved speaking your mind, being quick to express feelings, pushing for independence, and wanting a Western emotional style of communication at home. It is easy to understand how conflict developed in the home and how the narrative school counselor had to help Mimo navigate two relational landscapes.

Mimo slid into a deep depression caused by this clash of values and different ideas about emotional expression. Deconstructive work with Mimo and an elder sibling who initially upheld the traditions of the household enabled Mimo to learn how to better understand the emotional landscape she lived in within her home and the one outside of her home.

A salient example of the complexities of working across individualistic and collectivist contexts is also illustrated in Marie-Nathalie's counseling work with Angelica. Angelica was a Filipina middle-aged woman who was struggling in her relationship with her Australian husband, who engaged in ongoing emotional abuse. The only reason the emotional abuse did not turn into chronic domestic violence is that the first time he hit her, when she was pregnant with a daughter after their marriage, she immediately called the police and filed charges. The emotional abuse continued and increased in harshness but always remained verbal afterward. Marie-Nathalie helped Angelica connect to her *matatag na babae*, "brave feelings," which contributed to developing strong resilience in the face of her husband's abusive attacks and her growing nervousness. Using an externalization in her native language ensured it would resonate with as much embodied experience as possible. Angelica shifted from seeing herself as a failure to understanding the challenges she and her husband were facing relationally because of a problematic cycle of engaging each other. With new insights and understandings, Angelica progressively gained a stronger sense of self-worth, with increasing self-respect, but the relationship at first remained challenging, as he refused to participate in any form of counseling.

For practitioners, it is tricky to navigate collectivist cultural values and

Western individualistic cultural values. Angelica was raised in a collectivist context, unlike the two authors of this book, who were raised in more Western individualistic environments. In an interaction with Angelica, as therapy was progressing, Marie-Nathalie asked, "Is your relationship more equal now that you have less nervousness and are connecting with your *matatag na babae* inside?" Most Western therapists have ideas about the importance of equality in couples and it is common for us to encourage it, with the assumption that it is a better style of relationship. In this case, Angelica stated, "*It's becoming not more equal but more balanced.*" Marie-Nathalie was humbled, aware of her assumption, didn't press further, and asked instead about her view of "balance." Angelica described equality as being more self-centered, where each person calculates whether things are fair for themselves, which, in her situation, would just make things worse. Marie-Nathalie was careful to not further insert her own values here, as she was aware of the cultural difference and remembered that Angelica had been through hardships in other therapies where she had been pressured to be more assertive. All of these therapist-centered interventions had shamed her and contributed to demeaning her in the eyes of her husband, solidifying the problem story that their problems were due to her shortcomings as a wife.

Another major turning point came in the counseling work when Angelica realized that speaking her opinion was helpful to both herself and her husband. Having originally immigrated from a collectivistic culture, she was more motivated to do something that would benefit both of them rather than just her own well-being, an individualistic concept. When Angelica responded that she felt the relationship was more "balanced," she explained that balance "was about a whole that is functioning better and contains space for everyone." Marie-Nathalie supported Angelica to listen to her *matatag na babae* and find her own ways. The counseling work culminated in Angelica developing a preferred way of being that didn't entirely solve the relational problems but made them much more manageable and significantly reduced the frequency, duration, and intensity of the emotional abuse. Even when hurtful words were said, she was able to dismiss them and hold herself with a restored dignity.

Cultural Consultants and Bridge People

Sometimes it is difficult to traverse cultural divides across collectivist and individualistic cultural communities. The ethnic, linguistic, and gender differences are so great between therapists and clients, it is a gift when paraprofessionals and cultural translators can get alongside Indigenous or collectivist healers to facilitate understanding.

Collaborative and Indigenous Mental Health Therapy, coauthored by Maori healer Wiremu NiaNia, his psychiatrist colleague Allister Bush (NiaNia et al., 2017), and David Epston, shows the path forward in strengthening the ties with narrative therapy and poststructural approaches to knowledge and practice and the significant contributions to mental health healing embedded in *tikanga (things)* Maori. David has taken full advantage of helping promote the work of cultural consultants by showing how Maori knowledge and practice can be bridged with Western psychiatry. In this text, David lays out the important elements by which a Maori healer and a psychiatrist build a collaborative partnership, which is an illustration of *tataihono (strong sense of order and organization)* between a Maori spiritual teacher and healer and a *Pakeha* (white) psychiatrist (NiaNia et al., 2017).

This collaborative process harnesses what are described here as cultural consultants and bridge people to facilitate the success of the healer partnership. We find that in exclusively Western contexts for delivering mental health services, middle-class mental health professionals don't usually participate in direct unmediated access to collectivist communities; rather, talking therapy is delivered in an office or over a video monitor with a complete stranger uninformed of the cultural sensibilities of the client(s). The cultural worlds of the mental health professionals and clients who are typically underrepresented in the mental health arena benefit from intermediaries, or what Cho (2019) terms "bridge people" and Waldegrave calls "cultural consultants." In the story of Adriana struggling in a school where the school staff and her peers don't know her cultural communities and her history, there is a great need of bridge people and cultural consultants in the school.

Waldegrave (2012) suggests that there is great value to people who reside in communities that are underserved to receive services, where possible, from someone from that community. Cultural consultants are often not trained or licensed in a particular mental health field but are likely to have an important role in the community and are well placed to work alongside the licensed practitioner. The cultural consultant often speaks the native language of the client, has the necessary relational skills, and understands cultural metaphors, so they can play a constructive part in the therapy.

For example, in a Maori context, the rituals associated with welcome and respect can be followed and will be in alignment with that cultural community. In this way there is a person or persons who can enter the private world of the client or client family, as it feels to the clients that the cultural consultant is an "us" with the family. Waldegrave suggests this enables family members to speak freely without having to translate their personal experiences into the language and conceptual framework of the practitioner's dominant social group.

Cho (2019) writes about health and social-care services provided in the United Kingdom for older Chinese immigrants, and found that the role of "bridge people" was essential for these immigrants to access and benefit from the services provided (Liu et al., 2017). Cho comments that bridge people can come from a variety of backgrounds (e.g., family, friends, public servants, and paraprofessionals) and bridge access to services. Bridge people are typically bilingual, understand intimately the cultural contexts of the clients, and are "support people" who are trusted and whose services can be accessed with minimal financial resources. Bridge people are often an untapped resource who possess rich cultural knowledges about their communities. Cultural consultants and bridge people can assist therapists to engage clients from collectivist communities in making meaning of important mind–body connections that are otherwise not accessed by monolingual and monocultural therapists working in middle-class, Western contexts.

Somatic Expression

For practitioners to be effective with clients within Indigenous and collectivist communities, it is important to note clients' cultural relationship with the expression of affect. Our bodies are always performing in response to interactions with others. When there are very different "others" required to engage with one another, the relational flow is not always conducive to comfort and relaxation. Human interaction at times can be more menacing than comforting. Griffith and Griffith (1994) state that when the outward performance of a body is forbidden, human beings present a "somatized expression by the body" (p. 61). They suggest that forbidden outward expressions of the body can contribute to chronic somatic symptoms and other bodily manifestations of significant psychological distress.

Maffini and Wong (2014) found that a range of somatic states were expressed in Asian American ethnic communities. There were different meanings made of the symptoms and approaches to addressing somatic suffering across diverse ethnic communities. In many ethnically diverse communities, somatized pain with no organic origins can occur throughout the body, including the head, back, joints, and chest, and can also show up as pseudoneurological symptoms. In this case, hallucinations, double vision, dizziness, and seizures driven by psychological stress rather than organic causes can present in therapy. Maffini and Wong argue for a more benign interpretation of somatized responses within particular ethnic communities. He noted that in some Asian American communities it is preferable to suppress emotions and experience physical distress in other parts of the body, as it is less culturally acceptable to display strong emotion, which is registered by one's community as a sign of weakness, lack of control, and immaturity.

According to Maffini and Wong's (2014) research, Asian Americans often seek help from a holistic healer or doctor who can treat physical and mental reactions at the same time and can understand the client's primary language to explain their symptoms and cultural idioms, words, and phrases. Maffini and Wong write about the value of gently building rapport while explaining the structure of counseling roles and expectations, and the importance of emphasizing confidentiality to build a strong therapeutic alliance.

Paying attention to affect and bodily responses assists narrative therapists to build important therapeutic connections, and to introduce mindfulness and integrate somatic work with clients experiencing somatic symptoms. An example of somatic work occurred when a therapist worked intensely with a Tibetan man who had endured knee pain for many years and the breakthrough in the therapy came when the man linked his knee pain to witnessing, as a child, the violent murder of his mother after her knees were crushed by a soldier during the Chinese invasion of Tibet.

Connecting Specific Indigenous Mind–Body Practices With Contemporary Mental Health Approaches

Many people from ethnically and linguistically diverse communities in need of mental health services do not feel comfortable meeting with a stranger over a video screen or in a counseling office where the rituals of engagement require the client to share deeply personal information in a middle-class counseling vernacular. There are numerous healing practices developed in many Indigenous and collectivist contexts that do not start with verbal intimate disclosure. Rituals are engaged with that help facilitate trust and confidence between healer and the person seeking help for their distress. Many of these practices have been translated from a variety of Indigenous collectivist cultures into Western contexts for mental health treatment.

Within richly diverse Native American communities in North America there are numerous mind–body healing practices that have been used for centuries and have highly positive healing properties, such as sweat lodges and synchronized-movement gatherings.

Sweat Lodge

Christopher Webb was discharged from the U.S. Army in 2006 after being wounded in combat in Afghanistan. He had suffered from hypervigilance, anxiety, depression, nightmares, and a number of other distressing symptoms accompanying a "posttraumatic stress disorder." Shortly after being discharged he participated in the American Lake Veterans Affairs sweat lodge in Washington State, held by Lakota elders (Shore et al., 2009).

Christopher describes the process:

As we waited for stones to heat up in the sacred fire, elders and experienced participants taught me how to make prayers, wrapping offerings of tobacco in diverse colors of cloth, which are used for different kinds of prayer. They patiently explained how to show respect to the sacred fire burning near the entrance to the sweat lodge before taking me in to sit in a tight circle with other participants. (Most were Native American, but there were a few other white veterans like me.)

One by one, several red-hot grandfather stones were brought into the lodge and placed in the center. The flap to the lodge was closed, and we were enveloped by complete darkness, except for the dim red glow of the heated stones. Medicinal herbs and water were sprinkled over the hot stones. The lodge filled with the scent of the burning herbs, and our lungs inhaled the hot, pungent steam. Drummers in the lodge began to drum and sing, and over the next several hours, we sang and gave passionate prayers. That first ceremony was intense—almost overwhelming—but it was the first of many and the beginning of a healing journey that would change my life. (Webb, 2020, para. 6)

It was explained that the sweat-lodge ritual would last for about three hours, and prayers, songs, and teachings inspired by the Lakota traditions were shared with participants, providing the opportunity to restore and repair broken relationships with significant others around them. He learned to take on a new point of view that was shaped by a "spirit-oriented perspective." This new perspective invited Chris to engage in reflecting on his life as a spirit who comes into the temporal world to live and cycle out and return to another realm. The institution of the sweat lodge, a healing practice that goes back many centuries, is currently used with highly beneficial effects in addressing mental health challenges and trauma today.

Dozens of Native American tribes have adopted the use of the sweat lodge. The sweat-lodge ritual of the North American Plains Indians typically begins by gathering at a fire pit for a beginning ceremony. In most instances, participants smudge with sage as a cleansing ritual. We discussed the effects of smells in Chapter 6. The powerful scent of the sage can transport the person toward welcome bodily associations activated by the smudging process. Scent oils and herbs on their own can have healing properties and then, when associated with healing experiences in the sweat lodge, kick-start those positive memories. A "talking stick" is sometimes used by participants to acknowledge their intentions before entering into the ceremony. The sweat-lodge ceremony involves being subjected to intense heat for varying amounts of time. Lex (1979) reports that the rituals accompanying the sweat lodge shift the *"mode of consciousness characteristic of the right cerebral hemisphere, associated . . . with perceptions of unity and holism. Hence, individuals, eager or reluctant, are integrated into a group, not only by the sharing of pleasurable emotions through participation in formalized, repetitive, precisely performed interaction forms, but also by a mode of thought that reinforces feelings of solidarity"* (p. 144). These states are excellent examples of the relational flow that Siegel (2023) describes as an essential element in brain functioning and health.

When clients have gone through such powerful bodily experiences such as participating in a sweat lodge, we as practitioners may then be meeting them over a video screen in more typical practitioner–client interactions. Emphasizing mind–body work in our therapeutic conversations, we can engage the client in preferred-story accounts that not only track the narrative cognitive reflections of the experience in the sweat lodge but also support the client to give voice to the physiological story of the heart and gut.

Dance and Drumming

Healing rituals and life transitions within some Indigenous knowledges, not unlike most cultures around the world, harness powerful rhythms of music and dance. Many communities, both traditional and modern, use the combination of music, dance, and drumming not just for entertainment but for mental rejuvenation and emotional and spiritual healing. The exceptional value of these practices, in many instances, is backed up by neuroscience and medical research.

Basso et al. (2021), writing about the value of dance, speak of the interactive effects of brain–body connectivity and how the brain influences human movement as well as how the body's movement affects brain development. They remark that when human beings hear music, there is an invitation to move in time and respond to the beat, leading to a positive affective state. Basso et al. explain:

> Dance evolved as a form of interpersonal coordination, which includes both imitation and synchrony. Imitation . . . refers to the matching of movement, whereas synchrony refers to the matching of time. Interpersonal coordination has an important role in social cohesion or bonding; these behaviors help connect the self to others, and recent studies have shown that they drive neural coupling. (p. 3)

Basso et al. (2021) write about the centrality of dance in creating social alignment in extended families and in our work and lives.

> Dance incorporates many aspects of interpersonal coordination, including touch, eye gaze, sensory–motor interactions, rhythmic or in tandem movement, physical movement coordination, facial expressions, or emotional qualities, and even synchronization with other physiological parameters, such as breathing, heartbeat, and sympathetic tone. (p. 5)

Basso et al. (2021) discuss how imitation in dance activates portions of the mirror neuron system described in Chapter 3. Dance in all its forms has a strong influence on human emotion and the movement involved produces elevated dopamine levels (Foley & Fleshner, 2008). It is, of course, a source of emotional self-expression through the movements and gestures exhibited by the body. Dancing is a way to perform our internal affective state with others, and Basso et al. suggest that while in motion, we are in a strong position to be apprised of another's affect, intentions, and actions, creating an opportunity for neural synchrony—a coupling of different people's neurocognitive systems. Thus, dance is another example where the social dynamics of the brain emphasize attunement with another and help us think about how neuroscience can be as much a social–relational process as it is an approach that exclusively focuses on individual brain processes. Northrup (2016) described the healing properties of explosive, energetic rhythmic activity. Her research showed that drumming released dopamine, enkephalins, and alpha waves in the brain, which are associated with general feelings of well-being and even euphoria. Her research showed that intense rhythmic-activity sessions reduced stress hormones, and provided an opportunity for a felt sense of "synchronicity"—contributing to a sensory connection to nature and a greater sense of peacefulness and well-being. There are many dance and drumming expressions that can be harnessed to celebrate living one's preferred story and embracing the preferred self. As a brief example of harnessing movement in facilitating change, Marie-Nathalie invites some of her clients to develop a simple dance movement or hand gesture, with an accompanying sound, to concretize and symbolically mark successes with preferred-self-expressions.

Conclusion

The founders of narrative therapy, and the narrative therapy community in general, have been at the forefront of finding ways to partner with local community approaches to addressing community mental health needs in many places around the globe. We think this work can be expanded as we fold in closer attention to the mind–body connection in therapy, and the study of affect in therapeutic conversations, while harnessing advances in neuroscience. In addition, exploring the role of music, art, dance, and other embodied rituals of engaging with human experience, narrative practitioners can honor these traditions as processes supporting healing and the therapeutic endeavor. We believe that engaging with affect and the body carries a decolonial spirit that attends to the histories of healing within communities that dominant Western health and medical practices have historically ignored.

CHAPTER 8

Harnessing Bodily Resources With Specialized Practices

In this final chapter, we focus on recruiting the brain's experiential network with additional considerations of mindfulness, touched upon periodically throughout the book, and deactivating states of hypo- and hyperarousal with practices using the eyes, such as eye movement desensitization and reprocessing (EMDR). We believe these approaches can augment a narrative practitioner's therapeutic range when addressing certain recalcitrant problems and the grip of serious traumatic histories that have plagued clients, sometimes for most of their lives.

Mindfulness

The Source of Mindfulness
Mindfulness is one of the most potent bodies of knowledge derived from 2,500-year-old Buddhist traditions and has profoundly shaped influential mental health treatment approaches in contemporary times. These contemplative practices approach the problem of human suffering with a disciplined focus on human responses to mental events. In the West, some of these ancient practices were appropriated and translated into a method to cultivate well-being, removing their connection to spiritual dimensions. We would like to respectfully acknowledge some of the premises informing these practices.

Buddhist traditions emphasize the importance of noticing that all sensations, thoughts, and emotions are impermanent and that the self is merely based upon ongoing interrelationships of mental formations and physical sensations (Wallace, 2011). To put it another way, Buddhism shows how personhood is produced within a cultural and social meaning-making system. Percy and Paré (2021a) noted that Buddhism invites a viewpoint where the self is always in draft form, a contextualized self constantly in the process of becoming other than how it most recently appeared.

As discussed earlier, the mind constructs stories about our experiences, over- and underfocuses on selective aspects, and falls into a veracity trap of assuming our thoughts and stories are "true," which leads to suffering. There are many forms of mindfulness training and they all intend to free us from this tendency, along with cultivating compassion, kindness, perspective, and awareness.

The Value of Mindfulness Meditation

The practice of mindfully engaging the experiential network can lead to immediate temporary biochemical changes in the body, and long-term structural modifications (increased cortical thickness) after 8 weeks of daily engagement (Lazar et al., 2005). Compelling research supports the value of mindfulness in many areas of life and in particular with emotion regulation (Creswell & Khoury, 2019; Singleton et al., 2014). From a biological perspective, when a person is experiencing chronic stress from a perceived or actual threat, the body is continually flooded with the hormone cortisol, which maintains the body in "fight-or-flight" mode, to provide protection. Blood pressure is increased, digestion is shut down, and levels of blood sugar increase. Mindfulness meditation has been proved to result in a drop in cortisol levels immediately following a session, providing protection from a chronic overreaction (Miodrag et al., 2013).

Khaddouma et al. (2015) suggest that mindfulness helps improve attunement within close relationships, as people become more aware of others' bodily signals and words, in the same way a musician might be attuned to the notes of their instrument. Barnes et al. (2007) report that mindfulness can lead to better communication and higher satisfaction within relationships and better connectedness with others. While this state typically requires training, new findings in IPNB and specialized breathing techniques can put it more readily within reach of children and adults, making them more interested in practicing afterward (Beaudoin, in press; Beaudoin & Maki, 2020).

Two Pathways in Applying Mindfulness and Narrative Therapy

Narrative therapists have been writing about using mindfulness in their narrative practice since the early 2000s (Beaudoin & Zimmerman, 2011; Percy, 2008). Percy and Paré (2021a, 2021b) use mindfulness to examine the entire scope of human experience, including sensations, images, thoughts, emotions, and memories, and share the following:

> The unpacking of dominant and problematic storylines of people's lives requires that bodies do the actual living of what happened, and they are present in the remembered telling and retelling of what happened. Likewise, the body is always present when bringing to the fore overlooked helpful responses to problems. . . . [There are] diverse ways in which we experience affective embodiment. Just as there are multiple stories available for making sense of our lives, there are multiple readings of sensations and gestures available to us. These acts of meaning may be shaped into stories which, in turn, produce other gestures and sensations and so on. (p. 8)

Marie-Nathalie has published numerous articles and books showing how mindfulness approaches can be integrated with narrative therapy using an interpersonal neurobiological approach. Since, in the brain, *attention gives power to the object of its gaze*" (Beaudoin & Maki, 2020, p. 76), inviting clients to pay attention in a certain way to their externalized experiences helps them observe thoughts as constructions of the mind, avoid the certainty trap discussed in Chapter 4, and consequently change the neural networks associated with problems. Similarly, giving attention to embodied experiences associated with preferred notions of the self strengthens those neural networks, makes those lived moments more readily available, and can infuse them with satisfying emotions (Beaudoin, 2017b, 2019; Beaudoin & Maclennan, 2021). This process can also be facilitated with children through various creative and artistic projects (Marlowe, 2017).

Similarities, Differences, and Overlaps Between Mindfulness and Narrative Therapy

Narrative therapy and mindfulness work are committed to reducing human suffering, and taking a step back to observe the effects of what is happening around us. Both approaches invite clients in choosing ways of being, developing control, finding meaning, being aware of an ethical lifestyle, and attending to their personal values.

Characteristics	Mindfulness	Narrative
Intention	Reduce suffering	Reduce suffering
View of people	Enslaved by mind & cravings	Enslaved by stories & culture
Focus	Attentional choice	Story choice
Process	Observe the unfolding activity of the mind	Observe externalization
Emotions	Detach from all	Disentangle from the problem
Action	Practice being present to life	Practice living preferred ways
Brain rewiring	Experiential network	Default network
Outcome	Presence	Preference
View of life	Comprehensive—body, mind, emotion	Discursive
Relationships to others	Compassion, kindness	Appreciation, preferred patterns

TABLE 8.1 **Similarities and differences between mindfulness practice and narrative therapy.**

Incorporating Mindfulness With Narrative Work

Being skillful in the application of mindfulness approaches when engaging in narrative practice provides advantages for both practitioners and clients.

For practitioners, mindfulness

- provides pre-session grounding,
- cultivates presence and attuned listening,
- enhances compassion and clarity,
- reduces the likelihood of reacting,
- facilitates the "right-to-right" hemisphere regulation of clients' intense emotions, and
- reduces vicarious trauma and burnout.

For clients, mindfulness

- offers new perspectives on problems,
- provides regulation skills and control,
- increases awareness of embodied triggers,
- enhances access and embodied experiences of preferred self, and
- creates embodied transition opportunities from problem experiences to preferred ones.

Using Mindfulness in Narrative Conversations

EXTERNALIZING

There is a helpful alignment between narrative therapy and mindfulness when both approaches help the clients dis-identify with the problem(s) they are struggling with. We are familiar with how narrative therapy creates a linguistic shift in therapeutic conversation, leading the client to be in touch with the notion that the person is not the problem but rather the problem is the problem. Mindfulness practice leads to a similar effect in that it trains people to be "both an observer who is aware and that which is observed" (Ogden, 2021, p. 224), therefore facilitating diverse perspectives.

As an example, Marie-Nathalie worked with a woman who struggled with debilitating moments of depression and suicidality and incapacitating anxiety about her baby not meeting society's developmental milestones. Pediatricians she consulted said the baby was thriving. In the end, Marie-Nathalie externalized "intensity" as the problem and most of the work was on recognizing those sensations building up, mapping "intensity's" disruptive effects, and discrediting its associated certainty trap. Incorporating mindfulness into the conversation encourages a similar dis-identification with the problem by supporting the client to connect to and experience the fleetingness of all experience. As Percy and Paré (2021a, pp. 7–8) articulate:

> Mindfulness offers a refinement of externalizing by locating it in moment-by-moment awareness; narrative offers practices for ethical living by recalling and developing story lines associated with one's pre-ferred values. There are many fertile possibilities for mindfulness to enhance narrative work and for the constitutive power of story-making to enhance mindfulness in everyday life.

Incorporating Mindfulness in Problem-Story Exploration

Sometimes clients keep getting stuck in a problem story and feel compelled to keep paying attention to the same troublesome sensations, emotions, and images associated with the problem they are discussing. The client can get locked into these sensations, which they replay again and again in their thinking, feelings, and behaviors. When these events happen in problem-story exploration and in the mapping-effects phase of therapy it is helpful to move from what Percy and Paré (2021a, 2021b) call narrative and attentional capture and attend to attentional choice. Having attentional choice is being able to decide what to pay attention to rather than be attentionally cap-tured, which is essentially being trapped by repetitive sensations and images. In this phase of therapy, the mindful narrative practitioner can switch from problem exploration to adopting a moment-by-moment attention to what-ever momentarily arises. At a pace the client is comfortable with, the client is invited to notice and name sensations, emotions, and images associated with the problem right there and then, avoiding the impulse to move on. If the client is running from the problem, being in the moment with awareness and observation invites the client to resist the impulse to avoid it—thus facing the problem in real time.

Incorporating Mindfulness in Preferred-Story Development

Mindfulness helps the clients notice the physiological aspects of their preferred selves, increases their likelihood of being able to enter those states at will, and affords them another way to activate those experiences. As an example, Marie-Nathalie helped a client discern and recognize her ignored gut feeling before a romantic date that turned sour. Even though the client eventually regretted the decision to date and sought therapy to recover from its negative effects, revisiting her sensations before the moment of decision revealed that her gut feeling had been accurate, which was comforting and an antidote to the problem story that she could not trust herself (Zimmerman & Beaudoin, 2015).

Acquiring attentional choice, or mindful intention, helps clients be more present when sensations occur, moving away from being on automatic pilot and following ingrained problem reactions. Marie-Nathalie illustrates this process with a couple experiencing anxiety and anger problems in the clinical example below.

Clinical Illustration of Mindfulness at Many Steps of a Narrative Process

Marie-Nathalie started therapy with Mr. Toms, who presented as being very thoughtful and attentive but struggled with distressing levels of anxiety. He worked as an engineer in the construction of a large hospital and had to shoulder the weight of many responsibilities and a large group of employees. He said, "There are always unexpected situations and problems to solve. I go from one to the next and never accomplish everything I set out to do in a day." I (MN) explored anxiety and its effects on Mr. Toms, and discussed his experience of his racing heart, which was now creating health issues for him. When asked about moments he could relax, he revealed that there weren't any because he went from the stress of work to the stress at home, where he was cautious because his wife had "serious anger issues." I asked if his wife might be willing to join the counseling sessions and he wasn't sure, as he had requested this many times before and she had refused. Given the significant health issues of Mr. Toms, I explored how he handled the stress, what helped him the most, and whether he might be interested in learning a mindfulness exercise. He was very interested, especially when he was offered the opportunity to use a Muse headband, a biofeedback device that functions as a tiny EEG and measures neural activity. Being an engineer, he loved the experience of meditating with the headband, which gave him auditory feedback on how well he succeeded in not thinking and just focusing on sensations. He felt immediately calmer within 10 minutes of the exercise and was pleased with the device's scores and histograms of the session. He then incorporated the device into his daily life, during lunch and after work in his car before entering his home.

Two weeks later, Mrs. Toms agreed to meet with me. Mrs. Toms noticed that her husband was a bit calmer and was intrigued as to how therapy could help her. She said she was from a culture that didn't believe in mental health services but was willing to meet me once.

Mrs. Toms was very charming and expressive and we immediately connected. She reported with embarrassment that as a child she was known for terrifying tantrums that left her soft-spoken parents, community, and schoolteachers hesitant to set limits. She reflected that her anger problem had been present most of her life. She had always been incredibly successful at school, having the best grades, getting numerous awards, and later being admitted to two top universities. She was now very successful, working as a lawyer for a high-tech company. She expressed that no one would oppose her opinions and she had quick, stunning replies for people challenging her, which left people speechless. While she was successful at getting her way, she reflected that this came at a cost. Anger would get her to scream, insult, demean, judge, and hold grudges for sometimes two weeks, and this long recovery period left the couple with very few moments of closeness. When we examined together the effects of this anger on her relationships, she choked up a little bit as she acknowledged having lost connections with so many close friends and family members. Marie-Nathalie used "numeral questions" to gently increase the action potential of the motivation to change and we listed, one by one, a total of 26 friends and family members lost to an anger outburst. She was dumbfounded by the number, and the distressing emotions contributed some determination to address the intensity of this anger. Mrs. Toms reported promising herself vehemently many times that she'd stop the anger, but without success, as its speed of onset was extremely fast, intense, and physically overwhelming. She felt she was condemned to be "an angry person." She described the anger as "an upward surge of fury" that would flood her body, leading to her shouting loudly. She realized that this anger contributed to her husband's anxiety and health problems, and was damaging to their relationship and their toddler's feeling of safety.

Mrs. Toms reported that her husband would leave the house regularly to go smoke outside (which she hated) to escape the yelling and said he wanted to protect his son from further exposure to conflicts. Mrs. Toms became a bit tearful reporting on how horrible she felt as she tried to fall asleep knowing how damaging her behavior had been, but she felt powerless. When asked to break down the sequence of sensations in her body, Mrs. Toms described a flash of heat moving from her chest to her face and then a big inhale in preparation for yelling. Since she was now externalizing anger, was very clear about the significant effects of this problem, and seemed to genuinely desire change, I asked if she'd be willing to try an experiment. She agreed eagerly. I wondered if changing the breathing pattern involved in the anger would help neutralize a habit that had been deeply ingrained. She listened attentively as I taught her and explained the uyajii breath. I had done research on different patterns of breathing for some time (Beaudoin & Maki, 2020) and had continued to develop breathing methods applicable to various problems. The uyajii breath consists of mobilizing the muscles in the neck into a contraction as one exhales slowly, making a sound similar to "Ahhh," or figuratively sounding like an ocean wave breaking on shore. We practiced it a few times in the office and Mrs. Toms really liked the approach. She felt very empowered to have an anger-controlling method, which she was now determined to use. She had clarity from the verbal externalization and map of effects *and* a method to control the biological freight train of nonverbal activation that trampled her best intentions.

By the following meeting, Mrs. Toms had made remarkable progress, dramatically reducing the frequency, intensity, duration, and range of hurtful episodes. She had diligently used the ujjayi breath nearly every day (after warning her husband of this peculiar strategy). Over the subsequent two to three meetings, we engaged in classic narrative therapy and explored a wide range of unique outcomes articulating how she replaced the angry yelling with other responses. Now that the biological freight train of anger activation was under control, progress unfolded very quickly. The final step eventually involved helping the couple co-develop their flourishing identity individually and as a family. This process was facilitated in particular by working with their mutual love of sunsets, and encouraging them to mindfully live and dwell on these moments of closeness. In nature, they found peace, intimacy, and especially the experience of awe. Awe is a unique form of "positive" emotion, as it physiologically activates the experiential network and triggers important biochemicals associated with thriving (Van Elk et al., 2019). It shifts the self-referential activity of the mind and broadens awareness to engage with an inspiring sight much bigger than oneself, changing our experience of our relative size. When shared with others, the experience of awe enhance closeness and synchronicity.

In this example, Marie-Nathalie demonstrated how the therapeutic work was significantly accelerated by mindfulness and breathing practices, as it placed the narrative reauthoring on more solid ground. In the second section of this chapter we turn to various ways of helping clients with intense emotions by using their eyes. We will introduce the research on the connection between eyes and emotions, then mention a few interesting practices using eyes, and elaborate on eye movement desensitization and reprocessing (EMDR), which complements narrative therapy. Working with these practices supports the development of preferred emotional states and identity stories, especially when people are trapped by complex traumatic events difficult to address with classical narrative work alone.

Hyper- and Hypoarousal–State Deactivation

States of hyper- and hypoarousal associated with intense emotions typically involve older areas of the brain, such as the brain stem and midbrain, and structures such as the amygdala and periaqueductal gray (PAG), which activate very quickly under threat, before we are even consciously aware of a danger. Interestingly, there is an area in the back of the eye that connects directly to the PAG. Van der Kolk (online workshop, April 4, 2022) shares that how the PAG "lights up specifically determines whether you have a more hyperactive or a more dissociative response." It comes as no surprise, then, that working with intense emotions, especially those associated with traumatic experiences, might benefit from practices involving the eyes.

Marie-Nathalie had been exposed to EMDR and mindfulness in the 1990s, and also studied a few somatic approaches such as Brainspotting (Grand, 2014). In a nutshell, EMDR involves moving the eyes bilaterally to deprogram an association between terror and the body (Shapiro, 2013). Brainspotting involves noticing where a client's eyes fixate when talking about a traumatic experience, exploring memories encoded with this position, and, afterward, engaging in movements that can be freeing of the stuckness. Little did she know that all these studies would become critical tools during a serious medical situation with her daughter Emilie.

Unbeknownst to Marie-Nathalie, her daughter, at 12 years old, had encoded an implicit traumatic memory associated with a feverish state when a large group of nurses panicked and yelled loudly about a vomiting accident in the lab while her blood was being drawn. A couple of years later, as a teenager, Emilie had another fever and was required to have an urgent blood test, as it was feared she had an acute appendicitis. On exiting the examining doctor's office, Emilie collapsed in tears and became adamant that she could not do this. Marie-Nathalie externalized the fear and mapped the effects, to no avail. No amount of discussion or logical argument around the potential life-threatening condition Emilie was experiencing would convince her to have the test. Explaining the seriousness of her health condition only worsened her terror, and she became unable to walk, progressively heading from a state of hyperarousal to one of hypoarousal. At a loss, Marie-Nathalie proceeded to combine everything she knew at that time about implicit affect and deprogramming traumatic influences. She first reminded Emilie of a breathing exercise she had taught her before, which consists of moving the two main sheets of muscles in the abdomen, the diaphragm and abdominal wall, to their inner limits. This exercise, the Two Blankets of

Power (Beaudoin & Maki, 2020), inspired by ancient yogic traditions, generally leaves people feeling significantly calmer and grounded. It can physiologically neutralize hyperarousal in a few minutes. The abdominal sheet is pushed all the way down in the abdominal cavity on the inhale and the abdominal muscles press toward the spine on the exhale. Both movements trigger sensations in the lower back and waist area. Once this was reviewed, and Emilie was slightly more able to engage verbally, Marie-Nathalie proceeded to help her visualize the present-time microsteps needed to get the blood test done, while deactivating her physiologically as soon as a surge of emotions threatened to overwhelm her.

> **Marie-Nathalie (very slowly, holding her hand, and paying close attention to Emilie's face):** *We will walk to the car . . . get in the car . . . drive to the lab . . . open the door . . . get out of the car . . .*
>
> **Emilie (with a surge of terror and crying):** *I can't!*
>
> **Marie-Nathalie:** *It's okay, let's breathe together, right now . . . we will practice the steps again, but a little differently. When we get to that scene and the fear is overwhelming, we will do the Two Blankets of Power and at the same time you will follow my finger left and right with your eyes only, like this, without moving your head. Let's try it. Doing all these things together will deprogram the fear.*
>
> **Emilie (hopeful):** *Okay.*

The eye deactivation involved moving the eyes left and right, slowly making a figure eight, following a finger at about one foot from the face and going out for about six inches on each side. Involving gentle movement, especially of the eyes or the body, keeps the person connected to the present-time physical location. The breathing and movement done together as a joint relational activity allows the ventral branch of the vagal system to remain online, which can prevent the slip into autonomic arousal and dissociation. This process essentially substituted the terrifying implicit sensations from the past (which were entirely bottom up and did not even include images) with a present-time sense of safety and control.

Every time we revisited going to the lab we could inch much further, and eventually, after a couple of hours, Emilie walked bravely into the lab. She still had some anxiety, but it was no longer a debilitating terror and she had the breathing exercise to control some of it. Marie-Nathalie then encouraged Emilie to write down her new story of getting the blood test done, what was helpful and to list the strategies that were most effective if some nervousness came back for future blood tests. The intent was to thicken her preferred self, create a written document about the successful process, and articulate more thoroughly who she had become. Marie-Nathalie also knew that this success in the feverish brain state may not be easily generalizable to getting a blood test without a fever, and that more work would be needed to clear the past encoding of this issue. She started explaining to Emilie that a follow-up with an EMDR specialist would be valuable.

Eye Movement Desensitization and Reprocessing (EMDR)

There are occasions where the vividness of people's recollections of traumatic events is so heightened that all of their senses, including sounds, tastes, smells, and bodily sensations, are reactivated, taking them back to the site of the trauma as though it had just happened, or they disconnect completely in an attempt to reclaim their lives, as seen in Chapter 5. All practitioners have worked with clients who, despite their best efforts, just do not respond to the practices they have used effectively with others, including talented applications of classical narrative work.

Several narrative therapists we know of have written unpublished papers on the subject (Haegert & Moxley-Haegert, 2021; Jacobs & Moxley-Haegert, 2020; L. Rosen, personal communication, May 8, 2018; L. Storm, personal communication, December 10, 2022). We believe there are compelling reasons why on some occasions the integration of narrative therapy with EMDR is advantageous, and we make a case for this in the rest of the chapter.

EMDR was first developed by Francine Shapiro in the 1980s when she noticed that her upsetting emotions accompanied by disturbing thoughts disappeared when her eyes moved rapidly back and forth on their own. She began experimenting with this and found that when others moved their eyes rapidly back and forth their upsetting emotions seemed to dissipate too. The idea that eye movements could alter thinking patterns and emotional responses led to Shapiro conducting a more formal research program, which has revealed that EMDR is a highly effective approach to helping people get past acute and chronic traumatic memories (Shapiro, 2013).

Shapiro makes the argument that the rapid bilateral eye movement replicates what the body does naturally in the REM stages of sleep. During this time, new learning and new neural connections are made when new information is consolidated and integrated into other memories. This process parallels narrative practitioners' work where they help clients connect to moments of lived experiences that have not been connected before, thus forming preferred narratives that clients can embrace. Shapiro suggests that distressing memories persist when the level of disturbance is so great that the brain's natural healing functions are overwhelmed and the brain cannot by itself integrate the experiences into existing memories. When abruptly awakened by a nightmare, one is in the middle of the brain's attempt to incorporate new information—sometimes unsuccessfully in this disrupted state.

Today, EMDR has become a combination of a set of processes that can be integrated into other counseling approaches such as narrative therapy. The formal EMDR protocol involves eight phases. If narrative therapists seek to include EMDR in their clinical work, we strongly recommend they receive quality training in the theory and practice of it. There are important intricacies to become proficient in before adapting the essential elements into narrative work.

Much of the work on EMDR is about learning how to keenly observe an experience without attaching oneself to judgment. Many of the guidelines in the practice of EMDR invite the client to notice their reactions and try not to force an alternative response to habitual actions. As with mindfulness practice, the client using EMDR to directly address trauma pays attention to what is occurring in the immediate present in the session rather than following a narrative line of inquiry not immediately connected with bodily sensations, emotions, and in-the-moment thoughts.

Bilateral Stimulation

In the late 1980s and early 1990s the focus on rapid eye movement was extended to other forms of bilateral stimulation. In her 2013 book, *Getting Past Your Past*, Shapiro expressed the wish that she had first described her work as reprocessing therapy, as the focus began to move away from the centrality of eye movement desensitization and more toward bilateral stimulation and reprocessing. Today, bilateral stimulation is engendered by light signaling producing rapid eye movement, bilateral cognitive attention to alternate-hand tapping on thighs, tactile pulsing, auditory signaling, and sweeping finger movements. All of these tools assist the brain in refocusing attention while looking at traumatic memories during bilateral stimulation.

Emilie's Experience With EMDR

A couple of years after facing the blood-test trauma, Emilie faced another traumatic experience while training for track. She inadvertently fell, and twisted her spine to regain balance, which herniated discs in her spine and left her unconscious on the street, alone, with a paralyzed foot. For a long time while being rehabilitated, Emilie would check visually many times per hour whether her foot was still there, as she couldn't feel it at all. The severe concussion also altered her cognitive state into an unusual mindset, encoding the scary experience of checking visually that her foot was still at the end of the unfelt leg.

After many months of physical therapy and various treatments, Emilie recovered; she started to walk again and the day came when she could start running! Yet, as she got back into her running groove, flashbacks of falling would occur, taking over her conscious awareness, and she would unexpectedly lose sensation in her foot at odd moments. Changes in consciousness were difficult to attain with narrative linguistic practices alone, so Marie-Nathalie found a therapist Emilie liked who offered EMDR.

Over the course of eight weeks, EMDR helped her overcome the traumatic experiences associated with the altered states of consciousness, dissociation, and flashbacks around her foot mobility and, as a bonus, completely normalized her ability to get a blood test! When reflecting on how EMDR had helped, Emilie made the following statements:

I was surprised at how effective it was. The process felt very safe, but it was much more tiring than I expected, probably because of all the emotions and the challenges of having to keep looking at the fast-moving green light signals. What worked best was when I spoke of a memory for a very short moment, or briefly just imagined a difficult scene, and then I was quickly switched to talking about something enjoyable in my life. It was like just touching or poking at a scene, and then giving lots of attention to positive things in my life. This was definitely a turning point. The therapist using EMDR desensitized my left elbow where the blood test had been drawn the two times I was sick. I had developed a habit of covering the scar there whenever I was anxious or in any stressful situation. Finally, it was nice to share all the exciting things in my life with another adult, outside of people in my family.

Shapiro (2013) states that many of our responses come from the part of the brain not governed by the rational mind. Our automatic reactions that usually control our emotions arise from neural connectivity within our memory networks that are occurring independently of our higher thinking power. That is why we can witness ourselves engaging in behaviors that we know we will regret later.

EMDR With Maria

Maria was an undocumented 28-year-old female, first-generation Mexican American who, as an eight-year-old, had escaped drug-related violence in central Mexico with her mom and sister. Maria was completing a graduate program in counselor education in a southern California university and kept being triggered by flashbacks of violence she had witnessed when her clients or peers would talk about traumatic events involving violence. These flashbacks would bring up many emotions and reactions that made it hard for her to manage on a day-to-day basis. Maria had come across EMDR in her training and wanted to try it out. She was referred to a narrative therapist (Rochelle) who had completed the EMDR training and become qualified in the method. Rochelle was able to integrate her practice of narrative therapy with EMDR, and consulted with Gerald.

In the first phase of therapy, or what EMDR therapists call "history taking," Maria reported symptoms associated with the traumas that presented as nightmares, irritability, insomnia, and troublesome images of loved ones dying.

From an EMDR perspective, memories contain the feelings, physical sensations, and perceptions that we experience at the time of the turbulent unprocessed event. Tightness in the chest, fear, knots in the stomach, powerlessness, and shame were all tied to Maria's early memories. Maria also reported somatic symptoms that included dizziness and intense pain in her arms, hands, head, and neck. Furthermore, she spoke of suffering from a sense of emptiness and hopelessness. Rochelle, the narrative therapist, had explored some of the central problem-saturated stories that were affecting Maria's ability to be present in her interactions with colleagues and clients. Externalizing conversations occurred around shame and guilt for not being able to protect her family and especially her mother from the violence that was at times all pervasive.

Maria grew up witnessing domestic violence, particularly when her father was inebriated. Her father regularly became physically violent toward her mother and Maria's male siblings, with a misguided idea of toughening up her brothers. Maria witnessed this violence for most of her early childhood. She spoke of many instances of comforting her mother and brothers when they had been assaulted. On one occasion she ran to the neighbors after she witnessed a brutal assault by her father against her mother, and was immediately punished by her father for trying to involve others outside of the family. The narrative therapist engaged Maria in telling about these acts of bravery and together they coauthored stories of Maria's resilience and courage. In the early phases of therapy, stories of Maria's extraordinary capacity to love others and be so attentive and caring to her loved ones were documented, even toward her father when he was sober and struggling with depression. These accounts were in an alignment with her emerging preferred self as an advocate for women and children who were being subjected to violence. While clear progress was made in therapy, Maria experienced certain frozen memories that continued to plague her just when she thought she was becoming calm and having feelings of "tranquilidad."

When talking about earlier traumatic events, Maria recalled how at around 6 years of age her mother fell to the ground screaming in their small kitchen as Maria was told by her sister that her oldest brother had been found dead on the side of the road nearby. He had fallen victim to the drug cartel's violence and had been badly tortured.

A year later was the event that precipitated the escape of members of her family to the U.S.–Mexico border: Maria's second-eldest brother, who was 14 years old, disappeared on his way home from school and his body was never found. Maria's mom, using nearly all their savings, paid a *coyote* (human smuggler) to help her leave her husband and take her two remaining children to the United States to escape the violence in her community and the domestic violence episodes that had become the norm in her household.

Rochelle, combining EMDR and narrative therapy, did not ask the details of these horrific events that had been so present with Maria in the early phase of therapy. She did not want to retraumatize Maria by asking her to recount these events. On the other hand, there was no use merely avoiding these frozen memories that haunted Maria most days. EMDR, when skillfully implemented, builds in robustly tested safeguards to process disturbing trauma events, which greatly alleviates traumatic distress.

One of the great advantages of EMDR is that it does not require the client to talk explicitly about the details of the trauma because the practice helps the client process the fragmented memories internally, using bilateral stimulation, at the client's own pace. This is particularly important when the client experiences great shame and culpability when verbalizing the details of the trauma to the therapist. The aim of the EMDR interventions is to process traumatic memories of the past, identify and process present everyday triggers, and facilitate a privately focused approach that encodes new memories of success. The goal is to integrate disturbing memories into something more manageable. Once engaging in EMDR, it is common for formerly unconscious memories to emerge. This is particularly important as many early childhood memories (formerly unconscious) continue to drive somatic suffering and unregulated harmful emotions that often keep pushing people in directions they don't want to go in.

In the second, "preparation," phase of the EMDR approach, the therapist prepares clients for the remaining phases. Psychoeducation was used to help Maria understand the importance of making connections between traumatic events and troublesome somatic responses. Like other interventions discussed in other chapters, EMDR integrates relaxation techniques, mindfulness, guided visualizations that involve creating a calm safe place, progressive muscle relaxation, breath work, and grounding techniques into therapeutic practice. In preparing to work on her somatic pain, Maria engaged in the safe/calm state exercise, a hallmark guided-memory activity in EMDR.

In phase three, an EMDR therapist reviews some dominant negative and positive cognitions held by the client. This is called the "assessment" phase. For a narrative therapist, this phase can involve helping the client identify the central themes or headlines of problem stories and alternative preferred stories. As we know, problem stories that form from traumatic events often create distorted ideas, leading to the pathologization of the self. From an EMDR perspective, the memories associated with the trauma are inadequately processed or maladaptively stored.

In "desensitization," phase four, many guardrails have been put in place by the EMDR protocols, which are too numerous to document here. The focus is on physiologically desensitizing the triggers and some of the painful touchstone memories. For example, Maria chose core themes based upon these touchstone memories of violence. With her, Rochelle mapped the effects of the problem story of powerlessness Maria experienced as a child and Maria quickly identified thematic headlines that all related to the cause of the family's suffering. The EMDR protocol asks clients to identify what they call core positive and negative cognitions associated with the trauma and the progress on being freed from it. We believe there is value in first learning the protocol from certified EMDR trainers; once accomplished in the method, one can adapt the practice to integrate it more with narrative work. Narrative practitioners don't typically use language derived from cognitive psychology. However, when narrative therapists use the EMDR protocol, they can adapt the language to be more fitting with narrative practice. The key point, though, is to use brief thematic descriptions that characterize problem and preferred stories, as clients need to hold this information in their thinking while engaging in bilateral stimulation. Clients can be given a menu of choices from which to select problem-story descriptions that relate directly to their lives and/or co-generate headlines with their therapist. Maria identified "fault finding," "not being good enough," "worthless," "not in control," and "incompetence" to describe dominant problem narratives when thinking about the traumatic events that had occurred in her life.

When tracking the preferred stories of the self, Maria, with the help of the narrative practitioner, headlined "I am a strong woman" and "I overcome hardships." Clients shaped by more collectivist cultural communities often do not like to emphasize the "I" and can claim a collective association with preferred-identity descriptions such as "We are worthy." Maria emphasized the collectivist nature of preferred stories of the self. She named "We are resilient" as the preferred title of her story. These headlines were shaky at best to hold on to, and when she was triggered by the problem-saturated traumas, the preferred-story headlines were eclipsed by the problem stories once more. Maria needed to have the intellectual ideas she had about herself as worthy anchored to her physiology as a body that was truly courageous, loving, and resilient.

When getting close to the traumatic memories of the kind Maria was experiencing, it is critical to follow all the elements of the EMDR protocol. In this phase the client must be able to access preferred-story themes and have the ability to scan the body for physical sensations.

In "installation," phase five, the therapist uses bilateral stimulation (in the case of Maria, bilateral tactile pulses by two held objects, one in each hand, that pulse in a steady bilateral sequence). Using EMDR, Maria identified some reprocessing targets, which were memories associated with the death of her oldest brother, the kidnapping and disappearance of her 14-year-old brother, and the earliest touchstone memories, which were associated with the powerlessness of being a young child seeing her mother beaten and not being able to do anything to stop it.

Guided imagery techniques are used while the bilateral stimulation is occurring, such as the metaphor of the client being on a train and noticing the traumatic events out the window and seeing thoughts and feelings as part of the scenery going by. Phases six, seven, and eight are of equal importance and don't necessarily go in any particular order. The purpose in these last phases is to continue to desensitize the client to the intensity of the traumatic sensations, thoughts, and feelings and to "integrate" (what narrative therapists might call promoting preferred-story associations) unprocessed material that is held in conscious memory, as well as having the ability to scan the body to eliminate hangovers of somatic pain still associated with unprocessed old memories. EMDR uses phrases such as "installation of preferred memories," "conducting body scans to clear old unprocessed material," completing a "closure protocol," and then conducting a "reevaluation phase." The EMDR work is languaged in this fashion to guide the therapist to ensure the client is free from ongoing unprocessed traumatic memories. Maria completed the eighth phase of the standard EMDR protocol. Her somatic symptoms improved and the anxiety that seemed like it came from nowhere significantly diminished. She reported that she no longer held on to her initial negative thematic problem headlines such as "not good enough," "worthless," "not in control," and "incompetent" when old memories started to visit. Essentially the EMDR work had unfrozen all of these negative associations, leading to a lasting embodied embrace of her preferred self. These old problem-saturated ideas were replaced by embodied preferred-story headlines. Working with clients like Maria, who have frozen trauma stories that are understandably overwhelming, can become overwhelming for practitioners too. In Appendix 3, we have laid out a decision tree to organize important dimensions to consider when determining which level of therapeutic engagement may be most helpful when addressing the biopsychosocial dimensions of trauma. Maria was a great candidate for EMDR and successfully graduated from her counselor-education program.

Conclusion

In this final chapter, we have given accounts of two specific practices that add to the repertoires of narrative practitioners who work beyond the typical verbal therapeutic practices of classical narrative therapy. The chapter's emphasis is placed upon using the elements of mindfulness and EMDR, which attend to the somatic and embodied expressions of human action.

We have targeted practices that use bodily sensation and "in-the-moment" attention to the body to help clients break through stuck, frozen, or rigid problem stories. These are the problem accounts that don't seem to respond right away to the explicit re-storying process of narrative work that most clients benefit from. Through clinical stories and theoretical discussion we have interwoven both verbal and nonverbal conversational practices that provide unique pathways to overcome debilitating emotional and somatic problems often present in traumatic experiences. A diagram of factors to consider when determining which practices can support the development of resilient identities with clients who have overcome traumatic experiences is compiled in Appendix 3. We hope this book has offered narrative practitioners concrete ways to support emergent neural pathways associated with flourishing identities and preferred ways of living.

40+ Examples of Practices and Questions From Classic and Contemporary Narrative Work

Examining Contextual Contributors

	Problem-focused questions	**Reauthoring questions**
Macrocontext deconstruction	Where did the idea that a bad relationship is better than no relationship come from? Are there some messages in the media that promote that belief? What are the problems with that belief and what effects does it have on people?	Are there some communities that have been intriguing to you? What is it like for you when you read about the feminist community or LGBTQ+ articles? What would it be like for you to look into that? Might it help with self-hate?
Microcontext influences	What else was happening when you had the reaction? Was your mind busy with other things?	In which context are you most likely to be able to act in your preferred ways?

Working With the Process of Storying Identity

De-storying	Is your mind making the problem about you? Is it possible that it is simply a reaction of your body, about which you had no control?
Reauthoring	When you stopped yourself from saying something mean to your friend, is it possible that it reflected something about you?
Remembering	Is there someone in your life who inspired that value for kindness?
Grafting	Which other emotion comes up for you about this successful turn of events? Can you tell me a story about your past connection to this emotion?
Intensifying	Since you are currently feeling pride, can you imagine breathing in more of it and intensifying it to another level?
Embodying	Where in your body do you feel this determination? Can you feel its headquarters . . . epicenter . . . border . . . shape . . . texture . . . color . . . temperature?
Sustaining	What are small things in your daily life that can contribute to sustaining this well-being that you now cherish?
Expanding (magnanimous self)	Now that you have overcome depression and are more content with your life, are you seeing the suffering of others with different eyes? Are there issues that touch you more?
Summarizing	We've explored how the lying habit is getting you to misrepresent events to please other people, to avoid conflicts, and sometimes to protect others from stress. This habit is misleading you into thinking you'll have better relationships and less trouble, but it seems that it has damaged relationships with family and friends. On the other hand, you've expressed a desire to improve your relationships and have started making efforts to be more in line with your intentions and values. You've shared a few examples of challenging yourself to be "honest" and the energizing effects this has on many aspects of your life, including relationships. What do you wish to remember from our conversation?

Including Information From the Body: Landscape of Affective Physiology

Beaudoin, M. N. (2020). Affective double listening: 16 dimensions to explore affect, emotions and embodiment in narrative therapy. *Journal of Systemic Therapies*, 39(1), 1–28. Reproduced by permission. © 2020, JST Institute.

	Problem-focused questions	Reauthoring questions
Speed	Does the shame come on really fast, or does it build up slowly?	How quickly were you able to activate that sense of confidence after the initial moment of fear?
Intensity	On a scale of 1 to 10, how intensely did you experience anger?	How intensely did you live the joy of getting this promotion you've been working for?
Valence	Sensing energy building up in you before going to class, is that a helpful and satisfying experience, or is it more anxiety provoking?	When you stop and pay attention to your partner's facial expression, does it feel like something positive-ish or negative-ish is stirring inside?
Action potential	What is it in particular that shame intensely wants you to avoid?	You mentioned avoiding self-hate yesterday by being kind to yourself. What gave emotional power to that kindness?
Frequency	How many times per day, on average, would you say panic assails your mind?	How often, roughly, did you experience moments of contentment this week?
Duration	You mentioned that depression took over all of your free time on Saturday. How many hours, roughly, are we talking about?	You shared feeling pride when your daughter received the dance award. For how long were you able to keep this feeling active and alive?
Recovery	After self-doubt sabotaged your concentration at work, how long did it take, roughly, to be able to concentrate on the task again?	You shared feeling really excited about your weekend until barely escaping the car accident. How long did it take to be excited again?
Range	Does this have to be labeled anxiety or could it also be called a form of excitement?	You mentioned feeling good. If we added nuance to that, would it be joy, happiness, satisfaction . . . ?

Including Information From the Body: Landscape of Affective Embodiment

Beaudoin, M. N. (2020). Affective double listening: 16 dimensions to explore affect, emotions and embodiment in narrative therapy. *Journal of Systemic Therapies*, 39(1), 1–28. Reproduced by permission. © 2020, JST Institute.

	Problem-focused questions	Reauthoring questions
Kinesthetic tension	When anxiety takes over, which areas of your body become tensed and which areas are not at all on the radar?	How are your facial muscles different when you are feeling spontaneous and relaxed?
Visceral activation	What happens deep down in your abdomen when the fear bubbles up?	How does your chest progressively change as the sense of satisfaction settles in?
Sensory dominance	Are you aware of what you see, hear, smell, or touch when that critical voice turns you inward, against yourself?	When you have a moment of tenderness with your son, do your eyes see more of him than usual?
Spatial awareness	Is there a difference in how you are walking when the hyper-energy is building up?	What is the likelihood that shyness takes over if you are standing tall, feet hips-width apart, arms crossed, and feeling entitled to this space, as you did when you were angry today?
Relational attunement	When you were out on this first date with him, did you have a feeling about this guy and how he was treating you?	As you sang the duo side by side, you mentioned feeling some synchronicity with her. Can you tell me more?
Aesthetic	You felt like you were standing tall and powerful like a volcano ready to erupt if this lady dared criticize your child. What might be the headquarters of this power? What does it mean that you found this powerful state in your body?	You mentioned "pleasing" made you wrap everything you said in a "hard grain sugar." What kind of sweetener or condiment describes your message when you embody the Strong Confident Woman?
Time	When embarrassment startles you, does the time seem to pass slower or accelerate?	When you are fully immersed in contentment, does time slow down?

| Presence | Does this experience of sadness take you inward in a way that you're no longer present with the people around you? | Do you feel more present, in the now, when you let go of the worries? |

Other Practices Including the Body

Tend to unique outcomes	When you were able to speak up with your manager, can you describe how your voice, eyes, posture, and feet were different than when fear sculpted all these body areas?
Transform the construction	When you watch a movie and your heart accelerates, can this be called something other than anxiety? Could it be associated with something else going on?
Transfer the activation	Before walking on stage, would it be helpful to tweak the agitation and live it as excitement instead of fear?
Transition between two states	There is now confidence when you do a meeting on Zoom but when you walk to your supervisor's office, self-doubt creeps up on you. Is it possible to stop and get a sip of cold water, or take a long way there to walk more, and shake this out of your body?
Teach (create an experience)	Are you interested in doing an experiment with me, and exploring a breathing exercise?
Table, brain map, puzzle image	Let's list on paper the effects of disgust on your body and life and check how all these items are different when you are in the nonjudgmental mindset that you prefer to cultivate.
Move	I can see from the tears that there are lots of feelings going on right now. How about we take a walk and talk about it?
Identify dominant sense	If you had one sense that dominated your awareness more than the others, which one might it be: vision, audition, taste, olfaction, touch, or something else?
Umwelt	How would you describe what it's like to live in your shoes? What do you tend to notice, linger on, be drawn to, what energy level, etc.?
Sound	When you're feeling at your best, are there specific types of music or sounds that resonate with you, and sustain you?

Sight	You mentioned becoming completely disconnected from care for your toddler when exasperation is rising. When that happens, what is it that you stop *seeing* about his body? What might your eyes no longer notice about him?
Touch	When self-hate makes you tempted to cut yourself and reach for the razor blade, I wonder if there's something else that could be touched to change the intense sensations in your body. What kind of texture would be associated with self-forgiveness? Is there something about water, ice, sand, wood, plant, walls, etc. that could be helpful to touch? Tell me the story of when you discovered the pleasantness of this contact.
Taste	If, as you said, the pleasing habit feels like "too much sugar," what dish or food would represent pride?
Smell	You mentioned feeling so content at the flower market this weekend. How would you describe the different scents that floated around you? Do you think they contributed to the experience of contentment?

Addressing Emotions

	Problem-focused questions	Reauthoring questions
Loiter	Help me understand how this problem happens.	Walk me through what led to this situation you ended up resolving.
Externalize	You mentioned jealousy. Do you think that this might be behind many of the conflicts?	What would you call the state you were in when you decided to let go of worrying? Was that a form of trust?
Mapping effects (thoughts, feelings, behaviors, relationships, body, identity, etc.)	How does the craving affect what you do, think, and feel at dinnertime? Where might you feel it in your body?	When you have a wave of gratitude, how does that affect how you are in relationships?

Evaluation	We've listed all the effects of "longing" (stealing) on your life. What is it like to look at all of this?	We summarized all the implications of you adjusting to feeling alone as a parent now that your daughter is in college. Do you have any reaction that arises from seeing the "alone feeling" as just a transition state?
Justification	You say that you are realizing the sneakiness has more negative effects than you thought, and you don't want it in your life anymore. Tell me what in particular stands out. Is there anything specific that makes you wish to change this pattern?	You commented on how you prefer to be fearless. Can you share why that seems important and what this motivates you to do?
Cross the border of the WOT	You mentioned not caring about the fact that your anger injures other people. Let's go back to the moment in that scene when your fist slammed into the other student's belly. Can you tell me more about what was happening for you and how that felt?	Would you say this situation is one of the hardest you've handled? Is it revealing something about how far you've come in standing up to this problem?
Dwell inside of the WOT's border	When annoyance is intense and threatens to spill over in your actions, what dominates the most? Does it involve something about your body, or your thoughts?	Jealousy often makes you tempted to take a permanent marker and draw on your mother's favorite dress, but you haven't done it yet. At the moment when that urge is very intense, what helps you hold it back?
Lining (simultaneous questions)	Can you tell me about the hardest moment of this situation and what you did to help yourself?	
Neutralize emotions	Let's do X together, at the same time, and press the floor gently but equally with both of your feet.	How did you keep the intensity of your emotions down when in this dire situation?

Contrast	So, panic wanted you to look away, and instead, you used your determination to look straight at his eyes.	Last time, you forced yourself out of shyness by imagining you were like this actor you admire, and this time you moved out of shyness by pretending you were someone else speaking. What's similar and different between these two strategies?
Granularize	When you share with me that you "felt bad," can you describe a little more what you mean by that? Different people mean different things when using those words.	You mentioned feeling more confident. If two or three other emotions were to also come up or be associated with feeling confident, what might those be?
Tap	Where is the embarrassment in your body right now? What would it be like to tap it gently just as you tapped the back of your baby to comfort her this morning?	The excitement of your upcoming marriage is getting your heart to race. What would it be like to just tap it with joy to stabilize its beat?
Shake	Your hands are shaking from talking about this. Let's intentionally shake them to further let the stress go and slowly settle your body.	The thrill of this unexpected promotion is making you jittery. How about we intentionally shake our bodies to release some of that pent-up surprise.
Liquify	We've been talking about this knee pain that appears when things feel out of control. Would you be interested in trying a mindfulness exercise where we will slowly try to liquify and flush out some of this pain?	Would you be interested in doing an experiment with me to see if we can expand this experience of self-compassion?
Zoom out	Let's step away from the scene you are sharing, and imagine you are seeing it from far away, as if a movie on a TV screen at a distance from you. Can you stay connected to the present and see this scene in a small container? What does it look like now?	When you imagine yourself in the clouds or in the sky, and watching over your family life as if in a movie, what is it that triggers the most love or gratefulness? What kind of music would a film maker add to this scene?

Left-Hemisphere Activation

	Problem-focused questions	Reauthoring questions
Languaging	Whenever you have a glass of wine with your husband, memories of your high school friend's suicide attempt flood your mind and get you to cry. Have you ever told the story of what happened?	You shared how traumatic this period of your life was and how you don't like talking about it. Can I ask you about the skills you may have developed because of these events or if they might have contributed to you developing something you like about yourself?
Numeral question	What percentage of the time do you actually fail an exam as predicted by the worries?	Can you put a number on how much taller you felt?
Speculation	The depression is making you feel hopeless right now, but what if there was a way other than hurting yourself that would solve the situation?	Is it possible that you making this choice might lead to a completely different outcome?
Certainty trap	Anger makes you convinced that your friend did this on purpose. Let's just imagine for a second that there was another explanation. What could it be?	After you've had so much fun with your boyfriend, do you see the jealous thoughts differently? They make you very certain of his intent to leave sometimes. Would you like to remember to question that certainty?
Focusing poles	Is it possible that the pleasing habit is making you overfocus on one thing, and underfocus on something else?	When you get a break from the terror, do you see things in a broader way? Would you say your focus is wider?

Right Hemisphere

	Problem-focused questions	Reauthoring questions
Lining distress with agency (simultaneously)	When you heard the doctor say your sister had leukemia, what happened for you at that moment and what helped you?	The grief felt engulfing and yet you kept your composure. Did the two coexist in a form of balance?
Metaphor	When you say the despair is like a dark cloak, can you describe the cloak a bit more?	If, as you said, self-hate was like a poison running through your veins, how would you describe the feeling of acceptance that's coming up right now?
Brain map	Let's draw and organize everything we talked about in this brain-map illustration.	

Therapeutic Posture

	Problem-focused questions	Reauthoring questions
Centering	Based on what I heard, I believe you meet the diagnostic criteria for disorder x.	I think you did a great job and you are an amazing mother.
Decentering (verbal)	What do you think about this stealing habit?	Is there something you like about being honest with your friends?
Co-centering	The sadness is very strong right now and making it difficult to talk. Let's try to breathe at the same pace, together.	I can feel that you have more enthusiasm. Would you call this state something else? Tell me more about it. . . . I'm also delighted to hear that this exam went so well for you.

Native and Indigenous Knowledge

Relational flow (Expressions such as *aroha* and *manaakitanga*)
Bridge people
Somatic manifestations
Shared experiences of embodied rituals
Synchronicity

Specialized Nonverbal Practices

Mindfulness
Breathing exercises
State deactivation
EMDR

Narrative Therapy Definitions

Deconstructing Deconstructing involves taking apart or examining the cultural ideas affecting clients in a usually negative way. The practice harnesses therapeutic curiosity and persistence where clients come to identify discourses as cultural ideas rather than as truths. When problem discourses are deconstructed, clients attain more clarity about what they are up against when committed to change and identify more clearly what the effects are of the discourses on peoples' lives.

De-storying The process of helping a client recognize that a problematic experience is related to a physiological process rather than to a dominant story or problematic identity.

Discourses Cultural ideas or beliefs held by a large community of people that intimately affect human behavior in communities identified by race/ethnicity, sexuality/gender, class, religion, geographical location, and so on.

Externalizing the problem/externalizing conversation A way of talking used by a narrative practitioner to separate the client from their problem. This approach opens up new opportunities for the client to see the problem as not their essence but something that can be targeted and diminished by their emerging preferred self. This fits with the narrative mantra: "The problem is the problem and the person is not the problem."

Grafting The practice of finding a completely unrelated but meaningful story of life and connecting it to the therapeutic work to heighten the intensity of the emerging preferred self.

Mapping the effects This is a practice of helping clients identify what the problem-saturated story is doing to them. It is built upon Gregory Bateson's ideas of creating "news of difference." When the therapist methodically explores the history of the problem-stories' effects on the client and others, the information generated by doing this mapping usually becomes motivating for the client to be even more committed and want something different in their lives.

Preferred self/selves and identity(ies) As clients begin to recognize and embrace their preferred stories that were previously untold or in the shadows of their lives, these stories invite a new posture or life position and direction that becomes integrated into how they see themselves in the world.

Preferred story/stories With their clients, narrative practitioners track life events and memories that were not previously connected together. Their focus is on coproducing with their clients a story or stories that promote an identity and a way of living in the world that provides strength and robustness to face life challenges and live a life of one's own design.

Problem-saturated and thick problem stories Negative or harmful narratives that people tell about themselves or that significant others tell about them that are diminishing of their lives and cloud the opportunities to think about stories and lived experiences that can be life enhancing.

Reauthoring conversations These conversations are coproduced by the therapeutic interactions that take place between the practitioner and client. The practitioner and client become coauthors in the storying process. As unique outcomes are woven together, they become part of a restorying process that constructs the preferred story.

Thickening rich stories Narrative practitioners use a range of interventions to have clients attend to multiple lived events experienced by clients in both the present and the past and also in the contemplated future that can be woven together in therapeutic conversations that bolster their preferred selves.

Unique outcomes These are like the solution-focused concept of "exceptions." They are lived moments clients can embrace that stand outside of a problem-story description. When unique outcomes are connected together, they become plot points that form the basis of a preferred story.

Zone of proximal development Proposed by Lev Vygotsky, this is the optimal space between the boundaries of what a learner can grasp without assistance and what a learner can do with guidance from and collaboration with knowledgeable others.

Practice Decision Tree to Foster Agency and Resiliency When Working With Traumatic Experiences

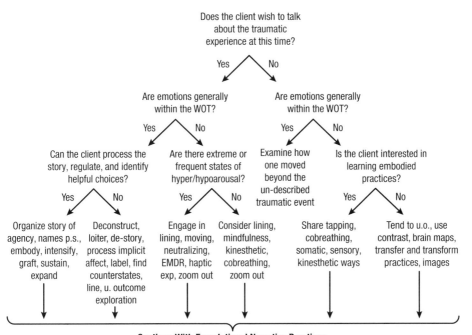

Does the client wish to talk about the traumatic experience at this time?

Yes / No

Yes → Are emotions generally within the WOT?

No → Are emotions generally within the WOT?

(Left branch — Yes path)
Yes / No

Yes → Can the client process the story, regulate, and identify helpful choices?

No → Are there extreme or frequent states of hyper/hypoarousal?

Yes / No (under "Can the client process...")
- **Yes →** Organize story of agency, names p.s., embody, intensify, graft, sustain, expand
- **No →** Deconstruct, loiter, de-story, process implicit affect, label, find counterstates, line, u. outcome exploration

Yes / No (under "Are there extreme or frequent states of hyper/hypoarousal?")
- **Yes →** Engage in lining, moving, neutralizing, EMDR, haptic exp, zoom out
- **No →** Consider lining, mindfulness, kinesthetic, cobreathing, zoom out

(Right branch — No path)
Yes / No

Yes → Examine how one moved beyond the un-described traumatic event

No → Is the client interested in learning embodied practices?

Yes / No (under "Is the client interested in learning embodied practices?")
- **Yes →** Share tapping, cobreathing, somatic, sensory, kinesthetic ways
- **No →** Tend to u.o., use contrast, brain maps, transfer and transform practices, images

Continue With Foundational Narrative Practices

Key: p.s. = preferred self   u.o. = unique outcome

References

Almås, I., Cappelen, A. W., Sørensen, E., & Tungodden, B. (2020). *Fairness across the world Preference and beliefs* [Presentation]. FAIR workshop, Deaton Review, University of Stockholm.

Almås, I., Cappelen, A. W., & Tungodden, B. (2020). Cutthroat capitalism versus cuddly socialism: Are Americans more meritocratic and efficiency-seeking than Scandinavians? *Journal of Political Economy, 128*(5), 1753–1788.

Anderson, H. (2012). Possibilities of the collaborative approach. In T. Malinen, S. J. Cooper & F. Thomas (Eds.), *Masters of narrative and collaborative therapies.* Routledge.

Anderson, H., & Goolishian, H. (1992). The client is the expert: A not-knowing approach to therapy. In S. McNamee & K. J. Gergen (Eds.), *Therapy as a social construction*, pp. 25–39. Sage.

Baars, B. (2019). *On consciousness: Science and subjectivity.* Nautilus Press.

Bach, D., Groesback, G., Stapleton, P., Slims, R., Blickhaeuser, K., Church, D. (2019). Clinical EFT (Emotional Freedom Techniques) improves multiple physiological markers of health. *Journal of Evidence-Based Integrative Medicine.* https://doi.org/10.1177/2515690X18823691

Badenoch, B. (2011). *The brain-savvy therapist's workbook.* Norton.

Badenoch, B. (2021). Becoming a therapeutic presence in the counseling room and the world. In D. Siegel, A. Schore, & L. Cozolino (Eds.), *Interpersonal neurobiology and clinical practice.* Norton.

Barnes, S., Brown, K. W., Krusemark, E., Campbell, W. K., & Rogge, R. D. (2007). The role of mindfulness in romantic relationship satisfaction and responses to relationship stress. *Journal of Marital and Family Therapy, 33*(4), 482–500.

Barrett, L. F. (2017). *How emotions are made: The secret life of the brain.* Houghton Mifflin Harcourt.

Basso, J. C., Satyal, M. K, & Rugh, R. (2021). Dance on the brain: Enhancing intra- and inter-brain synchrony. *Frontiers in Human Neuroscience,* 7(14). https://doi.org.10.3389/fnhum.2020.584312

Bateson, G. (2000). *Steps to an ecology of mind: Collected essays in anthropology, psychiatry, evolution, and epistemology.* University of Chicago Press.

Bateson, G. (2002). Mind and nature: A necessary unity. Hampton Press.

Beaudoin, M.-N. (2004). Stabilizing therapeutic progress with anchors to preferred selves. *Journal of Brief Therapies, 3*(2), 139–152.

Beaudoin, M.-N. (2005). Agency and choice in the face of trauma: A narrative therapy map. *Journal of Systemic Therapies, 24*(4), 32–50.

Beaudoin, M.-N. (2010). *The SKiLL-ionaire in every child: Boosting children's socio-emotional skills using the latest in brain research.* Goshawk Publications.

Beaudoin, M.-N. (2014). *Boosting ALL children's social and emotional brain power: Life transforming activities.* Thousand Oaks, CA: Corwin Press Publications.

Beaudoin, M.-N. (2015). Flourishing with positive emotions: Increasing clients' repertoire of problem counter-states. *Journal of Systemic Therapies, 34*(3), 1–13.

Beaudoin, M.-N. (2017a). Helping clients thrive with positive emotions: Expanding people's repertoire of problem counter-states. In M.N. Beaudoin & J. Duvall (Eds.), *Collaborative therapy and neurobiology: Evolving practices in action.* Taylor & Francis.

Beaudoin, M.-N. (2017b). Tapping into the power of the brain-heart-gut axis: Addressing embodied aspects of intense emotions such as anxiety. In M.N. Beaudoin & J. Duvall (Eds.), *Collaborative therapy and neurobiology: Evolving practices in action* (pp. 75–86). Routledge.

Beaudoin, M.-N. (2019). Intensifying the preferred self: Neurobiology, mindfulness and embodiment practices that make a difference. *The International Journal of Narrative Therapy and Community Work, 2,* 1–10.

Beaudoin, M.-N. (2020). Affective double listening: 16 dimensions to explore affect, emotions, and embodiment in narrative therapy. *Journal of Systemic Therapies, 39*(1), 1–18.

Beaudoin, M.-N. (2023). *Thinkitis: Reclaiming your life from overthinking, worrying, self-doubt and anxiety using the power of neuroplasticity* [Manuscript in preparation].

Beaudoin, M.-N., & Duvall, J. (Eds.). (2017). *Collaborative therapy and neurobiology: Evolving practices in action*. Routledge.

Beaudoin, M.-N. & Estes, R. (2021). Benefits of "decentered and influential" practices during telehealth: Establishing, slipping and re-establishing position in a therapeutic conversation. *Journal of Systemic Therapies*, 40(2), 26-42.

Beaudoin, M.-N., & Maclennan, R. (2020). Mindfulness and embodiment in family therapy: Overview, nuances, and clinical applications in poststructural practices. *Family Process*, 60(4), 1555–1567.

Beaudoin, M.-N., & Maki, K. (2020). *Mindfulness in a busy world: Lowering barriers for adults and youth to cultivate focus, emotional peace, and gratefulness*. Rowman and Littlefield.

Beaudoin, M.-N, Moersch, M., & Schnare, B. (2016). The effectiveness of narrative therapy with social and emotional skills development: An empirical study of 835 children's stories. *Journal of Systemic Therapies, 35*(3), 42–60.

Beaudoin, M.-N., & Zimmerman, J. (2011). Narrative therapy and interpersonal neurobiology: Revisiting classic practices, developing new emphases. *Journal of Systemic Therapies*, 30(1), 1–13.

Beetz, A., Kotrschal, K., Hediger, K., Turner, D., & Uvnäs-Moberg, K. (2011). The effect of a real dog, toy dog and friendly person on insecurely attached children during a stressful task: An exploratory study. *Anthrozoös, 24*, 349–368.

Bird, J. (2004). *Talk that sings: Therapy in a new linguistic key*. Edge Press.

Blumenrath, S. (2020). *How taste and smell work*. BrainFacts.org. https://www.brainfacts.org/thinking-sensing-and-behaving/taste/2020/how-taste-and-smell-work-011720

Bradley, R., Greene, J., Russ, E., Dutra, L., & Westen, D. (2005). A multidimensional meta-analysis of psychotherapy for PTSD. *American Journal of Psychiatry, 162*(2), 214–227.

Brewer, J., Worhunsky, P., Gray, J., Tang, Y., Weber, J., & Kober, H. (2011). Meditation experience is associated with differences in default mode network activity and connectivity. *Proceedings of the National Academy of Sciences of the United States of America, 108*(50), 20254–20259.

Brown, D., Rodgers, Y. H., & Kapadia, K. (2008). Multicultural considerations for the application of attachment theory. *American Journal of Psychotherapy, 62*(4), 353–63.

Bruner, E. M. (1984). *Text, play and story: The construction and reconstruction of self and society*. American Anthropological Association.

Bruner, E. M. (1986). Introduction: Experience and its expressions. In V. Turner & E. M. Bruner (Eds.), *The anthropology of experience* (pp. 3–30). University of Illinois Press.

Bruner, J. S. (1990). *Acts of meaning: Four lectures on mind and culture* (Vol. 3). Harvard University Press.

Bruner, J. S. (2009). *Actual minds, possible worlds.* Harvard University Press.

Burton, R. (2009). *On being certain: Believing you are right even when you're not.* St. Martin's Griffin.

Campbell, D., & Doman, A. (2012). Healing at the speed of sounds. Plume-Penguin group.

Carey, M. (2017). From implicit experiences to explicit stories. In M.N. Beaudoin & J. Duvall (Eds.), *Collaborative therapy and neurobiology: Evolving practices in action.* Taylor & Francis.

Carey, M., Walther, S., & Russell, S. (2009). The absent but implicit: A map to support therapeutic inquiry. *Family Process, 48*(3), 321–323.

Carlson, H., Leitao, J., Delplanque, S., Cayeux, I., Sander, D., & Vuilleumier, P. (2020). Sustained effects of pleasant and unpleasant smells on resting state brain activity. *Cortex, 132,* 386–403.

Carlson, J. G., Chemtob, C. M., Rusnak, K., Hedlund, N. L., & Muraoka, M. Y. (1998). Eye movement desensitization and reprocessing (EMDR) treatment for combat-related posttraumatic stress disorder. *Journal of Traumatic Stress, 11*(1), 3–24.

Carson, J., Carson, K., Gil, K., & Baucom, D. (2004). Mindfulness-based relationship enhancement. *Behavior Therapy, 35,* 471–94. https://doi.org/10.1016/S0005-7894(04)80028-5

Caves, E., Brandley, N., & Johnsen, S. (2018). Visual acuity and the evolution of signals. *Trends in Ecology and Evolution, 33*(5), 358–372.

Chamberlain, S. (2012). Narrative therapy: Challenges and community of practices. In A. Lock & T. Strong (Eds.), *Discursive perspectives in therapeutic practices* (pp. 106–125). Oxford University Press.

Childre, D., & Martin, H. (2000). *The HeartMath solution: The Institute of Heart-Math's revolutionary program for engaging the power of the heart's intelligence.* Harper Collins.

Cho, W. L. (2019). *Context filtering: Clinical and linguistic practices of Asian American multilingual mental health clinicians* [Doctoral dissertation, Claremont Graduate University].

Christoff, K., Gordon, A., Smallwood, J., Smith, R., & Schooler, J. (2009). Experience sampling during fMRI reveals default network and executive system contributions to mind wandering. *Proceeds of the National Academy of Science USA, 106*(21), 8719–8724.

Chun, M., Golomb, D., & Turk-Brown, N. (2011). A taxonomy of internal and external attention. *Annual Review of Psychology, 62*(1), 73–101.

Church, D., Yount, G., Brooks, A. (2012). The effect of emotional freedom technique: A randomized controlled trial on stress biochemistry. *Journal of Nervous & Mental Disease, 200*(10), 891–896.

Cozolino, L. (2016). *Why therapy works: Using our minds to change our brains.* Norton.

Craig, A. D. (2002). How do you feel? Interoception: Senses and the physiological condition of the body. *National Review of Neuroscience, 3,* 655–666.

Craig, A. D. (2015). *How do you feel? An interoceptive moment with your neurobiological self.* Princeton University Press.

Creswell, J. D., & Khoury, B. (2019). *Mindfulness meditation: A research-proven way to reduce stress.* American Psychological Association.

Critchley, H. D., & Garfinkel, S. N. (2017). Interoception and emotion. *Current Opinion in Psychology, 17,* 7–14.

Crivelli, C., Jarillo, S., Russell, J., & Fernandez-Dols, J. M. (2016). Reading emotions from faces in two indigenous societies. *Journal of Experimental Psychology, 147*(7), 830–843.

Cromby, J. (2012). Narrative, discourse, psychotherapy—neuroscience? In A. Lock & T. Strong (Eds.), *Discursive perspectives in therapeutic practices* (pp. 288–307). Oxford University Press.

Cromby, J. (2015). *Feeling bodies: Embodying psychology.* Palgrave Macmillan.

Csikszentmihalyi, M. (2000). *Beyond boredom and anxiety.* Jossey-bass.

Damasio, A. R. (1994). *Descartes' error: Emotion, reason and the human brain.* Putnam.

Damasio, A. R. (2018). *The strange order of things: Life, feeling, and the making of cultures.* Pantheon.

Davis, P. (2021, May 26). *Why does anger make us stronger, yet we become weak with laughter?* New Scientist.

de Jongh, A., Amann, B. L., Hofmann, A., Farrell, D., & Lee, C. W. (2019). The status of EMDR therapy in the treatment of posttraumatic stress disorder 30 years after its introduction. *Journal of EMDR Practice and Research, 13*(4), 261–269.

de Jongh, A., Holmshaw, M., Carswell, W., & van Wijk, A. (2011). Usefulness of a trauma-focused treatment approach for travel phobia. *Clinical Psychology & Psychotherapy, 18*(2), 124–137.

Demuth, C., Keller, H., & Yovsi, R. D. (2011). Cultural models in communication with infants: Lessons from Kikaikelaki, Cameroon and Muenster, Germany. *Journal of Early Childhood Research, 10*(1), 70–87.

Denborough, D. (Ed.). (2006). *Trauma: Narrative responses to traumatic experiences.* Dulwich Centre Publications.

Denborough, D. (2019). Narrative practice, neuroscience, bodies, emotions and the affective turn. *International Journal of Narrative Therapy, 3*(1), 13–53.

Derrida, J. (1972). *Positions.* Nouvelles Editions Latines.

Derrida, J. (2001). *Writing and difference.* Routledge.

Duffy, M. (2012). The body, trauma, and narrative approaches to healing. In A. Lock & T. Strong (Eds.), *Discursive perspectives in therapeutic practices* (pp. 269–287). Oxford University Press.

Dunne, P. (2017). Insights on positive change: An exploration of the link between drama therapy and neural networks. In M.N. Beaudoin & J. Duvall (Eds.), *Collaborative therapy and neurobiology: Evolving practices in action* (pp. 62–74). Routledge.

Duvall, J. (2019). Transforming trauma and the migration of identity: Accepting the "call" from outside the cave. In M. Hoyt & M. Bobele (Eds.), *Creative therapy in challenging situations* (pp. 58–69). Routledge.

Duvall, J., & Beres, L. (2011). *Innovations in narrative therapy: Connecting practice, training and research.* Norton.

Duvall, J., & Maclennan, R. (2017). Pivotal moments, therapeutic conversations, and neurobiology: Landscapes of resonance, possibility, and purpose. In M.N. Beaudoin & J. Duvall (Eds.), *Collaborative therapy and neurobiology: Evolving practices in action* (pp. 15–27). Taylor & Francis.

Duvall, J., & Young, K., (2009). Keeping faith: A conversation with Michael White. *Journal of Systemic Therapies, 28*(1), 1–18.

Durant, M. & White, C. (1990). *Ideas of therapy with sexual abuse.* Dulwich Centre Publications.

Ecker, B., Ticic, R., & Hulley, L. (2012). *Unlocking the emotional brain: Eliminating symptoms at their roots using memory reconsolidation.* Routledge.

Eisenberger, N., Lieberman, M., & Williams, K. (2003). Does rejection hurt? An fMRI study of social exclusion. *Science, 302*(5643), 290–292.

Elbrecht, C., & Antcliff, L. (2014). Being touched through touch. Trauma treatment through haptic perception at the Clay Field: A sensorimotor art therapy. *International Journal of Art Therapy, 19*(1), 19–30.

Engels, A., Heller, W., Mohanty, A., Herrington, J., Banish, M., & Webb, A. (2017). Specificity of regional brain activity in anxiety types during emotion processing. *Psychophysiology, 44,* 352–363.

Epston, D. (1993). Internalizing discourses versus externalizing discourses. In S. Gilligan & R. Price (Eds.), *Therapeutic conversations.* Norton.

Epston, D. (1998). *Catching up with David Epston: A collection of narrative practice–based papers published between 1991 & 1996.* Dulwich Centre Publications.

Epston, D. (2008). *Down under and up over: Travels with narrative therapy.* AFT.

Epston, D. (2016). Re-imagining narrative therapy: A history for the future. *Journal of Systemic Therapies, 35*(1), 79–87.

Epston, D. (2020a). How Michael White came up with the idea of externalization: An educated guess. *Journal of Contemporary Narrative Therapy, 3,* 25–33.

Epston, D. (2020b). Re-imagining narrative therapy: An ecology of magic and mystery for the maverick in the age of branding. *Journal of Contemporary Narrative Therapy, 3,* 9–38.

Epston, D. and White, M. (1992) Consulting your consultants: The documentation of alternative knowledges. In D. Epston and M. White (Eds.), *Experience, Contradiction, Narrative and Imagination: Selected Papers of David Epston and Michael White* (pp. 11–26). Australia: Dulwich Centre, Adelaide.

Ewing, J., Estes, R., & Like, B. (2017). Narrative neurotherapy: Scaffolding identity states. In M.N. Beaudoin & J. Duvall (Eds.), *Collaborative therapy and interpersonal neurobiology: Emerging practices* (pp. 87–100). Routledge.

Farb, N. A. S., Segal, Z. V., Mayberg, H., Bean, J., McKeon, D., Fatima, Z., & Anderson, A. K. (2007). Attending to the present: Mindfulness meditation reveals distinct neural modes of self-reference. *Social Cognitive and Affective Neuroscience, 2*(4), 313–322. https://doi.org/10.1093/scan/nsm030

Fernald, A., Marchman, V., & Weisleder, A. (2013). SES differences in language processing skill and vocabulary are evident at 18 months. *Developmental Science, 16*(2), 234–248.

Finn, S., Perry, B., Clasing, J., Walters, L., Jarzombek, S. , Curran, R., & Rouhanian, M. (2017). A randomized, controlled trial of mirror therapy for upper extremity phantom limb paining male amputees. *Frontiers in Neurology, 8,* 267.

Foley, T. E., & Fleshner, M. (2008). Neuroplasticity of dopamine circuits after exercise: Implications for central fatigue. *Neuromolecular Medicine, 10,* 67–80.

Fosha, D. (2009). Emotion and recognition at work: Energy, vitality, pleasure, truth, desire, and the emergent phenomenology of transformational experience. In D. Fosha, D. Siegel, & M. Solomon (Eds.), *The healing power of emotion: Affective neuroscience, development, and clinical practice* (pp. 172–203). Norton.

Foucault, M. (1982). The subject and power. *Critical inquiry*, 8(4), 777–795.

Foucault, M. (1990). *The history of sexuality: An introduction* (R. Hurley, Trans., Vol. 1). Vintage.

Foucault, M. (2012). *Discipline and punish: The birth of the prison*. Vintage.

Foucault, M. (2013). *Archaeology of knowledge*. Routledge.

Fredrickson, B. (2009). *Positivity: Top-notch research reveals the 3-to-1 ratio that will change your life*. Harmony.

Freedman, J., & Combs, G. (1996). *Narrative therapy: The social construction of preferred reality*. Norton.

Furness, J. B. (2006). *The enteric nervous system*. Blackwell.

Gattinara, P. C. (2009). Working with EMDR in chronic incapacitating diseases: The experience of a neuromuscular diseases center. *Journal of EMDR Practice and Research*, 3(3), 169–177.

Geertz, C. (1988). *Works and lives: The anthropologist as author*. Stanford University Press.

Geertz, C. (2008). *Local knowledge: Further essays in interpretive anthropology*. Basic Books.

Gendron, M., Roberson, D., Van der Vyver, M., & Barrett, L. F. (2014). Perception of emotions from facial expressions are not culturally universal: Evidence from a remote culture. *Emotion*, 14(2), 251–262.

Gergen, K. J. (1990). Therapeutic profession and the diffusion of deficit. *The Journal of Mind and Behavior*, 11(3), 353–368.

Gergen, K. J. (1991). *The saturated self*. Basic Books.

Gergen, K. J. (2015a). *An invitation to social construction* (3rd ed.). Sage Publications.

Gergen, K. J. (2015b). The neurobiological turn in therapeutic treatment: Salvation or devastation? In D. Loewenthal (Ed.), *Critical psychotherapy, psychoanalysis and counselling: Implications for practice* (pp. 53–73). Palgrave-MacMillan.

Germer, C. (2014). *A mindful path to self-compassion*. Guilford.

Ginot, E. (2015). *Integrating brain and mind in psychotherapy*. Norton.

Goleman, D., & Davidson, R. J. (2017). *Altered traits: Science reveals how meditation changes your mind, brain and body*. Avery.

Goodman, R. D., Williams, J. M., Chung, R. C. Y., Talleyrand, R. M., Douglass, A.

M., McMahon, H. G., & Bemak, F. (2015). Decolonizing traditional pedagogies and practices in counseling and psychology education: A move towards social justice and action. In R. D. Goodman & P. Gorski (Eds.), *Decolonizing "multicultural" counseling through social justice* (pp. 147–164). Springer.

Gorman, T., & Gree, S. (2016). Short-term mindfulness intervention reduces the negative attentional effects associated with heavy media multitasking. *Scientific Reports*, 6, Article 24542. https://doi.org/10.1038/srep24542

Gorski, P. C., & Goodman, R. D. (2015). Introduction: Toward a decolonized multicultural counseling and psychology. In R. D. Goodman & P. Gorski (Eds.), *Decolonizing "multicultural" counseling through social justice* (pp. 1–10). Springer.

Grand, D. (2014). Brainspotting: *The revolutionary therapy for rapid and effective change*. Sounds True.

Griffith, J. L., & Griffith, M. (1994). *The body speaks: Therapeutic dialogues for mind–body problems*. Basic Books.

Guidarelli, L. (2021). *La questione della lingua* comes to therapy. In m. polanco, N. Zamani, & C. Kim (Eds.), *Bilingualism, culture, and social justice in family therapy* (pp. 25–31). Springer.

Hadhazy, A. (2010, February 12). Think twice: How the gut's second brain influences mood and well-being. *Scientific American*.

Haegert, C. M., & Moxley-Haegert, L. (2021). *Integrating eye movement desensitization and reprocessing therapy into narrative therapeutic conversations: Resisting abuse in childhood sport training* [Unpublished paper].

Hamkins, S. (2014). *The art of narrative psychiatry*. Oxford University Press.

Hansen, T., Aartsen, M., Slagsvold, B., & Deindl, C. (2018). Dynamics of volunteering and life satisfaction in midlife and old age: Findings from 12 European countries. *Social Sciences*, 7(5), 78.

Hanson, R. (2016). *Hardwiring happiness: The new brain science of contentment, calm, and confidence*. Harmony Books.

Healy, J. (2021, December 3). Behind the charges faced by the parents of the Michigan shooting suspect. *New York Times*.

Heath, T., Carlson, T., & Epston, D. (2022). *Reimagining narrative therapy through practice stories and autoethnography*. Routledge.

Hendricks, L., Bore, S., Aslinia, D., & Morriss, G. (2013). The effects of anger on the brain and body. *National Forum Journal of Counseling and Addiction*, 2(1), 2–5.

Hepi, T., & Denton, E. (2010). Secular science meets sacred art: The bi-cultural work of Tangi Hepi. *New Zealand Journal of Counselling, 30*(2), 1–22.

Hill, D. (2021). Dysregulation and its impact on states of consciousness. In D. Siegel, A. Schore, & L. Cozolino (Eds.), *Interpersonal neurobiology and clinical practice*. Norton.

His Holiness the 13th Dalai Lama, Tutu, D., & Carlton-Abraham, D. (2016). *The book of joy: Lasting happiness in a changing world*. Avery.

Hölzel, B. K., Carmody, J., Vangel, M., Congleton, C., Yerramsetti, S. M., Gard, T., & Lazar, S. W. (2011). Mindfulness practice leads to increases in regional brain gray matter density. *Psychiatry Research, 191*(1), 36–43.

Horton, R. (2006). Indigenous peoples: Time to act now for equity and health. *Lancet, 367*(9524), 1705.

Horowitz, A. (2016). *Being a dog: Following the dog into a world of smell*. New York: Scribner.

Horowitz, A. & Frank, B. (2020). What smells? Gauging attention olfaction in canine cognition research. *Animal Cognition, 23*(1), 11–18.

Hwang, J. H., Wu, C. W., Chou, P. H., Liu, T. C., & Chen, J. H. (2005). Hemispheric difference in activation patterns of human auditory-associated cortex: An FMRI study. *ORL, 67*(4), 242–246.

Iacoboni, M. (2009). Imitation, empathy, and mirror neurons. *Annual Review of Psychology, 60*, 653–670.

Iturria-Medina, Y., Pérez Fernández, A., Morris, D. M., Canales-Rodríguez, E. J., Haroon, H. A., García Pentón, L., Augath, M., Galán García, L., Logothetis, N., Parker, G. J., & Melie-García, L. (2011). Brain hemispheric structural efficiency and interconnectivity rightward asymmetry in human and nonhuman primates. *Cerebral Cortex, 21*(1), 56–67.

Jacobs, J., & Moxley-Haegert, L. (2020). *Narrative and EMDR with the Onkwehonwe-Original People: Kanien'kehá:ka's (Mohawk) transformational journey* [Unpublished paper].

Jaffe, A. E., Blayney, J. A., Bedard-Gilligan, M., & Kaysen, D. (2019). Are trauma memories state-dependent? Intrusive memories following alcohol-involved sexual assault. *European Journal of Psychotraumatology, 10*(1), Article 1634939. https://doi.org/10.1080/20008198.2019.1634939

Jarero, I., Artigas, L., & Luber, M. (2011). The EMDR protocol for recent critical incidents: Application in a disaster mental health continuum of care context. *Journal of EMDR Practice and Research, 5*(3), 82–94.

Jensen, E. (2008). *Brain based learning: The new paradigm of teaching*. Corwin Press.

Johnston, A., & Malabou, C. (2013). *Self and emotional life: Philosophy, psychoanalysis, and neuroscience*. Columbia University Press.

Kabat-Zinn, J. (1990). *Full catastrophe living: Using the wisdom of your body and mind to face stress, pain and illness*. Delacorte.

Kabat-Zinn, J. (2003). Mindfulness-based interventions in context: Past, present, and future. *Clinical Psychology: Science and Practice, 10*(2), 144–156. Kabat-Zinn, J. (2005). *Coming to our senses. Healing ourselves and the world through mindfulness*. Hachette Books.

Kahneman, D. (2003). A perspective on judgment and choice: Mapping bounded rationality. *American Psychologist, 58*, 697–720.

Kearney, B., & Lanius, R. (2022). The brain-body disconnect: A somatic sensory basis for trauma-related disorders. *Frontiers in Neuroscience, 16*, Article 1015749. https://doi.org/10.3389/fnins.2022.1015749

Keller, H. (2022). *The myth of attachment theory: A critical understanding for multicultural societies*. Routledge.

Kerr, F., Wiechula, R., Feo, R., Schultz, T., & Kitson, A. (2019). Neurophysiology of human touch and eye gaze in therapeutic relationships and healing: A scoping review. *Database of Systemic Reviews and Implementation Reports, 17*(2), 209–247.

Khaddouma, A., Gordon, K. C., & Bolden, J. (2015). Zen and the art of dating: Mindfulness, differentiation of self, and satisfaction in dating relationships. *Couple and family psychology: Research and Practice, 4*(1), 1.

Khoury, B., Knäuper, B., Pagnini, F., Trent, N., Chiesa, A., & Carriere, K. (2017). Embodied mindfulness. *Mindfulness, 8*, 1160–1171.

Kirmayer, L. J. (2012). Rethinking cultural competence. *Transcultural Psychiatry, 49*(2), 149–164.

Konig, N., Steber, S., Seebacher, J., von Prittwitzz, Q., Blien, H., Rossi, S. (2019). How therapeutic tapping can alter neural correlates of emotional prosody processing in anxiety. *Brain Science, 9*(8), 206.

Konuk, E., Epözdemir, H., Atçeken, Ş. H., Aydın, Y. E., & Yurtsever, A. (2011). EMDR treatment of migraine. *Journal of EMDR Practice and Research, 5*(4), 166–176.

Kornfield, J. (1993). *A path with heart: A guide through the perils and promises of spiritual life*. Bantam.Krahé, B. (2020). *The social psychology of aggression*. Routledge.

Krusemark, E. A., Novak, L. R., Gitelman, D. R., & Li, W. (2013). When the sense of smell meets emotion: Anxiety-state-dependent olfactory processing and neural circuitry adaptation. *The Journal of Neuroscience, 33*(39), 15324 –15332.

Kull, K. (2010) Umwelt and modeling. In P. Cobley (Ed.), *The Routledge companion to semiotics* (pp. 43–56). Routledge.

Lang, A., Craske, M., & Brown, M. (2001). Fear-related state dependent memory. *Cognition & Emotion, 15*(5), 695–703.

Lansing, K., Amen, D. G., Hanks, C., & Rudy, L. (2005). High-resolution brain SPECT imaging and eye movement desensitization and reprocessing in police officers with PTSD. *The Journal of Neuropsychiatry and Clinical Neurosciences, 17*(4), 526–532.

Lazar, S. W., Kerr, C. E., Wasserman, R. H., Gray, J. R., Greve, D. N., Treadway, M. T., & Fischl, B. (2005). Meditation experience is associated with increased cortical thickness. *Neuroreport, 16*(17), 1893–1897.

Levine, P. (2010). *In an unspoken voice: How the body releases trauma and restores goodness.* North Atlantic Books.

Levine, P. (2015). *Trauma and memory: Brain and body in a search for the living past: A practical guide for understanding and working with traumatic memory.* North Atlantic Books.

Lewis, P., & Critchley, H. (2003). Mood-dependent memory. *Trends in Cognitive Sciences, 7*(10), 431–433.

Lewis, T., Amini, F., & Lannon, R. (2000). *A general theory of love.* Vintage.

Lex, B. W. (1979). The neurobiology of ritual trance. In E. d'Aquili, C. D. Laughlin, & J. McManus (Eds.), *The spectrum of ritual* (pp. 117–151). Columbia University Press.

Lieberman, M. D. (2013). *Social: Why our brains are wired to connect.* Oxford University Press.

Liu, X., Cook, G., & Cattan, M. (2017). Support networks for Chinese older immigrants accessing English health and social care services: The concept of bridge people. *Health & Social Care in the Community, 25*(2), 667–677.

Lohrasbe, R. S., & Ogden, P. (2017). Somatic resources: Sensorimotor psychotherapy approach to stabilising arousal in child and family treatment. *Australian and New Zealand Journal of Family Therapy, 38,* 573–581.

Lomas, T. (2020). Towards a cross-cultural map of wellbeing. *The Journal of Positive psychology.* Advance online publication. https://doi.org/10 .1080/17439760.2020.1791944

Lomas, T. (2021). The dimensions of pro sociality: A cross-cultural lexical analysis. *Current Psychology, 40*, 1336–1347. https://doi.org/10.1007/s12144-018-0067-5

Lopez Yañez, I. (2022). *Under pressure: A study on the impact of cultural expectations on identity and emotional expression of Mexican children* [Unpublished paper]. San Diego State University.

Lutz, J., Brühl, A. B., Scheerer, H., Jäncke, L., & Herwig, U. (2016). Neural correlates of mindful self-awareness in mindfulness meditators and meditation-naïve subjects revisited. *Biological Psychology, 119*, 21–30.

Maclennan, R. (2019). An emotion management practice: A therapeutic process of reciprocal interpersonal and inner-personal engagement. *Journal of Systemic Therapies, 38*(3), 11–26.

Madigan, S., Ly, A., Rash, C. L., Van Ouytsel, J., & Temple, J. R. (2018). Prevalence of multiple forms of sexting behavior among youth: A systematic review and meta-analysis. *JAMA Pediatrics, 172*(4), 327–335.

Madsen, W. (1999). *Working with multi-stressed families.* Guilford Press.

Maffini, C. S., & Wong, Y. J. (2014). Assessing somatization with Asian American clients. In L. T. Benuto, N. S. Thaler, & B. D. Leany (Eds.), *Guide to psychological assessment with Asians* (pp. 347–360). Springer.

Majid, A., & Burenhult, N. (2014). Odors are expressible in language, as long as you speak the right language. *Cognition, 130*(2), 266–270.

Majid, A., & Kruspe, N. (2018). Hunter-gatherer olfaction is special. *Current Biology, 28*(3), 409–413.

Malinowski, P. (2013). Neural mechanisms of attentional control in mindfulness meditation. *Frontiers in Neuroscience, 7.* https://doi.org/10.3389/fnins.2013.00008

Marian, V., & Neisser, U. (2000). Language-dependent recall of autobiographical memories. *Journal of Experimental Psychology: General, 129*(3), 361–368.

Marlowe, S. (2017). Supporting young children visited by big emotions: Mindfulness, emotion regulation, and neurobiology. In M.N. Beaudoin & J. Duvall (Eds.), *Collaborative therapy and neurobiology* (pp. 50–61). Routledge.

Marsten, D., Epston, D., & Markham, L. (2016). *Narrative therapy in wonderland: Connecting with children's imaginative know-how.* Norton.

Martin, R. (2021). *Why we get mad: How to use your anger for positive changes.* Watkins Publishing.

Mason, M. F., Norton, M., Van Horn, J., Wegner, D., Grafton, S., & Macrae, C. N. (2007). Wandering mind: the default network and stimulus independent thought. *Science, 315*(581), 393–395.

Maxfield, L., & Hyer, L. (2002). The relationship between efficacy and method-ology in studies investigating EMDR treatment of PTSD. *Journal of Clinical Psychology, 58*(1), 23–41.

Mayer, E. (2011). Gut feeling: The emerging biology of gut-brain communication. *National Review of Neuroscience, 12*(8), 1038–1043.

McGilchrist, I. (2009). *The master and his emissary: The divided brain and the making of the western world.* Yale University Press.

McGonigal, K. (2021). *The joy of movement: How exercise helps us find happiness, hope, connection, and courage.* Avery.

Meier, B. P., Moeller, S., Riemer-Peltz, M., & Robinson, M. D. (2012). Sweet taste preferences and experiences predict prosocial inferences, personalities, and behaviors. *Journal of Personality & Social Psychology, 102,* 163–174.

Miodrag, N., Lense, M. D., & Dykens, E. M. (2013). A pilot study of a mindfulness intervention for individuals with Williams syndrome: Physiological outcomes. *Mindfulness, 4,* 137–147.

Monk, G., Winslade, J., Crocket, K., & Epston, D. (Eds.). (1996). *Narrative therapy in practice: The archaeology of hope.* Jossey-Bass.

Monk, G., & Zamani, N. (2018). Integrating emerging understandings of neuropsychology and affect for narrative therapy with couples. In M. B. Scholl & J. T. Hansen (Eds.), *Postmodern perspectives on contemporary counseling issues: Approaches across diverse settings* (pp. 233–260). Oxford University Press.

Monk, G., & Zamani, N. (2019). Narrative therapy and the affective turn: Part 1. *Journal of Systemic Therapy, 38*(2), 2–16.

Morgan, A. (2000). *What is narrative therapy?* Gecko.

Morton, B. E. (2013). Behavioral laterality of the brain: Support for the binary construct of hemisity. *Frontiers in Psychology, 4,* 683.Mullen, M. K., & Yi, S. (1995). The cultural context of talk about the past: Implications for the development of autobiographical memory. *Cognitive Development, 10*(3), 407–419.

Myerhoff, B. G. (1988). Surviving stories: Reflections on *Number our days.* In J. Kugelmass (Ed.), *Between two worlds: Ethnographic essays on American Jewry* (pp. 265–294). Cornell University Press.

Myerhoff, B. G., & Metzger, D. (1992). *Remembered lives: The work of ritual, storytelling, and growing older.* University of Michigan Press.

Myers, D. G. (2007). The powers and perils of intuition. *Scientific American Mind, 18*(3), 24–31.

Nader, K., & Einarsson, E. (2010). Memory reconsolidation: An update. *Annals of the New York Academy of Sciences, 1191*, 27–47.

Ncube, N. (2007). *The tree of life project* [Keynote presentation]. 8th International Conference for Narrative Therapy & Community Work, Kristiansand, Norway.

Nhat Hanh, T. (2003). *Creating true peace: Ending violence in yourself, your family, your community and the world.* Simon & Schuster.

Nia Nia, W., Bush, A., & Epston, D. (2016). *Collaborative and indigenous mental health therapy: Tātaihono—stories of Māori healing and psychiatry.* Routledge.

Niedenthal, P. M., Barsaloo, L. W., Winkielman, P., Krauth-Gruber, S., & Rice, F. (2005). Embodiment in attitude, social perceptions, and emotion. *Personality and Social Psychology Review, 9*(3), 18–211.

Noel, C., & Dando, R. (2015). The effect of emotional state on taste perception. *Appetite, 95*(1), 89–95.

Northrup, C. (2016). 10 health reasons to start drumming. https://www.drnorthrup.com/health-benefits-drumming/

Odendaal, J. S., & Meintjes, R. (2003). Neurophysiological correlates of affiliative behaviors between humans and dogs. *The Veterinary Journal, 165*(3), 296–301.

Ogden, P., Minton, K., & Pain, C. (2006). *Trauma and the body: A sensorimotor approach to psychotherapy.* Norton.

Ogden, P. (2021a). A healing context: Philosophical-spiritual principles of sensorimotor psychotherapy. In D. Siegel, A. Schore, & L. Cozolino (Eds.), *Interpersonal neurobiology and clinical practice.* Norton.

Ogden, P. (2021b). *The pocket guide to sensorimotor psychotherapy in context.* Norton.

Ostachuk, A. (2019). The organism and its *Umwelt*: A counterpoint between the theories of Uexküll, Goldstein and Canguilhem. In K. Köchy & F. Michelini (Eds.), *Jacob Von Uexkull and philosophy* (pp. 158–171). Routledge.

Parker, S. (2007). *The human body.* DK Publishing.

Percy, I. (2008). Awareness and authoring: The idea of self in mindfulness and narrative therapy. *European Journal of Psychotherapy and Counselling, 10*(4), 355–367.

Percy, I., & Paré, D. (2021a). Narrative therapy and mindfulness: Intention, attention, ethics. Part 1. *Journal of Systemic Therapies, 40*(3), 1–14.

Percy, I., & Paré, D. (2021b). Narrative therapy and mindfulness: Intention, attention, ethics. Part 2. *Journal of Systemic Therapies, 40*(4), 1–11.

Plews-Ogan, M., Ardent, M., & Owens, J. (2019). Growth through adversity: Exploring associations between internal strengths, post traumatic growth, and wisdom. *Journal of Value Inquiry, 53*, 371–391.

polanco, m. (2013). Cultural democracy: Politicizing and historicizing the adoption of narrative practices in the Americas. *International Journal of Narrative Therapy and Community Work, 23*(1), 29–33.

Porges, S. (2017). *The pocket guide to the polyvagal theory: The transformative power of feeling safe.* Norton.

Post, S. (2005). Altruism, happiness, and health: It's good to be good. *International Journal of Behavioral Medicine, 12*(2), 66–77.

Price, C., & Hooven, C. (2018). Interoceptive awareness skills for emotion regulation: Theory and approach of mindful awareness in body-oriented therapy (MABT). *Frontiers in Psychology, 9,* 798–799.

Raichle, M., MacLeod, A. M., Snyder, A., Powers, W., Gusnard, D., & Shulman, G. (2001). A default mode of brain function. *Proceedings of the National Academy of Sciences, 98*(2), 676–682.

Ren, D., Tan, K., Arriaga, X., & Chan, K. Q. (2015). Sweet love: The effects of sweet taste experience on romantic perceptions. *Journal of Social Personality Research, 32,* 905–921.

Reybrouck, M., Podlipniak, P., & Welch, D. (2021). Music listening and homeostatic regulation: Surviving and flourishing in a sonic world. *International Journal of Environmental Research and Public Health, 19*(1), 278.

Reynolds, G. (2010, August 25). Phys ed: Does music make you exercise harder? *New York Times.*

Rizzolatti, G., Fadiga, L., Fogassi, L., & Gallese, V. (1999). Resonance behaviors and mirror neurons. *Archives Italiennes de Biologie, 137,* 85–100.

Robinson, J., Moeke-Maxell, T., Parr, J., Slark, J., Black, S., Williams, L., & Gott, M. (2020). Optimising compassionate nursing care at the end of life in hospital settings. *Journal of Clinical Nursing, 29*(11–12), 1788–1796.

Robson, D. (2017, January 26). *The "untranslatable" emotions you never knew you had.* BBC Future.

Rost, C., Hofmann, A., & Wheeler, K. (2009). EMDR treatment of workplace trauma: A case series. *Journal of EMDR Practice and Research, 3*(2), 80–90.

Rothbaum, F., Weisz, J., Pott, M., Miyake, K., & Morelli, G. (2000). Attachment and culture: Security in the United States and Japan. *American Psychologist, 55*(10), 1093.

Sacks, O. (2010). *Musicophilia: Tales of music and the brain.* Vintage Canada.

Salzberg, S. (2015). *The kindness handbook.* Sounds True.

Salzberg, S. (2021). *Real change: Mindfulness to heal ourselves and the world.* Flatiron.

Schore, A. (2014). The right brain is dominant in psychotherapy. *Psychotherapy*, 51, 388–397.

Schore, A. (2019). *Right brain psychotherapy*. Norton.

Shapiro, F. (2013). *Getting past your past: Take control of your life with self-help techniques from EMDR therapy*. Rodale Press.

Shapiro, F. (2018). EMDR Institute basic training course. The EMDR approach to psychotherapy. Part One developed by Francine Shapiro, Hampton, CT. Trauma Recovery EMDR Humanitarian Assistance Programs.

Shin, R. Q. (2015). The application of critical consciousness and intersectionality as tools for decolonizing racial/ethnic identity development models in the fields of counseling and psychology. In R. D. Goodman & P. Gorski (Eds.), *Decolonizing "multicultural" counseling through social justice* (pp. 11–22). Springer.

Shore, J. H., Shore, J. H., & Manson, S.M. (2009). American Indian healers and psychiatrists: Building alliances. In M. Incayawar, R. Wintrob, & L. Bouchard (Eds.), *Psychiatrists and traditional healers: Unwitting partners in global mental health* (pp. 123–134). John Wiley & Sons.

Siegel, D. (1999). *The developing mind*. Norton.

Siegel, D. (2007). Mindfulness training and neural integration: Differentiation of distinct streams of awareness and the cultivation of well-being. *Social Cognitive and Affective Neuroscience, 2*(4), 259–263.

Siegel, D. (2010). *The mindful therapist: A clinician's guide to mindsight and neural integration*. Norton.

Siegel, D. (2020). *The developing mind: How relationships and the brain interact to shape who we are* (3rd ed.). Guilford.

Siegel, D. (2021). Interpersonal neurobiology from the inside out. In D. Siegel, A. Schore, I. Cozolino (Eds.), *Interpersonal neurobiology and clinical practice*. Norton.

Siegel, D. (2023). *IntraConnected: MWE (Me+We) as the integration of self, identity, and belonging*. Norton.

Siegel, D., Schore, A., & Cozolino, L. (2021). *Interpersonal neurobiology and clinical practice*. Norton.

Singleton, O., Hözel, B. K., Vangel, M., Brach, N., Carmody, J., & Lazar, S. W. (2014). Change in brainstem gray matter concentration following a mindfulness-based intervention is correlated with improvement in psychological well-being. *Frontiers in Human Neuroscience, 8*(33), 1–7.

Smalley, S., & Winston, D. (2010). *Fully present: The science, art and practice of mindfulness.* Gildan Press.

Söderkvist, S., Ohlén, K., & Dimberg, U. (2018). How the experience of emotion is modulated by facial feedback. *Journal of Nonverbal Behavior, 42,* 129–151.

Strong, T. (2017). Neuroscience discourse and the collaborative therapies? In M.N. Beaudoin & J. Duvall (Eds.), *Collaborative therapy and interpersonal neurobiology: Emerging practices* (pp. 116–127). Routledge.

Sujan, M.U., Deepika, Ak., Mulakaur, S., John, A., Babina, N., Sathyaprabha, T. (2015). Effect of Bhramari pranayama (humming bee breath) on heart rate variability and hemodynamic-a pilot study. *Autonomic Neuroscience, 192,* 82.

Tate, K. A., Rivera, E. T., & Edwards, L. M. (2015). Colonialism and multicultural counseling competence research: A liberatory analysis. In R. D. Goodman & P. Gorski (Eds.), *Decolonizing "multicultural" counseling through social justice* (pp. 41–54). Springer.

Tomm, K. (2018). Foreword. In J. Zimmerman, *Neuro-narrative therapy: New possibilities for emotion filled conversations.* Norton.

Tugade, M. M., Fredrickson, B. L., & Barrett, L. F. (2004). Psychological resilience and positive emotional granularity: Examining the benefits of positive emotions on coping and health. *Journal of personality, 72*(6), 1161–1190.

Turuki Pere, R. (1991). *Te Wheke: A celebration of infinite wisdom.* Ao Ako Global Learning.

Van Elk, M., Arciniegas Gomez, M., Van der Zwaag, W., Van Schie, H., & Sauter, D. (2019). The neural correlates of the awe experience: Reduced default mode network activity during feelings of awe. *Human Brain Mapping, 40*(12), 3561–3574.

van der Kolk, B. A. (1998). Trauma and memory. *Psychiatry and Clinical Neurosciences, 52*(S1), S52–S64.

van der Kolk, B. (2014). *The body keeps the score: Brain, mind, and body in the healing of trauma.* Viking.

Veenstra, L., Schneider, I., & Koole, S. (2015). Embodied mood regulation: The impact of body posture on mood recovery, negative thoughts, and mood congruent recall. *Cognition and Emotion, 31*(7), 1361–1376.

Vermeire, S. (2023). *Unraveling trauma and weaving resiliency with systemic and narrative therapy: Playful collaborations with children, families and networks.* Routledge.

Vik, B. M., Skeie, G. O., & Specht, K. (2018). Neuroplastic effects of playing piano within cognitive rehabilitation of patients with traumatic brain injury. *Archives of Physical Medicine & Rehabilitation.* https://doi.org/10.1016/j.apmr.2018.08.046

Vygotsky, L. S. (1987). *The collected works of L.S. Vygotsky: Problems of the theory and history of psychology* (Vol. 3). Springer Science & Business Media.

Vytal, K & Hamann, S. (2010). Neuroimaging support for discrete neural correlates of discrete emotions: A voxel-based meta-analysis. *Journal of Cognitive Neuroscience, 22*(12), 2864–2885.

Waldegrave, C. (2012). Developing a "just therapy": Context and the ascription of meaning. In A. Lock & T. Strong (Eds.), *Discursive Perspectives in Therapeutic Practice* (pp. 196–211).

Wallace, A. (2007). *Contemplative science: Where Buddhism and neuroscience converge.* Columbia University Press.

Wallace, B. A. (2011). *Stilling the mind: Shamatha teachings from Dudjom Lingpa's Vajra Essence.* Simon & Schuster.

Webb, C. (2020, December 10). How sweat lodge ceremonies heal war's wounds. Sapiens. https://www.sapiens.org/culture/ptsd-sweat-lodge/

Weingarten, K., & Worthen, M. (2017). Unreliable bodies: A follow-up twenty years later by a mother and daughter about the impact of illness and disability on their lives. *Family Process, 56*(1), 262–277.

Wein, D. (2015). How taste is perceived in the brain. NIH Research Matters. https://www.nih.gov/news-events/nih-research-matters/how-taste-perceived-brain

Wetherell, M. (2012). *Affect and emotion: A new social science understanding.* Sage.

White, M. (1989). *Selected papers.* Dulwich Centre Publications.

White, M. (1991). Deconstruction and therapy. *Dulwich Centre Newsletter* (3), 21–40.

White, M. (1994). A conversation about accountability. *Dulwich Centre Newsletter* (2–3).

White, M. (2001). Narrative practice and the unpacking of identity conclusions. *Gecko, 1*, 28–55.

White, M. (2004). Working with people who are suffering the consequences of multiple trauma: A narrative perspective. *The International Journal of Narrative Therapy & Community Work* (1), 45–76.

White, M. (2006). Working with people who are suffering the consequences of multiple trauma: A narrative perspective. In D. Denborough (Ed.), *Trauma: Narrative responses to traumatic experiences* (pp. 25–85). Dulwich Centre Publications.

White, M. (2007). *Maps of narrative practice.* Norton.

White, M., & Epston, D. (1990). *Narrative means to therapeutic ends.* Norton.

White, M., & Morgan, A. (2006). *Narrative therapy with children and their families.* Dulwich Centre Publications.

White, M. (2011). *Narrative practices: Continuing the conversation.* Norton.

Winston, D. (2019). *The little book of being.* Sounds True.

Xu, H., Bègue, L., & Bushman, B. J. (2014). Washing the guilt away: Effects of personal versus vicarious cleansing on guilty feelings and prosocial behavior. *Frontiers in Human Neuroscience, 8,* 97.

Young, K., Hibel, J., Tartar, J., & Fernandez, M. (2017). Single session therapy and neuroscience: Scaffolding and social engagement. In M.N. Beaudoin & J. Duvall (Eds.), *Collaborative therapy and interpersonal neurobiology: Emerging practices* (pp. 103–115). Routledge.

Zhou, Y., & Tse, C. S. (2020). The taste of emotion: Metaphoric association between taste words and emotion/emotion-laden words. *Frontiers in Psychology, 11,* 986.

Zimmerman, J. (2018). *Neuro-narrative therapy: New possibilities for emotion-filled conversations.* Norton.

Zimmerman, J., & Beaudoin, M.N. (2015). Neurobiology for your narrative: How brain science can influence narrative work. *Journal of Systemic Therapies, 34*(2), 56–71.

Zimmerman, J., & Dickerson, V. (1996). *If problems talked.* Guilford.

Index

About the Authors

Marie-Nathalie Beaudoin's lifelong passion for the immense possibilities offered by our brain and body has fueled an exploration of narrative therapy's intersections with other fields since the mid-1990s. As a result, she has prompted many clinical practices to respond to distressing emotions and traumatic experiences, and has published over 50 articles and books on these subjects. Her work is constantly inspired by the courage of her clients and clever questions from students in her California-based training program. With a background in improvisational theater, Marie-Nathalie is well-known internationally for her engaging presentations focusing on the concrete application of compassionate, respectful, and effective clinical practices.

A therapeutic fire was ignited in **Gerald Monk** after first participating in a workshop with the developers of narrative therapy, Michael White and David Epston, in the early 1980s. Since then, he has been an enthusiastic practitioner, teacher, author, and promoter of narrative therapy ideas and its evolution. Setting off controversy among traditional narrative therapy advocates, Gerald has argued for an integration of new developments within the study of affect in order to advance a contemporary version of narrative therapy. Gerald is a professor in the field of family therapy at San Diego State University and the codeveloper of narrative mediation.